THE GLOBAL BODY MARKET

The dark side of body part trading operates in a dynamic fashion, full of mystery, intrigue, and ambition. On the one hand, black and gray markets are illegal, but also pioneering and inventive; and although this type of criminal activity requires a level of dexterity and innovation, the point should not be lost that these markets thrive and flourish, sometimes in view of law. On the other hand, altruistic body part procurement is mired by low participation, which encourages black market transactions. Thousands of sick patients will die each year without the hope of receiving an organ or bone marrow donation through the altruistic procurement system, so they turn to the dark side.

This book offers a frank conversation about altruism in the global body market. It exposes how researchers exploit their patients' ignorance to harvest tissue samples, blood, and other biologics without consent for research and patent development. The book chronicles exploitation in the name of altruism, including the nonconsensual use of children in dangerous clinical trials, and analyzes social and legal commitments to the value of altruism - offering an important critique of the vulnerability of altruism to corruption, coercion, pressure, and other negative externalities.

Michele Goodwin is the Everett Fraser Professor of Law and Professor of Medicine and Public Health at the University of Minnesota. She holds joint appointments at the University of Minnesota Medical School and the University of Minnesota School of Public Health. Prior to teaching law, Goodwin was a Gilder-Lehrman Postdoctoral Fellow at Yale University. She serves on the editorial boards of several journals, including *Law & Social Inquiry* and the *Harvard/Stanford/Duke Journal of Law and the Biosciences*. She is the author or editor of four books and more than sixty articles and book chapters. Her editorials and commentaries have appeared in the *Los Angeles Times, New York Times, Forbes, Gene Watch, Christian Science Monitor, Cleveland Plain Dealer, Houston Chronicle, Chicago Sun Times,* and *Washington Post*. She is a columnist for "The Conversation" at the *Chronicle of Higher Education* and a blogger for the Harvard Bill of Health blog.

The Global Body Market

ALTRUISM'S LIMITS

Edited by

MICHELE GOODWIN
Everett Fraser Professor of Law and
Professor of Medicine & Public Health,
University of Minnesota

CAMBRIDGE
UNIVERSITY PRESS

CAMBRIDGE UNIVERSITY PRESS
Cambridge, New York, Melbourne, Madrid, Cape Town,
Singapore, São Paulo, Delhi, Mexico City

Cambridge University Press
32 Avenue of the Americas, New York, NY 10013-2473, USA

www.cambridge.org
Information on this title: www.cambridge.org/9781107024687

First published 2013

Printed in the United States of America

A catalog record for this publication is available from the British Library.

Library of Congress Cataloging in Publication data
Goodwin, Michele, editor of compilation.
The global body market: altruism's limits / Michele Goodwin.
p. cm.
Includes index.
ISBN 978-1-107-02468-7 (hardback)
1. Procurement of organs, tissues, etc. – Law and legislation – United States 2. Dead bodies (Law) – United States. 3. Procurement of organs, tissues, etc. – Moral and ethical aspects – United States. 4. Procurement of organs, tissues, etc. – Economic aspects – United States. 5. Altruism. I. Title.
KF3827.D66G66 2013
344.7303′21783–dc23 2012042941

ISBN 978-1-107-02468-7 Hardback

For Sage and Brooks

Contents

About the Authors

Dorothy A. Brown: dorothy.brown@emory.edu
Professor Brown is a Professor of Law at Emory University Law School with specialty focus in federal tax law and critical race theory. Professor Brown previously taught at Washington and Lee University School of Law, where she was also the director of the Frances Lewis Law Center. Professor Brown's editorials on tax policy have appeared in the *New York Times*. She completed her LLM at New York University School of Law and holds a JD from Georgetown University Law Center and a BS from Fordham University.

Donna Dickenson: d.dickenson@bristol.ac.uk
Professor Dickenson is a research associate at HeLEX Centre for Health, Law, and Emerging Technologies; an Emeritus Professor of Medical Ethics and Humanities at the University of London; and an honorary Senior Research Fellow at the Centre for Ethics in Medicine, University of Bristol. Professor Dickenson's research interests include commodification of the human body, genetic patenting, reproductive ethics and law, personalized genetic testing, and biobanks. She is a prolific author and holds a PhD from Open University in the United Kingdom, an MSc from the London School of Economics, and a BA from Wellesley College.

Naomi N. Duke: duke0028@umn.edu
Dr. Duke is an Assistant Professor of Pediatrics in the Department of Pediatrics, University of Minnesota, and the Medical Director of the West Suburban Teen Clinic in the greater Twin Cities Metro area of Minnesota. Dr. Duke is board certified in Internal Medicine, Pediatrics, and Adolescent

Medicine. She holds an MD from Harvard Medical School, an MPH from the University of Minnesota, and a BS from Wake Forest University.

Richard A. Epstein: r-epstein@uchicago.edu
Professor Epstein is the James Parker Hall Distinguished Service Professor Emeritus of Law and Senior Lecturer at the University of Chicago Law School, the Laurence A. Tisch Professor of Law at New York University, and the Peter and Kristen Bedford Senior Fellow at the Hoover Institution. Professor Epstein is also a member of the American Academy of Arts and Sciences and a Senior Fellow of the Center for Clinical Medical Ethics at the University of Chicago Medical School. He is the author of many books, including *Takings: Private Property and the Power of Eminent Domain* (1985) and *Mortal Peril: Our Inalienable Right to Health Care?* (1997). He holds an LLB from Yale Law School, a BA (Juris) from Oxford University, and a BA from Columbia College.

Michele Goodwin: mgoodwin@umn.edu
Professor Goodwin is the Everett Fraser Professor in Law at the University of Minnesota. She holds joint appointments at the University of Minnesota Medical School and the University of Minnesota School of Public Health. Professor Goodwin's research focuses on the role of law in the promotion and regulation of critical intersections of medicine, science, and biotechnology. She teaches Constitutional Law, Torts, Constitutional Torts, and a broad selection of health law courses. She is the author of *Black Markets: The Supply and Demand of Body Parts* (2006) and *Baby Markets* (2009). She was a Gilder-Lehrman Postdoctoral Fellow at Yale University after completing her LLM from the University of Wisconsin, a JD from Boston College Law School, and a BA from the University of Wisconsin.

Jamila Jefferson-Jones: jjefferson@mail.barry.edu
Professor Jefferson-Jones teaches at Barry University School of Law. She is a graduate of Harvard Law School and Harvard College. Prior to entering academia, serving as a Visiting Assistant Professor at the University of Denver Sturm College of Law, she was a staff attorney in the New Orleans Public Defenders office and an associate in the general business and energy section for Jones Walker, LLP in New Orleans. She was the Executive Editor of the *Civil Rights–Civil Liberties Law Review* and graduated with honors

from Harvard College as an undergraduate, presenting the English Oration at Harvard's 346th commencement.

Ray D. Madoff: ray.madoff@bc.edu
Professor Madoff is a Professor of Law at Boston College Law School and a regular commentator on matters of estate taxes, charitable giving, and the rights of the deceased. She completed her LLM at New York University School of Law and holds a JD from New York University School of Law and an AB from Brown University.

L. Song Richardson: srichard@wcl.american.edu
Professor Richardson is a Professor of Law at the University of Iowa Law School. Professor Richardson is an expert in criminal law and procedure, and her current research utilizes the science of implicit social cognition to study criminal procedure and policing. She holds a JD from Yale Law School and a BA from Harvard University.

Debora L. Spar: dspar@barnard.edu
Professor Spar is the seventh President of Barnard College. Professor Spar's scholarly research focuses on issues of international political economy, examining how rules are established in new and emerging markets and how firms and governments jointly shape the changing global economy. She is the author of *The Baby Business.* She holds a PhD from Harvard University, an AM from Harvard University, and a BS from Georgetown University.

Acknowledgments

The Global Body Market is a long time coming, and there was no better home for it than with John Berger at Cambridge University Press. Thank you, John. The book began as a symposium idea, during my visit at the University of Chicago Law School. Thus, I am grateful to Saul Levmore, Richard A. Epstein, and the John M. Olin Program in Law and Economics at the University of Chicago for support of the project that ultimately resulted in this edited volume. In addition to the fine authors who contributed to this book, there are many others whom I wish to thank, including my former student Nevin Gewertz and Professors Jake Linford and Shine Tu, as well as my former colleagues at the University of Chicago: Lee Fennell, Lainie Ross, Mary Anne Case, Lior Strahilevitz, and Anup Malani.

This book is about human flourishing and the ways in which that can be achieved through human biological exchanges. There are colleagues in the field who, for many years, have shared a passion for pursuing this ideal and their individual and collective voices have mattered to this work. I am grateful to Lori Andrews, Adrienne Asche, Naomi Cahn, June Carbone, Mary Anne Case, Glenn Cohen, Richard A. Epstein, Benjamin Hippen, Frances Kissling, Virginia Postrel, Radhika Rao, Dorothy Roberts, Sally Satel, Mary Simmerling, and Harriet Washington. In addition, I am indebted to the Tarrytown Meetings (and alumni) for three years of stimulating exchange with brilliant scholars, activists, journalists, and others and the Baby Markets "faculty" who keep the fire burning six years after our first meeting in Chicago with annual symposia.

I am also grateful to the late Senator Arlen Spector who courageously agreed to promote a dialogue about organ transplantation policy before departing Congress. He and his staff were helpful in thinking through steps forward to relieve the strain in the nation's organ transplantation system. That it has been nearly thirty years since Congress last took up organ transplantation policy in more comprehensive terms indicates how long overdue a meaningful dialogue remains.

My coauthors add pathbreaking value to this book. I thank each of them: Dorothy A. Brown, Donna Dickenson, Naomi N. Duke, Richard A. Epstein, Jamila Jefferson-Jones, Ray D. Madoff, L. Song Richardson, and Debora L. Spar. My gratitude for their commitment to this project and eagerness to engage in a long overdue conversation about the nuances of altruism, choice, incentives, and the externalities that attend each of those domains cannot be overstated. I am indebted to them.

David Wippman, Dean of the University of Minnesota Law School, provides generous support for my research, and I wish to thank him. My work benefits from the assistance provided by Professor Suzanne Thorpe of the University of Minnesota Library. I work closely with Suzanne and am grateful for her contributions on nearly all of my projects. This project could not have been completed without the aid of my former Executive Assistant, Jessica Kubis, who assisted in transcribing and proofing. I am also grateful to my research assistant, Allison Whelan, for her cite checking.

Finally, for a book positing *altruism's limits,* there is a subtle irony in closing my acknowledgments by thanking my family for their selflessness, support, kindness, and consideration. I am inspired by and ever grateful to them. I mark the growth, travels, and development of my children by their accomplishments as well as each of my book projects. As I finalize this book, Sage completes a first semester in college after a year in China and Brooks nears the end of his time at Fletcher, after a successful summer in Thailand. Their accomplishments place everything that their parents achieve in context as too often what we do pales in comparison. And to my husband, Gregory Shaffer, thank you for knowing what work is, for recognizing it, embracing it, and giving so very much with an indomitable kindness of spirit and soul.

The Global Body Market: Altruism's Limits

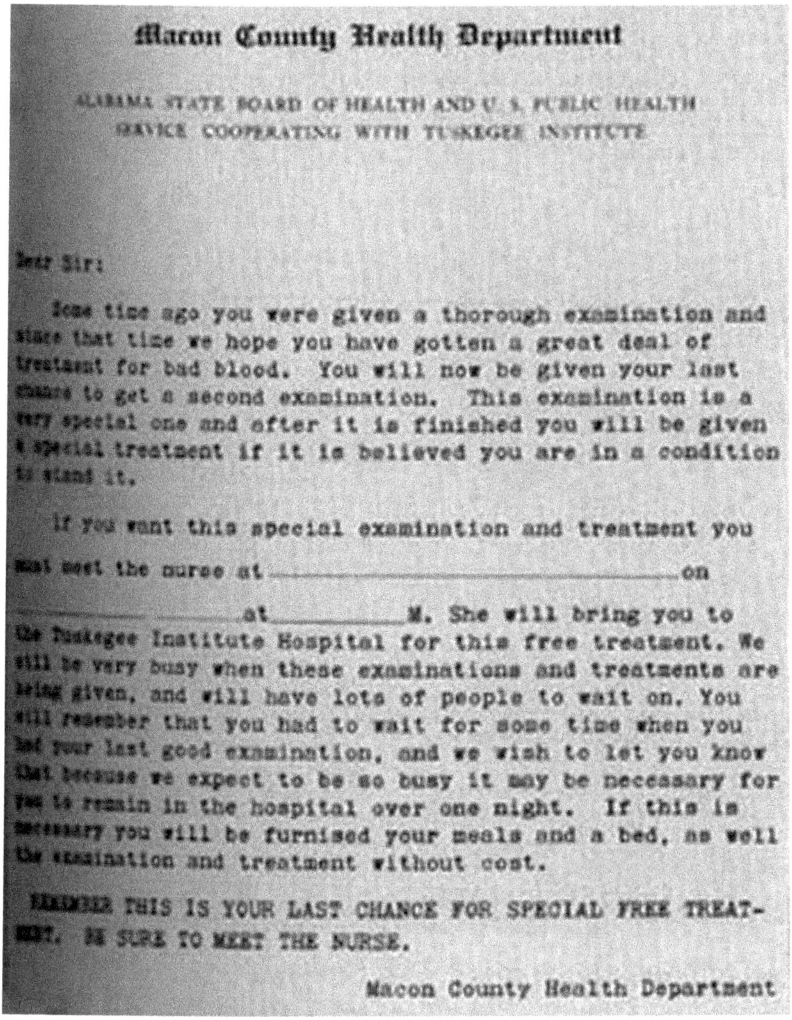

Macon County Health Department

ALABAMA STATE BOARD OF HEALTH AND U.S. PUBLIC HEALTH SERVICE COOPERATING WITH TUSKEGEE INSTITUTE

Dear Sir:

Some time ago you were given a thorough examination and since that time we hope you have gotten a great deal of treatment for bad blood. You will now be given your last chance to get a second examination. This examination is a very special one and after it is finished you will be given a special treatment if it is believed you are in a condition to stand it.

If you want this special examination and treatment you must meet the nurse at ________________ on ________________ at ________ M. She will bring you to the Tuskegee Institute Hospital for this free treatment. We will be very busy when these examinations and treatments are being given, and will have lots of people to wait on. You will remember that you had to wait for some time when you had your last good examination, and we wish to let you know that because we expect to be so busy it may be necessary for you to remain in the hospital over one night. If this is necessary you will be furnished your meals and a bed, as well the examination and treatment without cost.

REMEMBER THIS IS YOUR LAST CHANCE FOR SPECIAL FREE TREATMENT. BE SURE TO MEET THE NURSE.

Macon County Health Department

(U.S. Public Health Service; Tuskegee University Archives)

Eighty years ago a medical study, commonly referred to as the "Tuskegee Study," engaged hundreds of poor black farmers and day laborers in a human research project focused on their deaths from syphilis. The participants were syphilitic and many were sexually active with their wives, who later became infected. During the forty years that the study was conducted, treatments to cure the clinical trial subjects were withheld from them. Instead, under the guise of treatment, they were provided aspirin and subjected to painful spinal taps. Most interesting, however, are the dynamics and interplay of altruism. The U.S. Public Health Service and researchers involved emphasized that what the human subjects received was "special and *free.*" The research subjects were problematically portrayed as altruistic, rather than coerced and vulnerable. This book addresses these problematic framings.

Introduction

Michele Goodwin

There exists both the public and private negotiation processes for body part transactions, and both systems operate at crisis levels. These systems are characterized by incoherence, ambiguity, and sometimes fraud, coercion, clandestineness, and opportunity. Even more perniciously, there are black market transactions in the human body that involve direct exploitation, slavery, and even murder. Such are the scale and scope of the human body trade.

On one end of the spectrum exists an altruistic vision for human body part exchange, whether for organs, bone marrow, ova, sperm, corneas, heart valves, bones, or other highly profitable body parts. At the other end operate cold realities: medical school chop shops selling off abandoned and donated parts; creepy, mafialike organizations that sweep in after disasters like the tsunamis in Thailand and Japan or the devastating earthquake in Haiti to rob from the dead; rabbis hustling organs – conscripting poor Israelis to surrender kidneys for so-called cousins in the United States; and desperate delicensed doctors who figure the best way to make money these days is to open a biobank – and steal deceased persons' organs. These are the dark secrets of body part trading: hungry mafias taking while they can.

The dark side of body part trading operates in a dynamic fashion, full of mystery, intrigue, and ambition. On the one hand, black and gray markets are illegal, but also pioneering and inventive. It may be argued that criminal activity requires a level of dexterity and innovation. However, the point should not be lost; black and gray body part markets thrive and flourish, sometimes in view of law. Indeed, biobank companies often directly flout the rule of law.

On the other hand, our altruistic system of procurement is sadly predictable and quite conventional. For example, today we know that thousands of sick patients will die without the hope of ever receiving an organ or bone marrow donation. End-stage renal failure patients – those in need of kidneys – are the unfortunate victims in a system that demands altruism from any and all who will consider saving their lives. Only recently, in *Flynn v. Holder,* did the Ninth Circuit carve out an exception for bone marrow patients. In other words, as of 2012, those in need of bone marrow are no longer harnessed to a procurement scheme that necessitates altruism only; their donors may be compensated or receive a gift or some form of incentive as a reward for donating. The United States Justice Department threatens to appeal.

Predictably, the transplant waiting list will expand far beyond the capacity of organ donors to ever meet the demand. You might consider what this all means after a "gift of life" public service announcement airs on your local television station. Within the span of your favorite one-hour television show, a candidate on our organ transplant waiting list will likely die. Commentators are divided as to how this issue should be addressed. To change the altruistic procurement system by introducing market alternatives may ultimately lead to placing values on products from the body, thereby interfering with important societal notions of personhood according to Professor Margaret Radin. Acquiescence to an altruistic system of procurement might necessarily mean accepting its failures to generate an adequate supply of organs and the avoidable deaths that result.

In either case, formal law has yet to catch up with these new malleable biotechnological regimes, which operate both within the public sphere and underground. The public process is best characterized by our current organ procurement and allocation systems, which are regulated by Congress through the National Organ Transplantation Act (NOTA) and at the state level through the Uniform Anatomical Gift Act. However, those systems, relying upon pure altruistic transfers, are underserved and oversubscribed. Quite bluntly, demand for precious body parts – corneas, kidneys, hearts, lungs, livers, and the like – far outpaces altruistic supply. The private, underground systems involve individuals taking their chances on buying an organ through the black market and companies buying and selling human body parts and tissues from university hospitals, funeral homes, and organ procurement organizations.

These contemporary scenarios raise a multitude of issues, including the ethics of financial incentives in supplying resources from the body, the role of law in shaping the contours of body part exchanges, the limits of autonomy, the breadth of legitimate contractual agreements, morality, responsibility, and conflicts of interests. The strange narratives associated with body part corruption are animated by the tremendous demand for human biological supply and suppliers resorting to crafty – and often clandestine – measures to procure them. With more than one million allograft surgeries taking place each year in the United States, supply must come from somewhere.

Yet, recent body part scandals obscure the other contested and equally commoditized spaces mapped on the human body. Wombs, ova, sperm, embryos, and children represent the publicly marketized end of the spectrum. At this end of the scale, the essences of life – the building blocks – become regularly and intensely subjected to market norms. What contributes to the differences in how these spheres (organs vs. ova and the like) are perceived in society, regulated by legislatures, or adjudicated by the judiciary is conditioned by perceptions and normative understandings of the human body.

Quite restrictively, NOTA prohibits any "valuable consideration" to be exchanged for human tissues. Despite this broad language, reproductive markets flourish in direct view of the Justice Department. The law, crafted by Senator Al Gore in 1984, reflects a biotechnologically bygone era that predates robust ova and sperm markets, billion-dollar tissue markets, and the grave disparity between organ supply and demand in the United States and worldwide.

The Global Body Market: Altruism's Limits reaches beyond asking what is appropriately commodifiable and what is not. Those questions are important but fall short of a nuanced engagement on commensurability and altruism. The book considers the tremendous demands for substances like organs, ova, sperm, and other biological materials as well as information demands that can only be satisfied by rigorous research and analysis. Importantly, this book does not abandon legal pragmatism in search of a theory. Instead, the analysis breaks ground by taking a legal realism approach to study the history of body part transactions and then turns to the necessary conditions for a market in contestable commodities. The chapters vary by subject matter, casting a broad net querying the function of altruism and markets across a spectrum, encompassing organ commodification and baby markets to patents based on cell lines and tissues for research.

The Framework

The Global Body Market does not attempt to prove that black markets exist in human biological supply. Rather, this book is the next step. It considers how we should think about the markets that currently exist and what we should do about them. To accomplish this, I have enlisted experts in contracts, criminal law, tax law, trusts and estates, tort law, and property law, among others, to contribute to this important dialogue. The contributors consider how we might begin to create frameworks that move the discussion about incentives for human biological materials beyond hypothetical treatments in the literature to test them at the state and federal levels.

The book offers an important analytical framework for regulating markets in the human biological domain, thus distinguishing it from sociolegal accounts of the topic in recent years that call attention to human markets without offering a normative view. It analyzes demand and supply of human biologics by taking into account the need for law, the demands of biotechnology, and the role of bioethics. We do not debate whether there should be markets in the human biological sphere. Rather, we acknowledge body markets as a global phenomenon and probe how we should think about public and private regulations of body markets. Thus, we move beyond attempting to call public attention to rogue operations involving human body parts to interrogating the rule and role of law when body markets emerge.

The Global Body Market contributes to an emerging social discourse on the human body exchange in five distinct ways. First, it expands the conventional bioethics framework to include an examination of markets in human biological supply – an issue marginally explored by traditional bioethics scholarship. Second, it adds cultural value to bioethics and biotechnology scholarship by taking seriously the emerging discourses of race, socioeconomics, and politics in bioethics. Third, it engages tort law, articulating why a civil remedies approach should serve as a viable vehicle for redressing harms suffered by consumers of human biological supplies. Surprisingly, in the realm of human body politics, tort law is a spotty patchwork. For example, in some instances plaintiffs who claim that their (or a relative's) body parts were "stolen" by doctors and researchers can recover damages, and in other cases they cannot. In some instances those who have been harmed by the implantation of unhealthy human tissue can recover, while again others are without a remedy. The chapter entitled *Liberalizing Tort Law* critiques the judicial formalism that ultimately constrains the development of judicial frameworks to reorient legal consideration of body part claims. Fourth, this book engages criminal and tax law, shaping a prospective view of public regulation of human biological exchanges. The chapters on criminal law and tax law regimes provide compelling, original scholarship, which defines how policy makers should "police" human biological exchanges. Fifth, in *Situated Bodies in Medicine and Research,* Naomi N. Duke warns that those most likely to be harmed by judicial formalism and a blind adherence to altruism will be poor people of color.

This book examines a blind spot in the broader literature on the human body and its uses in the marketplace, medicine, and society. Authors in this volume urge a more nuanced approach to considering human biological exchanges. That is, they make the case that social justice, morality, and important sociolegal values do not derive exclusively from altruism. For example, a legal and social literature has developed, which associates commensurability and alienability in the human body with devaluing personhood, repugnance, and even claims that compensating people for organ sharing amounts to prostitution. Quite often, racial and economic statuses are deployed to argue that alienability or markets particularly hurt minorities. Assumed in this are the vulnerability and lack of capability (or incapacity) of the poor and people of color to steer themselves effectively out of the reach of hungry body "commodifiers" or brokers who seek to coerce and exploit them for their body parts. Such heuristics condemn all nonaltruistic body part exchanges as tainted by money or property exchanges.

Yet, altruism is corruptible, vulnerable to coercion, pressure, and threat. Indeed, that which is "free" does not always correlate to nor uphold foundational human values, such as honesty, love, compassion, integrity, dignity, empathy, respect, freedom, liberty, and dignity. Slavery remains the starkest example of that. However, one need not extend back to slavery in order to parse out the limits of altruism.

The Global Body Market avoids positioning and patronizing marginalized groups as "objects" within the broader discourse of human biological exchange. For example, for many years bioethicists rejected the use of incentives to procure more organs. Largely, their claims rested on beliefs that incentives disserve and harm minorities. In the United States, the claim was that African Americans would become the unwitting victims of wealthy white organ procurers. Bioethicists used race as a trope for discouraging proposals that might have led to regulated body-supply markets. Ironically, black markets in human body parts have flourished in the absence of regulated markets. Missing is a credible alternative view that documents the scope of human biological markets, articulates the importance of incentivized markets in those domains, and explains why regulation of human biological industries makes more sense than an unwavering commitment to altruistic human biological exchanges. The collection of voices in this volume fills this void.

Authors in this book scrutinize the law's role in demarking the boundaries of commodification and the human body. By no means are their chapters uniform; indeed the diversity of opinion and varying insights are quite refreshing. The authors challenge the notion that markets necessarily violate personhood, while also debating the relevance of socioeconomics, status, race, politics, influence, power, and gender in biological exchanges. Their chapters are perceptive, constructive commentaries about body part supply and demand in a global economy.

For example, Ray D. Madoff reminds us that the global economy in human biologics predates the contemporary questions with which we struggle: to commodify or not to commodify. Simply harnessing supply became an eighteenth- and nineteenth-century challenge, which necessarily led to coercion, corruption, and surreptitious body part theft. The rise of the U.S. medical school model depended on grave exploration and pillaging. Medical students sometimes stole the bodies on which they would later research. Medical school deanships rose and fell on how well a supply of cadavers could be maintained for entering classes. Thus, the business of body part procurement is not a new predicament. Rather, this problem is quite old, and still seemingly unresolved.

Dorothy A. Brown and L. Song Richardson offer compelling intuitions that help to answer the problem. Richardson proposes criminal sanctions to reign in those who abuse biological markets. Brown takes a different approach, urging pragmatic consideration of tax liability associated with biological markets. Where Richardson proposes retribution and punishment to curtail a rogue body market, Brown turns to the tax code. Brown's chapter emphasizes the importance of considering the pragmatic contours of markets, including the tax liability that flows with the sale of goods.

In his chapter, Richard A. Epstein describes the selling of kidneys, livers, hearts, blood, and eggs, as well as the selling or adopting of babies as provoking "the constant cries of 'commodification,'" which are not meant to show how market institutions introduced the standardization that makes voluntary exchange possible. Instead, as he notes, "the new use of the term 'commodification'... is intended to explain why those supposed efforts at standardization and voluntary exchange, especially for valuable consideration, run against the moral grain." Thus, Epstein takes to dispelling what he describes as "confusion" about behavior in body part markets. His chapter provides a sophisticated counternarrative to the concern that markets prevent human flourishing and can never protect individual rights. That said, he critiques and later praises the enormously insightful chapter authored by Debora L. Spar.

Debora L. Spar is equally concerned with questions regarding markets and rights, particularly reproductive rights. For example, she questions whether markets can ever protect reproductive rights. She acknowledges that "markets are about money and prices," and nevertheless, markets, she notes, "may still be able ... to provide [the] critical function" of protecting rights. Spar's chapter explores this counterintuitive proposition, examining whether – and how, and why – markets might be harnessed to the service of this particular right. She reminds us that "markets do not operate in a vacuum, and they can never be the only source of protection for rights, since any movement that they make in this direction happens only as an accident of their normal, profit-maximizing behavior." So what can markets provide? She observes that, "[i]n the end ... the only market that can fully protect reproductive rights is one that combines commercial forces with the tempering hand of government regulation.

Yet, not all authors in this volume agree that rights or choice frameworks provide the most useful frame for debating markets in human tissue. For example, Donna Dickenson urges a revised concept of exploitation – one that "can provide a more sophisticated analysis than the standard neo-liberal rhetoric of choice." She makes a compelling case that "while emphasis on respecting individual choice in liberal and utilitarian thinkers was originally intended to extend rights to oppressed groups, particularly women, and while it was put to use by feminist groups in the ongoing debates over abortion, it is now too laden with vagueness" to provide explanatory or prescriptive guidance.

Jamilla Jefferson-Jones takes up these thematic concerns – rights, choice, and exploitation – in her chapter. Specifically, she wrestles with an important question: when might or under what circumstances could a charitable deed becomes repugnant? For example, under what circumstances might connecting prison release programs with organ donations reek of repugnance? Could concerns about coercion be mitigated through formal process? Jefferson-Jones explains why a program that provides opportunity for early prison release can not only avoid coercion, but also achieve important societal goals.

Collectively, these chapters argue for greater transparency and pragmatism in the disposition, procurement, and transplantation of human biologics. The authors emphasize the importance of avoiding fraud and coercion in human body part transactions as well as the value in considering a spectrum of supply platforms ranging from mild incentive-based procurement to regulated commodification. In this way, equity, access, and antidiscrimination can be at the forefront in the retrieval and disposition of human organs and tissues.

PART I

Contestable Commodities

1 Free Markets, Free Choice?

A Market Approach to Reproductive Rights

Debora L. Spar

Can markets protect reproductive rights?

It sounds like a rhetorical question, or even a patently absurd one, because markets, we are tempted to respond, have nothing to do with reproductive freedom. Markets are about money and prices, about putting buyers and sellers together in a neutral and impersonal environment. Markets do not care about reproductive rights, or indeed about any rights at all. How could they possibly be used to protect them?

Yet the apparent absurdity of this connection does not necessarily make it untrue. For although markets are clearly not designed to advance reproductive rights, they may still be able, under some circumstances, to provide this critical function. In fact, the very impersonality of markets and their sheer lack of normative content might actually make them uniquely capable of protecting reproductive freedoms.

The remainder of this chapter will explore this counterintuitive proposition, examining whether - and how, and why - markets could be harnessed to the service of this particular right.

Of Rights and Markets

The first point to consider is the normative void that lies at the center of commerce. Markets, as already noted, are not inherently defined by a commitment to any set of rights. They have no goals aside from their own function and no particular commitment to any of those who operate along their structure. Instead, markets are entirely impersonal and mechanical constructs, drawing together buyers and sellers, supply and demand, in a chain of interactions mediated by price. As Douglass North has so eloquently elaborated, markets exist at the behest of governments and on the back of appropriate institutions. When they work best, they encompass an intricate bundle of rules, norms, and traditions, all of which are directed at the dual pursuits of efficiency and profit maximization. There is no room in this complex for societal goals like justice or equity, and no reason to suspect that markets will naturally produce these auxiliary benefits.

Just because markets are not committed to rights, however, does not mean that they are inimical to them: it simply makes them neutral. Sometimes, to be sure, markets do produce social "bads," outcomes deleterious to social welfare. If, for example, the global fashion industry develops a keen taste for baby seal fur, then the normal operation of the market will lead to an increase in the killing of baby seals. If the furniture industry likewise starts to prize rare tropical hardwoods, then the market will drive up the price of these woods, increasing incentives for loggers to fell as many trees as they can. In the United States, meanwhile, one might similarly argue that the private provision of health care has pushed prices to unaffordable levels and undermined the right of poor people to enjoy good health. In all of these cases, putting something into the market – be it seals, trees, or emergency rooms – arguably leads to a suboptimal, even harmful, outcome.

In other cases, however, the same kinds of markets, serving the same impartial dictates of supply and demand, can produce beneficial outcomes and social goods. Private farms and agribusinesses, for instance, provide nearly all of the world's food supply; private corporations supply an increasing amount of the world's fresh water.[1] Private markets generate the energy that lights our schools, the computers that teach our children, and the books we treasure as knowledge. Hospitals around the world are frequently run by for-profit corporations and most lifesaving drugs have been developed by private pharmaceutical firms – massive, undeniably commercial entities that make money while saving lives.

In practice, therefore, it seems difficult to argue that markets themselves are inherently good or bad, or that the development of a market in any

[1] Madue Barlow, Blue Gold: The Fight to Stop the Corporate Theft of the World's Water (2002).

specific area would necessarily be either protective or destructive of rights. Instead, markets drive only toward those purposes for which they are so perfectly suited: matching supply and demand, allowing firms to manufacture products and maximize profits, and offering customers the opportunity to buy. Sometimes this matching and these purchases are socially beneficial; sometimes they are not. But it is difficult, or at least unfair, to blame the market in either case for its social effect.

Markets and Reproduction

Let us turn, then, to a second consideration, and to the particular characteristics that are likely to define the market for reproductive products or services. Is there anything about these markets that will tend to make them more or less protective of rights? Anything that might push them toward either creating or destroying social value? If markets in general are inherently neutral, capable of creating both social goods and social bads, then we need to examine the specific circumstances under which reproductive markets are likely to exist, and the specific pressures that are most likely to operate upon them.

Historically and theoretically, we have a rather good idea of what causes markets to fail. We know, for example, that markets are not very good at delivering public goods - things like the classic lighthouse, or clean air, whose costs are borne by a small number of people but whose benefits are inevitably and uncontrollably shared by many.[2] Markets are also not very good at producing goods drawn from common pool resources - Atlantic cod, for example, or Scottish salmon. The markets will work in these cases, but they will tend to overproduce the commodity at hand, destroying the underlying resource and creating a clear social "bad."

Yet reproduction is neither a public good (at least in the customary economic use of that term) nor a common pool resource. Instead, reproduction is an innately *private* good, one that draws from a theoretically unlimited resource pool: ourselves.

So technically at least, we should expect a market in reproductive services or products to work very well - matching supply and demand through

[2] *See* R.H. Coase, *The Lighthouse in Economics*, 17 J. L. & ECON. 357 (1974).

the mechanism of price. Moreover, because competition in markets tends to increase supply over time and reduce price, we might also expect that an active and vibrant market for reproduction would allow individuals to have great access, at lower prices, to whatever reproductive options are commercially available. This is a critical and often overlooked point, because if we believe that one of the key aspects of reproductive freedom is access to reproductive choice, then markets - which tend naturally to produce both access and choice - are a natural ally of those who argue for reproductive rights.

Admittedly, a functioning market is not necessarily a "good" market in normative terms. We could, theoretically, imagine a vast reproductive enterprise composed of all sorts of nefarious and exploitative behavior - women being coerced to sell their wombs or eggs, for example, or desperate couples selling their infants or embryos for a supposedly fair price. Indeed, such stories already populate a whole subgenre of science fiction tales, including such classics as Margaret Atwood's *The Handmaid's Tale* and Aldous Huxley's *Brave New World*.[3] Economic theory, however, is more prosaic. It simply suggests that markets in the field of reproduction - markets for eggs, or sperm, or babies, or wombs, or embryos - are not particularly prone to either market failure or the destruction of limited resources. In commercial terms, these markets should work. Indeed, basic economics suggest that enabling and expanding markets for reproduction will simultaneously expand reproductive options and, in the process, the reproductive rights of those with access to those options. What kind of normative outcomes are produced as a result, however, is a more complicated question, and one that leads us directly to a third strand of inquiry.

Reproductive Sales: A Brief History

At a time when the reproductive market seems to be leaping into headlines around the world, it is tempting to believe that this market is brand new, a freshly born product of massive technological change. And to some

[3] Margaret Eleanor Atwood, The Handmaid's Tale (2006); Aldous Huxley, Brave New World (1998).

extent this is true. Thanks to technologies such as preimplantation diagnosis (PGD) and intracytoplasmic sperm injection (ICSI), would-be parents have far more options available to them today than they did even twenty years ago. Thanks to the Internet and other modern media, they also have a rapidly advancing stream of information about these new options. This combination of options and information makes it feel as if the market for reproduction – what I have elsewhere called the "baby business" – is a creation of the twenty-first century.[4] Yet the history here actually runs much deeper. In fact, there have been several earlier iterations of the market, instances in which buyers and sellers met together to exchange reproductive goods. How these markets evolved and how they interacted with reproductive freedoms provide an interesting insight into the connections between markets and rights in the reproductive sphere.

The Market for Contraception

Consider, for example, the case of contraception. Prior to 1873, when it became illegal, contraception was a flourishing industry in the United States.[5] In that year, however, the moral crusader Anthony Comstock convinced Congress to pass the "Act of the Suppression of Trade in, and Circulation of, Obscene Literature and Articles of Immoral Use."[6] Under the bill's provisions, contraceptives were grouped with other "obscene" items and banned as such.[7] Interstate transport of contraceptives was outlawed, as was the use of the postal system for sending contraceptives and related

[4] *See* DEBORA L. SPAR, THE BABY BUSINESS: HOW MONEY, SCIENCE, AND POLITICS DRIVE THE COMMERCE OF CONCEPTION (2006).

[5] Estimated at $30,000 in 1892. Andrea Tone, Making *Room for Rubber: Gender Technology and birth Control before the Pill,* 18 HIST. & TECH. 51, 60 (2002).

[6] Act of March 3, 1873, ch. 258, 17 Stat. 598.

[7] *Judicial Regulation of Birth Control under Obscenity Laws,* 50 YALE L. J. 682 (1941). In fact one source specifically points out: "The anti-contraceptive laws were not originally passed as a result of controversy over religious doctrine; they were passed as a by-product of an attempt to give legal support to a widespread attitude about obscenity. Carol Flora Brooks, *The Early History of Anti-Contraceptive Laws in Massachusetts and Connecticut,* 18 AM. Q. 3 (1966).

information.[8] The bill also forbade the importation of contraceptives[9] and stated that:

Whoever ... shall sell, or lend, or give away, or in any manner exhibit, or shall offer to sell, or to lend, to give away, or in any manner to exhibit, or shall otherwise publish or offer to publish in any manner, or shall have in his possession, for any such purpose or purposes, any obscene book, pamphlet, paper, writing, advertisement, circular, print, picture, drawing or other representation, figure, or image on or of paper or other material, or any cast, instrument or other article of immoral nature, or any drug or medicine, or any article whatever, for the prevention of conception, or for causing unlawful abortion, or shall advertize the same for sale, or shall write or print or cause to be written or printed, any card, circular, book, pamphlet, advertisement, or notice of any kind, stating when, where, how, or of whom, or by what means, any of the articles in this section hereinbefore mention, can be purchased or obtained, or shall manufacture, draw, or print, or in any way make any such articles, shall be deemed guilty of a misdemeanor.[10]

The sentence for such crimes was a minimum of hard labor for six months with a maximum of five years for each offense and a fine of between $100 and $2,000.[11]

In the wake of what became known as the "Comstock law," most U.S. states followed suit with their own "mini" or "little" Comstock laws.[12] Twenty-two states, for example, passed local obscenity laws that theoretically made birth control illegal, although the precise determination of illegality was left to the courts.[13] Twenty-four states explicitly passed laws forbidding contraception and including advertising or information related

[8] J.E. Leonarz, *Validity of Regulations as to Contraceptives or the Dissemination of Birth Control Information*, 96 A.L.R.2d 955 (2001). See also 18 U.S.C.S. § 1461(mailing); 18 U.S.C.S. § 1462 (importation); previously 18 U.S.C. § 334 (mail) and 18 U.S.C. § 336 (interstate commerce). Also the Tariff Code of 1930 Section 350(a) of the Tariff Act of 1930 (19 U.S.C.A. § 1305(a)) provided: "All persons are prohibited from importing into the United States from any foreign country any article whatever for the prevention of conception or for causing unlawful abortion." Apparently this was one of the first examples of how the Congress could use its interstate commerce and postal powers to regulate matters typically left to the states. *See, e.g.*, Harriet F. Pilpel & Theodore S. Zavin, *Birth Control*, 14 MARRIAGE & FAM. LIVING 118 (1952).

[9] Act of March 3, 1873, ch. 258, 17 Stat. 598.

[10] *Id.*

[11] *Id.*

[12] Leonarz, *supra* note 8, at 955.

[13] MARY WARE DENNETT, BIRTH CONTROL LAWS 7 (1926); *Some Legislative Aspects of the Birth-Control Problem*, 45 HARV. L. REV. 723, 726 (1932)

to birth control.[14] Connecticut went the furthest of them all and outlawed the actual use of contraception.[15]

Even as these laws were being imposed and extended, however, contraceptive sales remained strong, driven by the strength of demand from men and women determined not to conceive. Mainstream producers of rubber continued to sell condoms under vague names such as "sheaths, male shields, capotes ... or rubber goods ... for gents," while smaller entrepreneurs (known less generously as "smut peddlers") offered a wide range of "feminine hygiene" products, composed primarily of douches and crude spermicides.[16] By 1938, these products with "virtually no names" included more than four hundred options and generated annual revenues of roughly $250 million.[17] Yet technically, advertising these products and selling them across state lines was still illegal.

Writing at the time, many observers noted that the thriving underground industry for birth control had effectively rendered the laws meaningless. "If the purpose of the statutes be to minimize the use of contraceptives," reported a 1939 article in the *University of Chicago Law Review*, "the rapid growth of the industry, particularly in recent years, shows clearly that such purpose is not being achieved."[18] Others noted that the legal prohibitions had actually encouraged the development of a wholly unregulated market: "The notorious unenforceability of such statutes is evidenced by the flourishing bootleg industry which prospers in spite of them. These laws, by driving the industry underground, have impaired effective government regulation and thus indirectly promote the sale of worthless products at exorbitant prices."[19] There was also dismay that the laws prevented doctors from doing what the bootleggers were doing: "Year after year this vicious law legally tied the hands of reputable physicians while quacks and purveyors of bootleg contraceptives and 'feminine hygiene' articles and formulas flourished."[20]

[14] DENNETT, *supra* note 13, at 10; *Some Legislative Aspects of the Birth-Control Problem*, *supra* note 13, at 723.

[15] DENNETT, *supra* note 13, at 10.

[16] Tone, *supra* note 5, at 445–47.

[17] *The Accident of Birth*, 17 FORTUNE 83, 85 (1938).

[18] *Contraceptives and the Law*, 6 Univ. Chi. L. Rev. 265 (1939).

[19] *Judicial Regulation of Birth Control Under Obscenity Laws*, 50 YALE L. J. 682, 686–87 (1941).

[20] Margaret Sanger, *The Status of Birth Control*: 1938, 94 NEW REPUBLIC 324 (1938).

Meanwhile, of course, activists such as Mary Dennett Ware and Margaret Sanger were also attacking the prohibitions on more philosophical grounds. Ware, a middle-aged activist and grandmother, tried to get the Comstock laws revoked by striking "for the prevention of conception" from Section 1142 of the New York Penal Law, which made it a misdemeanor for "a person to sell, or give away, or to advertise or offer for sale, any instrument or article, drug or medicine, *for the prevention of conception*."[21] She failed and was instead convicted in 1929 of sending obscene material through the mail.[22] In 1918, Sanger similarly went before the New York Court of Appeals, arguing for a doctors-only bill that would have exempted physicians from the Comstock laws.[23]

Eventually, the activists' reasoning gained ground. In a landmark 1930 decision regarding condoms, the Court interpreted the Comstock laws to apply to intent rather than products, ruling, "There is no federal statute forbidding the manufacture or sale of contraceptives. The articles which the plaintiff sells may be used for either legal or illegal purposes."[24] Three years later, in *Davis v. United States*, the Sixth Circuit Court of Appeals likewise determined (again in a case concerning condom sales) that the sale or advertisement of contraceptive materials was not necessarily illegal – instead, illegality required proof that the contraceptives were to be used for contraception rather than for combating disease.[25] Finally, in 1936, the Court issued its most liberal ruling on contraception, determining in *United States v. One Package* that physicians could legally both import and prescribe birth control.[26]

[21] CAROLE R. MCCANN, BIRTH CONTROL POLITICS IN THE UNITED STATES: 1916–1945 68–69 (1994). *See generally* John M. Craig, *"The Sex Side of Life": The Obscenity Case of Mary Ware Dennett*, 15 FRONTIERS: J. WOMEN'S STUD. 145 (1995).

[22] United States v. Dennett, 39 F.2d 564, 569 (2d Cir. 1930); Craig, *supra* note 21, at 158.

[23] MCCANN, *supra* note 20, at 68–69.

[24] Young's Rubber Co. v. C.I. Lee & Co., 45 F.2d 103, 107 (2d Cir. 1930).

[25] Davis v. United States, 62 F.2d 473, 475 (6th Cir. 1933).

[26] United States v. One Package, 86 F.2d 737 (2d Cir. 1936).Section 334 referred to the mailing provision and made it "unlawful for anyone to deposit or cause to be deposited 'non-mailable matter,' and defines that phrase to include any printed circular giving information where and how things designed, adapted and intended for indecent or immoral use, or for preventing conception can be obtained." Section 396 was the similar provision for interstate commerce, making it "unlawful for anyone to knowingly deposit, or cause to be deposited, with any express company or other common carrier for carriage in interstate commerce, any 'article, or thing designed, adapted, or intended for preventing conception."

Clearly, this belated triumph for contraception was due in part to the efforts of activists like Ware and Sanger, and to the noble arguments they had raised on behalf of reproductive freedom and access to birth control. The changing legal status of contraception reflected a growing acceptance of women's rights, and of all people's rights to reproductive choice and privacy. Yet it is also critical to realize that much of the legal victory in this ostensibly intimate realm was actually achieved by private firms arguing on commercial grounds. The 1930 decision, for example, was technically a trademark case, brought by one condom manufacturer suing another for trademark infringement. And the Court's reasoning – which had the inevitable effect of widening access to contraception – was nevertheless entirely commercial in its reasoning, focusing, as noted, on "the article which the plaintiff *sells.*"[27] *Davis v. United States* was also a commercial suit, brought by a wholesale company that sold rubber goods to druggists. Again, the Court's ruling had the effect of widening access to birth control, but an intent based on markets – here, of confirming that the sale or advertisement of contraceptive materials was not necessarily illegal.[28] Finally, the *One Package* case, arguably the most important in terms of limiting the impact of the federal Comstock laws, was again a commercial case, this time involving a gynecologist who had ordered the "one package" of pessaries (diaphragms) from Japan. This time, the Court did make reference to what might be considered a social goal, arguing that federal law "embraced only such articles as Congress would have denounced as immoral if it had understood all the conditions under which they were to be used."[29] Yet the ruling was still undeniably economic in origin, responding to the doctor's commercial right to import and sell diaphragms. Significantly, after *United States v. One Package*, doctor-prescribed contraception was essentially legal everywhere in the United States except Massachusetts and Connecticut.[30] A year after *One Package*, the American Medical Association (AMA) "formally recognized birth control as an integral aspect of medical practice."[31]

[27] *Young's Rubber Co.*, 45 F.2d at 107 (emphasis added).

[28] *Davis*, 62 F.2d at 475.

[29] *One Package*, 86 F.2d at 739.

[30] David Loth, *Planned Parenthood*, 272 ANNALS AM. ACAD. POL. & SOC. SCI. TOWARD FAM. STABILITY 95 (1950).

[31] Although a 1936 study by the *Journal of the American Medical Association* showed that the laws had no effect on physicians. *Report of the Committee to Study Contraceptive*

The Market for the Pill

The development of the birth control pill, today one of the most important elements of female reproductive control, was likewise driven largely by private firms and market motives. Although activists and concerns for reproductive rights played a key part in its development, it was ultimately the market – buyers and sellers, supply and demand – that made the pill possible.

Preliminary work on what would become the pill began as early as 1937, when scientists began to demonstrate the potential for progesterone to prevent ovulation.[32] Because of the uncertainty surrounding the Comstock laws, however, the science of contraception was left entirely in the laboratories, with no one attempting to push it toward women or into the market.[33] After two pharmaceutical firms, Syntex and Searle, independently synthesized progesterone in the early 1950s, however, one lone researcher named Gregory Pincus started to use progesterone to experiment with contraception.[34] During this time, his research was funded entirely by the private fortune of Katherine Dexter McCormick, a widow who was determined to provide women with some means of contraception that they alone could control. As his research progressed, Pincus joined forces with John Rock, a pathbreaking Boston physician, who, in 1944, had quietly carried out the first critical steps in what would later become in vitro fertilization (IVF). In 1954, Rock and Pincus began experimenting with progesterone, technically exploring its efficacy in treating infertility, but really monitoring its ability to prevent contraception by stopping ovulation.[35]

When Rock and Pincus arrived at a formula that worked, they tested their new birth control pill in Puerto Rico, where a largely Catholic population had never found the need for explicit laws condemning contraception.[36]

Practices and Related Problems Appointed by the Board of Trustees of the American Medical Association, J. AM. MED. ASS'N 1911 (1936).

32 LORETTA MCLAUGHLIN, THE PILL, JOHN ROCK, AND THE CHURCH 100–01 (1982); Barbara Seaman, *The Pill and I: 40 Years On, the Relationship Remains Wary*, N.Y. TIMES, June 25, 2000, at 19.

33 MCLAUGHLIN, *supra* note 32, at 102; *see also* Martha Campbell & Malcolm Potts, *History of Contraception*, 6 GYNECOLOGY & OBSTETRICS 1, 17 (2002).

34 MCLAUGHLIN, *supra* note 32, at 115.

35 *Id.*

36 *Id.* at 128; Linda Grant, *A Laboratory of Women*, INDEP., Sept. 19, 1993, at 14.

After successful clinical trials there and in Haiti, the scientists published their results in *Science*, stating unequivocally that progesterone could be used for contraception.[37] Searle, which manufactured the progesterone that Rock and Pincus had used, struggled briefly to decide whether or not to sell progesterone for contraception.[38] But their struggles were short-lived.[39] In 1957, the Food and Drug Administration (FDA) approved Enovid, Searle's first commercial birth control pill, as a treatment for "gynecological disorders." In 1959, Searle returned to the FDA to market Enovid explicitly as a contraceptive, and in 1960 it received the formal approval. By this point, however, an estimated 500,000 women were already using the pill for contraception, taking their cue from information attached to the 1957 drug release, which warned about "possible contraceptive activity."[40]

By 1961, an estimated one million women were using the birth control pill, at a price that had recently fallen from $10 to $7 per month.[41] By 1963, prices had plummeted to $2.90 per month, and a reported 1.75 million American women were using the pill, producing annual revenues for Searle of roughly $61 million.[42] By 1973, just ten years later, the number of users had soared to 10 million and the market – including both the firms that were profiting handsomely from the pill and the consumers who were avidly purchasing it – had triumphed over any remnants of legal and moral opposition.[43]

The Market for IVF

A similar and even more pronounced commercial dynamic surrounded the development of in vitro fertilization, the essential precursor to today's growing range of reproductive options.

37 C.R. Garcia et al., *Effects of Certain 19-Nor Steroids on the Normal Human Menstrual Cycle*, 124 Sci. 891, 892 (1956).

38 McLaughlin, *supra* note 32, at 135–37.

39 *Id.*

40 Bernard Asbell, The Pill: A Biography of a Drug that Changed the World 163–64, 170 (1995); Irwin C. Winter, *Industrial Pressure and the Population Problem—The FDA and the Pill*, 212 J. Am. Med. Ass'n 1067, 1067–68 (1970).

41 *G.D. Searle Reduces Prices of Birth Control Pill to $7 a Month*, Wall St. J., Feb. 9, 1961, at 8.

42 *Birth Control Push*, Wall St. J., Nov. 1, 1963, at 1.

43 Sharon Snider, *The Pill: 30 Years of Safety Concerns*, FDA Consumer, Dec. 1990, at 8.

In 1974, four years before the birth of Louise Brown, the world's first "test tube baby," the U.S. Congress placed a temporary moratorium on the use of federal funds for fetal research.[44] Although no baby had yet been born from IVF, Congress was apparently concerned about what might happen to aborted fetuses in the wake of the Supreme Court's legalization of abortion and thus specifically forbade the federal government to fund any kind of fetal research.[45] Because federal regulations defined the fetus as "the product of conception from implantation until delivery," the funding ban technically extended to research on IVF as well.

In theory, this funding ban could have meant the end of IVF in the United States. Yet, as was the case with contraception, legal restrictions in this area did not, in the end, hamper the development of either IVF technologies or an IVF industry. On the contrary, after the birth of Louise Brown in England, the American IVF industry surged forward, fueled by demand from couples desperate to conceive genetically related children and facilitated by private doctors who were willing to supply them.[46]

In 1980, Drs. Howard Jones and Georgeanna Jones set up the first private IVF clinic in the United States, the Norfolk, Virginia-based Jones Institute for Reproductive Medicine. In December 1981, they helped to produce Elizabeth Jordan Carr, the country's first successful "test-tube baby."[47] By this time, four other U.S. fertility clinics had also begun to offer IVF services.[48] Their prices were not cheap: at the Jones Institute, for example, preliminary screening for IVF treatment cost $1,650 in 1983, and the total cost of an IVF procedure, including nonmedical expenses, was around $7,500.[49] Since

[44] National Research Act, Pub. L. No. 93-348, § 213, 88 Stat. 342 (1974).

[45] Exceptions were made for research designed to protect the fetus itself. *See id.*

[46] As one source explains: "The diffusion is likely to continue during the next 5 years, as judged by the demand of sterile couples and the heightened efficacies reported by established centers." Clifford Grobstein et al., *External Human Fertilization: An Evaluation of Policy*, 222 SCI. 12 (1983). For earlier history of IVF attempts, see generally, Barry D. Bavister, *Early History of in Vitro Fertilization*, 124 REPRODUCTION 181 (2002).

[47] Paul Clancy, *A Special Kind of Mother's Day; "In Vitro" Families Celebrate*, USA TODAY, May 12, 1989, at 3A; Sandy Rovner, *Making Babies: How Science Can Help Infertile Couples*, WASH. POST, Aug. 6, 1986, at 13.

[48] Clancy, *supra* note 47, at 3A; Rovner, *supra* note 47, at 13.

[49] Clifford Grobstein et al., *External Human Fertilization: An Evaluation of Policy*, 222 SCI. 130 (1983). The estimate of $7,500 is for a woman's first attempt at IVF. Subsequent attempts were less expensive: around $5,000.

success rates were quite low, the overall cost for a couple to have a 50 percent chance of delivering a baby via IVF was probably in the range of $38,000.[50]

High prices, however, exerted little downward pressure on demand. Indeed, by 1986, test-tube pregnancies had become nearly routine, and more than two thousand children had been born through this recently vilified method. In 1986, there were more than one hundred clinics in the United States, performing 10,000 cycles of IVF and related technologies each year and generating annual revenues of about $41 million.[51] Sperm donation and embryo donation had become somewhat routine, and even more intricate technologies like surrogacy were starting to emerge.[52] All of this work, meanwhile, was still occurring in the private sector and with wholly private funds.

Today, IVF and related technologies are estimated to generate revenues in the United States of more than $3 billion a year.[53] In 2010, the most recent year for which data are available, there were 443 clinics in the United States, which reported carrying out 147,260 cycles and producing as a result 61,564 babies.[54]

These three examples are not, of course, determinative. But they do suggest that when markets have encountered reproduction in the United States, their operation has tended to expand reproductive options and enable wider access to them. Commercial markets do not have this effect because they care in a normative sense about either reproduction or reproductive rights. Instead, they simply follow the course of commercial activity, generating a supply (in this case, of contraceptive devices, birth control pills, and babies)for those who deeply desire them.

The Problem with Producers

In the reproductive market, therefore, it seems relatively safe to conclude that commercial growth and expanded supply have historically yielded tangible benefits to the ultimate "consumer" - to couples hoping not to conceive,

[50] *Id.* Note that this figure is not adjusted for inflation.
[51] Spar, *supra* note 4, at 32.
[52] Rovner, *supra* note 47, at 13.
[53] Spar, *supra* note 4, at 32–33.
[54] *2010 Assisted Reproductive Technology Success Rates*, Ctr. Disease Control (2010), http://www.cdc.gov/art/ (last visited Dec. 26, 2012).

individuals trying to avoid sexually transmitted diseases, and would-be parents attempting to conceive a child. As the technologies of assisted reproduction advance, it is also becoming increasingly possible for some parents to use the market to produce a particular kind of child, arguably exercising a parental right (or at least an option) to have a child born without Tay-Sachs or cystic fibrosis, for example, or a child whose cord blood can be used to save a dying sibling.[55] In this context, one could easily argue that the market does indeed protect and expand a parent's reproductive rights.

At the same time, though, the exercise or enjoyment of these rights often drags other individuals into the equation, individuals whose rights are both murkier and more vulnerable to exploitation.

Consider, for example, the case of PGD (preimplantation genetic diagnosis). PGD is the pathbreaking technology that allows parents to select an embryo with particular genetic characteristics: one without the Tay-Sachs gene, for example, or with the blood type to match an older, dying child. In this procedure, parents first create several embryos using IVF. Then, when the embryos are at the eight-cell stage (so early, in fact, that they are traditionally not yet even considered embryos), technicians remove a single cell from each embryo and subject it to screens that reveal the genetic makeup of the child that embryo would become. With this intervention, parents who know they are at risk of passing on a genetic mutation to their offspring can instead produce a healthy child. And parents who already have a sick child can – occasionally – conceive a healthy, perfectly matched sibling to serve as a desperately needed donor. In these cases, and they are growing, parents understandably regard PGD as a godsend, a medical miracle that literally saves their children's lives.

Yet even if the "consumers" in this case are wholly enthusiastic supporters of the market for PGD, and even if they feel that their rights have been dramatically expanded by its use, the technology does nevertheless raise questions about the rights of others.

For instance, has the child born from PGD had her human rights compromised in some way as a result of her parents' choice? Will she suffer from having not been born from the same blind conception that defines most humans? And what about other children, whose parents chose not to choose? Are their rights being imposed upon? What about the disabled,

[55] Spar, *supra* note 4, at 97–127.

whose rights could be undermined by others choosing against their inherited traits? These are tough questions, and troubling ones.

Even more troubling is the realization that new types of producers are also being created in the market for reproduction. They are, of course, the "component suppliers": the men who "donate" sperm, the women who "donate" eggs and "lend" wombs. Are their rights being compromised by the reproductive market?

For all of these questions, it is easy to answer yes: yes, human rights are compromised when some humans can choose their children's traits; yes, we hurt disabled individuals by letting other individuals choose against disability; and yes, most strongly, we exploit men and (particularly) women when we allow them to sell their genetic material.[56]

It is not entirely clear, however, that yes is always the appropriate answer. Because how do we know, other than by assertion, that children will feel wronged by having been chosen? We cannot. We could wait until these children grow up, perhaps, and systematically poll their feelings and preferences; we could wait and see whether they, as a group, demonstrate beliefs or behaviors that distinguish them from their peers. But without such analysis it seems foolhardy to assert any wrong on their behalf. After all, a child consciously conceived to be free of Tay-Sachs or cystic fibrosis or sickle cell anemia is not inherently shorn of any rights we typically assign to individuals. Likewise, it is not obvious that a living deaf person is inevitably deprived of his rights if an unrelated couple decides not to give birth to a deaf child. True, if this couple's individual decision were multiplied thousands of times, creating a society where deafness was either exceedingly rare or concentrated among certain groups, then we would need as a society to ensure that the remaining deaf individuals were not deprived of their rights or existing benefits. But again, it is not inevitable that individual choices (even thousands or millions of them) would suffice to eliminate the random mutations that cause deafness or other disabilities, or that a reduced level of these disabilities would cause able-bodied people to behave any differently.

[56] Classic arguments along these lines include GENA COREA, THE MOTHER MACHINE (1977); LEON KASS, TOWARD A MORE NATURAL SCIENCE: BIOLOGY AND HUMAN AFFAIRS 31 (1985); MARGARET JANE RADIN, CONTESTED COMMODITIES: THE TROUBLE WITH TRADE IN SEX, CHILDREN, BODY PARTS AND OTHER THINGS 139 (1996); Michael Sandel, *The Baby Bazaar*, NEW REPUBLIC, Oct. 20, 1997, at 25.

We are left, therefore, with the most vexing question to emerge from the reproductive market – the question of whether or not the sale of reproductive components (eggs, sperm, womb, and embryos) constitutes exploitation, or at least commodification, of the sellers. Most observers of this field have argued that it does: that selling body parts, and particularly eggs and wombs, places the sellers (young women) in a relationship that is inevitably exploitative; that, as Margaret Jane Radin has famously argued, "conceiving of any child in market rhetoric wrongs personhood."[57] Yet it is not clear why this relationship necessarily holds, nor why elements of commodification – paying a price for things of value – are inherently wrong. Does paying for eggs demean the egg donors or the children born as a result? Maybe, in some cases. Do surrogate mothers or sperm donors lose dignity in some way that even they cannot identify? We simply do not know. Yes, a handful of surrogate mothers have subsequently regretted their experience and rallied against the practice. A tiny number of sperm donors have sought to discover the children they sired. But in the vast majority of cases, surrogates and egg and sperm donors seem either pleased with their contribution or emotionally unaffected.[58] By what right can we claim degradation on their behalf?

Moreover, since discussions of commodification are inherently subjective and ill-defined (just what is a commodity, after all? And how can we tell when it is bad?), the debate over reproductive components might more usefully be framed in terms of more objective and practical considerations. We could begin, for example, with a basic evaluation of safety, examining whether any given procedure is safe for the donor, the prospective parents, and the imagined child. If the procedure is not safe for the donor, or if it exposes her to any long-term risk, then donation, whether paid or not, clearly compromises the donor's human rights. This seems a simpler calculation than commodification, and also a more immediately important one.

[57] RADIN, *supra* note 56, at 139.

[58] For surrogates, see HELENA RAGONE, SURROGATE MOTHERHOOD: CONCEPTION IN THE HEART (1994); Lori Andrews, *Beyond Doctrinal Boundaries: A Legal Framework for Surrogate Motherhood*, 81 VA. L. REV. 2343 (1995). For sperm donors, see DAVID PLOTZ, THE GENIUS FACTORY: THE CURIOUS HISTORY OF THE NOBEL PRIZE SPERM BANK (2005); K. Daniels et al., *Short Communication: Previous Semen Donors and their Views Regarding the Sharing of Information with Offspring*, 20 HUMAN REPRODUCTION 1670 (2005); David Plotz, *No Nobels, One "Failure," a Few Regrets*, Mar. 30, 2001, http://www.

Next we should ask whether the donor is being coerced in any way: by money or praise, doctors or relatives, glossy pamphlets or a lack of information. If the donor is being coerced, then the transaction is unfair and would arguably constitute a violation of the donor's rights. But if it is not, and if the donor is willingly and knowingly entering into a contractual relationship, then it is not clear that this contract necessarily constitutes exploitation.

And finally we need to think about the relationship between the donor and the child. Too often, reproductive markets and the debates around them concentrate only on the relationship between donor and prospective parent, or between the would-be parents and the still unconceived child. We need to broaden this discussion to consider the born child, and particularly the child who becomes an adult. What rights do they have in this process, and what relationship will they want to maintain with the donors who provided raw material for their birth? Recent revelations by the grown children of sperm donors suggest that they want far more than their parents - contractual, social, and genetic - ever imagined.[59] Any discussion of rights, therefore, must include theirs as well.

The Role of the State

Occasionally, economists and others make the unfortunate mistake of assuming that markets exist in a vacuum, and that the only role of governments is to collect taxes and get in the way of business.

Clearly, though, that assumption is totally misplaced, and wrong in ways that are directly relevant to the topic at hand, because of course no one is arguing - or for sure this chapter is not arguing - that the reproductive market should exist without regulation. On the contrary, all markets, even ostensibly free and competitive markets, are regulated to some extent by government, and it seems obvious, given the sensitivities and social implications involved, that the reproductive market is particularly in need of firm if flexible rules.

If, for instance, a given society thinks that gender selection is bad, then they can simply ban that piece of the reproductive market or subject it to

slate.com/articles/life/seed/2001/03/no_nobels_one_failure_a_few_regrets.html (last accessed Dec. 26, 2012).

[59] Voices of Donor Conception—Behind Closed Doors: Moving Beyond Secrecy and Shame (Mikki Morrissette, ed., 2006).

some kind of queuing system. If people think that certain reproductive options – mitochondrial transfer, for example, or reproductive cloning – are too dangerous, they can prohibit them. Conversely, if people believe that other techniques – like IVF – are socially or individually beneficial, they can choose to subsidize them, as is already the case in countries such as Denmark and Israel.

Which brings us around to where we began, with a plea for the impartiality of markets. On their own and in the aggregate, markets remain wholly aloof from both rights and reproduction. They do not exist to protect rights and have no natural mechanism by which to consider them. Yet both theory and history appear to suggest that markets can indeed advance reproductive rights, largely by expanding the range of reproductive options available to individuals and by granting them access to these options through the mechanical operation of supply and demand.

But markets do not operate in a vacuum, and they can never be the only source of protection for rights, since any movement that they make in this direction happens only as an accident of their normal, profit-maximizing behavior. In the end, therefore, the only market that can fully protect reproductive rights is one that combines commercial forces with the tempering hand of government regulation.

2 Exploitation and Choice in the Global Egg Trade

Emotive Terminology or Necessary Critique?

Donna Dickenson

Introduction: Can't Regulate, Won't Regulate?

As the global trade in human eggs continues to expand with logarithmic momentum, it is frequently argued that we could not regulate it even if we wanted to. Not all commentators do want to, of course. Many view regulation as counterproductive: reports have suggested that FDA governance has had the perverse effect of increasing levels of reproductive tourism by *estadounidenses* to Latin America.[1] Most of the other chapters in this volume are broadly in favor of letting market forces take their course, with varying degrees of control. In the previous chapter, for example, Debora Spar asserts that market transactions serve the all-important function of enhancing reproductive freedom.

Later in this chapter, I will examine whether reproductive freedom and choice really are all-important. Before I begin that analysis, however, I need to clear away the argument that we cannot control black markets in human body parts, including eggs, even if we want to. This argument is common to commentators from many positions in the political spectrum. Some writers assert that "baby markets," comprising egg sale, surrogacy, and paid adoption, are so firmly established that prohibiting or regulating them

[1] *Clinics Offer Discount for Women Guinea Pigs*, Bio Edge 108, Jan. 16, 2004, *available at* http://www.australasianbioethics.org/Newsletters/108-2004-01-16.html#clinics; *Reproductive Tourism Springs Up as FDA Sets Limits*, Bio Edge 108, Jan. 16, 2004, *available at* http://www.australasianbioethics.org/Newsletters/108-2004-01-16.html#reproductive; see also Elise Smith et al., *Reproductive Tourism in Argentina: Clinic Accreditation and its Implications for Consumers, Health Professionals and Policy Makers*, 10 Developing World Bioethics 59 (2010).

salves our collective conscience but amounts to no more than hypocritical pretense.[2] Other commentators claim that the burgeoning demand for eggs simply makes even an honest attempt to ban markets unrealistic[3] or imply that the natural and laudable desire for "procreative liberty" would inevitably drive couples to defy paternalistic legal bans.[4] On any of these accounts, regulating global markets in human tissue is said to be a lost cause.

Although those who rely on the argument from impossibility of regulation frequently claim to be pragmatic,[5] this style of argument actually contradicts common sense and legal precedent. Regulating murder is also a lost cause: people will no doubt continue to kill each other under any legal system - at least, they always have so far - but we do not generally consider that to be a valid argument for abolishing criminal laws against homicide.

Underneath the supposedly empirical and practical argument from impossibility of regulation lies a value judgment: while we can (almost) all agree that it is important to have laws against murder, even though legislation will never prevent all killings, we do not agree on the value of laws regulating black markets in eggs and other forms of human tissue. "Can't regulate" is actually a covert expression for "won't regulate."

Those who argue in favor of markets in tissue are correct, however, when they note that in most jurisdictions, only donors are expected to act altruistically, while brokers and corporations are permitted to make profits from trade in tissue. But from the argument that only donors are expected to act altruistically - what I call the argument from one-way altruism - we could move in one of two directions. The usual move is to conclude that the imbalance requires that *no one* should be expected to act

[2] Kimberly D. Krawiec, *Price and Pretense in the Baby Market, in* BABY MARKETS: MONEY AND THE NEW POLITICS OF CREATING FAMILIES 41 (Michele Bratcher Goodwin ed., 2010).

[3] David B. Resnik, *Regulating the Market for Human Eggs* 15 BIOETHICS 1 (2001).

[4] John A. Robertson, *Embryos, Families, and Procreative Liberty: The Legal Structure of the New Reproduction*, 59 S. CAL. L. REV. 939 (1985).

[5] Sonia Sutter, *Giving In to Baby Markets, in* BABY MARKETS: MONEY AND THE NEW POLITICS OF CREATING FAMILIES 278 (Michele Bratcher Goodwin ed., 2010); Guido Pennings, Difficulties in the Development of Legislation and Guidelines for Using Human Reproductive Tissues, Paper Presented at the PEALS 12th Annual Symposium on The Uses of Human Reproductive Tissue in Research and Treatment: Principles and Practice, Newcastle, UK, Feb. 23, 2011.

altruistically.[6] But it is equally possible to derive the conclusion that *everyone* should be expected to act altruistically, if justice is to be served.

Another way of putting this crucial point is to note that the usual conclusion from the one-way altruism argument suffers from what philosophers call the naturalistic fallacy, an illicit move from *is* to *should*. The empirical fact that the market in tissue *is not* purely altruistic does not entail the normative conclusion that it *should not* be altruistic. Neither does it entail the conclusion that it *should* be altruistic. The facts of the situation are not sufficient in themselves to determine the moral and political turn of the argument. Rather, we have to develop specifically ethical arguments, as I intend to do in the rest of this chapter by analyzing the two contrasting concepts of exploitation and choice.

Because it is not sufficient to say that markets should not be altruistic merely because they are not now altruistic, the argument from one-way altruism actually has to fall back on further implicit premises: for example, the assertion that it is impractical to run a system in which everyone is expected to be altruistic, or the claim that markets will inevitably undermine a not-for-profit system. But despite the adage to the contrary, markets can be "bucked." Kieran Healy, himself an advocate of limited organ markets, describes the shift in the U.S. blood donation system from the largely market-centered model described in Richard Titmuss's *The Gift Relationship* to a system that incorporates considerable altruism.[7]

France, which has consistently banned the sale of eggs from the earliest days of its bioethics legislation, renewed the prohibition against markets in oocytes in the latest revision of the laws, completed in June 2011. While the concepts underpinning the French model of regulation also have their provenance in Western political philosophy, like the laissez-faire liberalism and utilitarianism that dominate U.S. and UK debate, they embody a very different set of social attitudes and suggest that there is indeed a politically viable alternative to letting the market decide.

Although France also faces a problem of reproductive tourism, together with a shortage – estimated by the Agence de la Biomédecine (Biomedicine

[6] I take this to be Michele Goodwin's style of argument in BLACK MARKETS: THE SUPPLY AND DEMAND OF BODY PARTS 18 (2006).

[7] KIERAN HEALY, LAST BEST GIFTS: ALTRUISM AND THE MARKET FOR HUMAN ORGANS (2006); RICHARD TITMUSS, THE GIFT RELATIONSHIP: FROM HUMAN BLOOD TO SOCIAL POLICY (Ann Oakley & J. Ashton eds., 1997).

Agency) – of about seven hundred egg donors a year, the French were more concerned about medical risks to and exploitation of donors if markets were permitted. Nor is this policy merely paternalistic. It reflects genuine popular concern, evident in the two-day deliberations of a people's panel that debated questions about reproductive medicine. The group condemned any attempt to pay for eggs or sperm, consistently with the long-standing recommendations of the French National Ethics Committee – indicating that distrust of the market is not just the opinion of a metropolitan elite, but rather a widespread view.[8] Commercial surrogacy will also continue to be prohibited, along with private umbilical cord blood banking – the latter on the grounds that it takes away a valuable resource from the public banks, undermines solidarity, and risks exploitation of parents at a vulnerable time.[9]

That the French use the term "exploitation" without embarrassment is indicative, as is the marked absence of the words "autonomy," "choice," and "procreative liberty" from their debates. While we in the Anglophone world tend to view "exploitation" as emotive terminology, I want to examine the premise that if properly elucidated, it offers a necessary critique of the global egg trade.[10] Conversely, I will argue, "reproductive autonomy" and "choice" are not the knockdown arguments that many commentators assume they are. Indeed, if anything deserves to be called emotive terminology, it is the blind and unthinking rhetoric of choice.

Exploitation: Disparity, Dignity and Degradation

Given the particular economic and historical context in the United States, it is unsurprising that the debate on payment for eggs has already coalesced

[8] La synthèse de PresseGénéthique, Mar. 26, 2010, *available at* http://www.genethique.org/revues/revues/2010/Mars/20100326.1.asp (accessed July 4, 2010); Comité Consultatif National d'Éthique (CCNE), Opinion No. 21: *That the Human Body Should Not Be Used for Commercial Purposes* (1990).

[9] This discussion summarizes a lengthier treatment in my article, *Regulating (or Not) Reproductive Medicine: An Alternative to Letting the Market Decide*, 8 Indian J. Med. Ethics 175 (2011).

[10] Some of these arguments about exploitation were originally developed in collaboration with Heather Widows, although we have each published their results separately: Donna Dickenson, Bioethics: All That Matters 20 (2012) and in this current chapter; Heather Widdows, *Border Disputes Across Bodies: Exploitation in Trafficking for Prostitution and Egg Sale for Stem Cell Research*, 2 Int'l J. Feminist Approaches to Bioethics 5 (2009)

there into the question of "how much to pay," with "whether to pay" attracting almost exclusively affirmative votes - as in the present volume.[11] As we have already seen, the French take a different view, while the Indian activist group SAMA insists that "the practice of egg donation should not be legalized, as it has the potential to run like a market, leading to exploitation of women at cost price."[12] Yet when everyone else is making a profit from women's tissue, as some U.S. commentators assert,[13] is it not exploitative to expect them to undergo the laborious and risky procedures in egg donation out of pure altruism? After all, as I have pointed out elsewhere, one-way altruism is better known as exploitation, even when clumsily camouflaged by the language of gift.[14]

This argument from one-way altruism does have the merit of recognizing that what women do in providing eggs is a form of purposeful labor, performed under potentially hazardous circumstances, and not merely a natural bodily function. It is certainly an improvement on the view expressed in a *Nature* editorial that a human egg has no value "when it is just one of those ovulated each month by billions of women and that [*sic*] perish unfertilized."[15] That is not how eggs are provided for IVF - through a process estimated to take sixty hours, comprising the three stages of ovarian function suppression, ovarian hyperstimulation, and egg extraction under anesthetic - as anyone writing an editorial for *Nature* really ought to know.

As purposeful work involving a certain level of risk, this labor could justifiably confer a property right,[16] although not necessarily a right to

[11] Josephine Johnston, *Paying Egg Donors: Exploring the Arguments*, 36 Hastings Ctr. Rep. 28 (2006), Charis Thompson, *Why We Should, in Fact, Pay for Egg Donation* 2 Regenerative Med. 203 (2007).

[12] SAMA Resource Group for Women and Health, *Response to Human Fertilisation and Embryology Authority Consultation* on Donating Eggs for Research: Safeguarding Donors (2007).

[13] Debora Spar, The Baby Business: How Money, Science, and Politics Drive the Commerce of Conception (2006); Bonnie Steinbock, *Payment for Egg Donation and Surrogacy*, 71 Mt. Sinai J. Med. 55 (2004).

[14] Donna Dickenson, Body Shopping: Converting Body Parts to Profits 161 (2009); Donna Dickenson, *Commodification of Human Tissue: Implications for Feminist and Development Ethics*, 2 Developing World Bioethics 55 (2002).

[15] Editorial, *Safeguards for Donors*, 442 Nature 7102 (2006).

[16] Donna Dickenson, Property, In the Body: Feminist Perspectives (2007); Donna Dickenson, Property, Women and Politics: Subjects or Objects? (1997)

compensation. Compensation is only one aspect of the "bundle" of rights that constitute property in jurisprudential terms.[17] In my view, and in the expressed view of plaintiffs in crucial cases such as *Moore*[18] and *Greenberg*,[19] the right to control the uses of the object of property is more important in issues of property in the body than compensation. I will not discuss this argument at greater length here, however, since I have done so frequently elsewhere.[20]

Although some of its advocates might not recognize its parentage, the argument from one-way altruism is actually descended from the Marxist concept of exploitation as *disparity* of compensation. In the classic Marxist analysis of exploitation, there is an external standard of disparity that overrides subjective interpretations, including those of the workers themselves (so that it is entirely possible for someone to be exploited even if she denies it). That standard famously has to do with the imbalance, extracted under conditions of subordination, between the labor value invested in producing an object by the worker and the price the worker is paid for his labor. (It is always *his* labor in Marx; only the male worker has the ironic liberty of selling his labor freely in the first place, whereas women's reproductive labor is not recognized *as* labor.)[21] Where there is an objective disparity between the surplus value added by the worker's labor and the wages paid to him, exploitation can be said to exist. Substitute "her" for "him," and the parallel to the argument about egg sellers being exploited when they donate altruistically becomes evident.

Just as early capitalism and its agricultural revolution predecessor were funded by the accumulation of value in labor and land taken from underpaid industrial workers and displaced peasants, so modern commercial biotechnology can be seen as underpinned by systematic and exploitative underpayment of the women who provide the crucial "components" and labor of artificial reproduction. This systematic transfer of surplus value

[17] A. M. Honoré, *Ownership*, *in* Making Law Bind: Essays Legal and Philosophical 161 (1987), originally published in Oxford Essays in Jurisprudence (Anthony Gordon Guest eds., 1961).

[18] Moore v. Regents of Univ. Cal., 793 P.2d. 479 (Cal. 1990).

[19] Greenberg v. Miami Children's Hosp. Research Inst., Inc., 264 F. Supp. 2d 1064 (2003).

[20] *See, e.g.*, Dickenson, *supra* note 14, at 205–17.

[21] Carole Pateman, The Sexual Contract (1988); Susan Dodds, *Women, Commodification, and Stem-Cell Research*, *in* Biomedical Ethics Reviews: Stem Cell Research 149 (James Humber & Robert F. Almeder eds., 2003)

on a global scale is bolstered by neoliberal governmental policies, in the view of the sociologists Catherine Waldby and Melinda Cooper: "What neo-liberalism seeks to make available is not merely a permanent surplus of labour power but also a surplus of reproductivity – a reserve of low-cost suppliers of reproductive services and tissues who perform unacknowledged reproductive labour within the lowest echelon of the bioeconomy."[22] Although this analysis may not seem so applicable in the United States, where professional-class college-student egg sellers may command substantial prices,[23] it does fit the phenomenon of "reproductive tourism" across borders: for example, the much lower payments made by international brokers to Eastern European and Latin American women on behalf of their Western European and North American clients. This updated version of the Marxist "reserve army of labor" thesis involves what Waldby and Cooper call "the purchase of fertility from poor women in the developing world."

A modern non-Marxist variant of this objective standard of exploitation is offered by Alan Wertheimer,[24] for whom exploitation essentially means extracting a nonstandard price, from either buyers of goods or sellers of labor. In biotechnology markets, however, there are as yet few if any standard prices. The markets are still too "undeveloped," and the amounts buyers are willing to pay too variable – particularly in the highly differentiated U.S. egg markets, where subjective preferences in hair color, musicality, and athleticism all factor into the price that buyers are willing to pay, despite substantial uncertainty about heritability of these phenotypical traits. But there are also deep difficulties in determining what a standard or just price ought to be, which go beyond the mere newness of markets in tissue.

Viewing exploitation as disparity between the price of the labor put into a product and the price for which it is sold rests on the labor theory of value, usually attributed to Marx but originally derived from Locke. In this view, it is "mixing one's labor" with the raw material that endows a product with

[22] Catherine Waldby & Melinda Cooper, *The Biopolitics of Reproduction: Post-Fordist Biotechnology and Women's Clinical Labor*, 23 Austl. Feminist Stud. 57(2008).

[23] Susan Weidman Schneider reported amounts of up to $50,000 per cycle. Susan Weidman Schneider, *Jewish Women's Eggs: A Hot Commodity in the IVF Marketplace*, 26 Lilith 22 (2001).

[24] Alan Wertheimer, Exploitation (1996).

value and gives the laborer title to it. The person in whom the natural property right is vested is primarily the person who has put work into it, particularly in the agricultural model used by Locke. But as Kieran Healy points out, exploitation under capitalism is masked because "capitalist markets lead people to believe that commodities possess value in their own right, rather than because of the social labor that goes into producing them. This is commodity fetishism."[25] Injustice and exploitation in other economic systems, Healy argues, at least have the merit of being obvious (unless obscured by religious precepts, perhaps – as in the hymn words "The rich man in his castle / The poor man at his gate / God made them high and lowly / And ordered their estate.") But because under capitalism people are primarily linked through the exchange of goods for money, they lose sight of the original source of value of the goods they purchase.

This sets up a major difficulty in establishing a just or fair price for human tissue, which, I would add, is exacerbated in the case of female tissue. Frequently there is little or no recognition that women's tissue is even involved in biotechnological processes, and even less awareness that women have labored to create the "product." When Hwang Woo Suk falsely claimed to have created tissue-matched stem cell lines using the somatic cell nuclear transfer (SCNT) process, which requires human ova in large quantities,[26] I, along with other feminists, was struck by the absence of discussion about how many women's eggs were used – more than twenty-two hundred, as it turned out. Many commentators made no inquiries about where the ova might have come from; others showed no awareness that ova were required at all. I call this phenomenon "the lady vanishes": what women do in the process escapes attention.[27]

Another difficulty in establishing a "fair" price for tissue, if any price is fair, is the muddiness of the distinction in tissue markets between objects external to ourselves and that which is a part of us. Modern biotechnology has blurred the line between things external and things internal. Mechanical

[25] Healy, *supra* note 7, at 4. For Marx's own analysis, see *The Fetishism of Commodities and the Secret Thereof, in* 1 Capital § 4 (1867).

[26] Woo-Suk Hwang et al., *Patient-Specific Embryonic Stem Cell Lines Derived from Human SCNT Blastocysts,* 308 Sci. 1777 (2005); Woo-Suk Hwang et al., *Evidence of a Pluripotent Human Stem Cell Line Derived from a Cloned Blastocyst,* 303 Sci. 1669 (2004).

[27] Donna Dickenson, *The Lady Vanishes: What's Missing from the Stem Cell Debate,* 3 J. Bioethical Inquiry 45 (2006).

ventilators or pacemakers can be incorporated from outside into our bodies, while parts of our bodies, such as deoxyribonucleaic acid (DNA) swabs or blood, may be removed from us and disaggregated.[28] The extent to which separated tissue continues to be "us" varies from our general feeling that we are not our nail clippings to the ongoing identification with the tissue and its recipient that has been reported by many living organ donors (and sometimes purposefully consolidated through donor-recipient reunions or other mechanisms designed to raise donation rates).[29] Likewise, egg donors and "surrogate" mothers often report having been encouraged by brokers to feel that they would be part of the recipients' families.[30]

Only objects separate from the self can be objectified or commodified, as Margaret Radin has pointed out[31] – in a distinction that goes back to Kant and Hegel, although it also influenced Marx. But we have not yet reached agreement on what tissues are genuinely separate from the self, if any. After the Alder Hey scandal in the United Kingdom, when a pathologist retained large numbers of tissue samples from dead children without their parents' consent, the Retained Organs Commission was set up to provide models of governance for tissue collections. Although the original revulsion against the pathologist's actions centered on the retention of an entire brain from an eleven-year-old, the commission found itself bogged down in questions about whether even tissue blocks and slides retained the identity of the donor. Scientists and pathologists complained, understandably enough, that they would be unable to perform their work if such a strict standard prevailed, but bereaved parents and other members of the public wanted to hold out against a "slippery slope" approach that might have resulted in another Alder Hey.

Marx also distinguished between attributing "use value" to something, *objectifying* it, and additionally making it an object of exchange,

[28] Catherine Waldby & Robert Mitchell, Tissue Economies: Blood, Organs and Cell Lines in Late Capitalism (2006).

[29] See Diane Tober, *Semen as Gifts, Semen as Goods: Reproductive Workers and the Market in Altruism*, 7 Body & Soc'y 137 (2001), which includes a discussion of imagined relationships between egg donors and egg recipients, as well as of the much more instrumental motivations of sperm donors; *see also* Helena Ragone, Surrogate Motherhood: Conception in the Heart (1996).

[30] Healy, *supra* note 14, at 33.

[31] Margaret J. Radin, Contested Commodities: The Trouble with Trade in Sex, Body Parts, and Other Things 34 (1996).

commodifying it. Objectification is just the process by which something external to ourselves is made to satisfy our wants and needs, which is not inherently wrong: merely necessary to sustain life. Although some analysts contend that Marx viewed commodification, by contrast, as wrong in itself, others assert that neither objectification nor commodification is intrinsically malign in Marx or anywhere else.[32] What is wrong is making a salable object of something that should be treated as having value in itself, irrespective of what use might be made of it. While the factory goods that were Marx's primary focus do not generally have such value in themselves – only insofar as they satisfy human needs – human beings (and possibly their body parts) do. This consideration leads naturally into a second potential meaning of exploitation, concerned with *dignity* rather than disparity.

Unless I conceive of my body and its tissues purely instrumentally, as radically exterior to me – a position that Marx might well term alienated – there are objections to my selling my tissues that have little or nothing to do with whether I am offered a price for them that fairly reflects the labor I have put into providing them. If I sell my eggs or my kidney, then I am objectifying those parts of my body and additionally commodifying them, turning them into objects of trade. The argument from human dignity might well be concerned at the diminution of self-worth that the process of commodification entails. This concern would not necessarily extend to objectification alone: giving away these tissues could be permissible, even meritorious – but only if the gift is genuine. In commercial egg economies, sellers may profess altruism to increase their chances of success in a competitive buyer's market[33] but are usually motivated mainly by monetary gain, while "the gift of life" has become merely a marketing concept.[34]

Another way of stating the objection from dignity is to ask the prior question of whether bodies and their parts are the sorts of things that have value

[32] Carolyn McLeod & Francoise Baylis, *Feminists on the Inalienability of Human Embryos* 21 HYPATIA 1 (2006).

[33] Laura Crimaldi, *Stalled Economy Fertile Ground for Baby Business*, BOS. HERALD, Jan. 25, 2009.

[34] Financial motivations were found to be paramount for egg providers in Andrea M. Braverman, *Exploring Ovum Donors' Motivations and Needs*, 1 AM. J. BIOETHICS 16 (2001). *See also* Karla Momberger, *Breeder at Law*, 11 COLUM. J. GENDER & L. 127 (2002) (describing the way she negotiated with several egg brokerage agencies to obtain the highest price). For the idea that the gift of life has become a marketing concept, see GOODWIN, BLACK MARKETS, *supra* note 6, at 25.

in themselves, beyond the realm of commerce. If human tissue cannot be turned into a commodity without harming people's worth as persons, then *any* form of tissue sale, including but not exclusive to female tissue such as eggs, is in a sense exploitative, *whatever price is offered for it*. This position is actually more Kantian than Marxist: it is consistent with the particular formulation of the categorical imperative that insists that we must never treat others merely as means. It is inherently degrading to human beings, as subjects who have dignity and value in themselves, to be treated as commodities, because commodities are mere means. An extended Marxist account like Waldby and Cooper's begins from the disparity perspective but also implicitly incorporates the Kantian affront to dignity involved in failing to acknowledge women's reproductive labor.

It is interesting to speculate whether when people deny that they are being exploited, even in the face of a huge disparity between what they put in and what they get out, they are actually asserting their dignity against perceived assault. If so, then they are interpreting exploitation as an affront to dignity and thus concentrating on this second meaning of the concept. In Robert Tressell's iconic novel of the skilled British working class, *The Ragged-Trousered Philanthropists*,[35] the protagonist, Frank Owen, is constantly running up against his workmates' fierce antipathy to the notion that they are being exploited. Although Owen sets out in clear monetary terms the way in which the workers are actually subsidizing their employer, Mr. Sweater, through accepting wages that do not reflect anything like the value of the work they put into the finished product – hence their ironic title of "philanthropists" – they refuse to accept that their situation could be bettered. Their passivity arises neither from religious fervor, for the most part, nor from active support of the "sweating" system. It simply seems their last resort, in the face of continual assaults on their dignity, is to assert that this very dignity requires them to accept their lot.

Similarly, a UK study of women enrolled in an "egg-sharing" program to obtain IVF at a reduced price found that they typically rejected the language of exploitation, even though they candidly described themselves as "desperate."[36] Because there is widespread noncompliance with the

[35] Robert Tressell, The Ragged Trousered Philanthropists (Peter Miles ed., 2005).

[36] Erica Haimes & Ken Taylor, An Investigation of Women's Experiences of an IVF Egg-Sharing Scheme for Somatic Cell Nuclear Transfer Research, paper presented at

official National Institute of Health and Clinical Excellence recommendation that infertile couples should receive three free cycles of treatment on the National Health Service, these women had no other means of obtaining IVF at a price they could afford except by part-exchanging their eggs. They professed a sense of free choice, yet insisted that they did not want to give up any of their eggs. Some admitted that they were being exploited but accepted the situation anyway. Perhaps by asserting their freedom of choice, they were reclaiming a sense of agency and dignity that was denied by the objectively exploitative facts of their situation.

Another modern interpretation of exploitation links disparity and dignity through the additional concept of degradation. Ruth Sample defines exploitation as the act of reaping unfair benefit from conditions that fail to recognize the inherent worth of another, and that thereby degrade the other.[37] This definition, Sample asserts, is consistent with some aspects of Marx's account but is more "moralized." Whereas some Marxists, according to Sample, regard exploitation as a relatively "thin" technical concept, her own definition, she claims, is a "thick" moral concept. Here she appears to agree with the assessment that Marx does not regard commodification as inherently good or bad. Similarly, even exploitation seems inherently neutral in Marx[38] until the element of coercion enters in, when choices are forced upon us when our options are illegitimately narrowed.[39]

The additional concept of degradation helps to capture the demeaning nature of exploitation and enables us to understand responses like that of an Indian "surrogate" mother who denied she was being exploited because her contract pregnancy was far better than her normal job, crushing glass for fifteen hours a day.[40] Crushing glass for fifteen hours a day is exploitation, but that does not itself make "surrogacy" exploitation-free. Yet compared to such bone-breaking and demeaning labor, contract pregnancy may well appear less exploitative not merely in monetary terms, but also in

the PEALS 12th Annual Symposium on The Uses of Human Reproductive Tissue in Research and Treatment: Principles and Practice, Newcastle, UK, Feb. 23, 2011.

37 Ruth Sample, Exploitation: What It Is and Why It's Wrong (2003).

38 Steven Lukes, Marxism and Morality (1993).

39 Sample, *supra* note 37, at 6.

40 Abigail Howarth, *Surrogate Mothers—A Womb for Rent*, Marie Claire, July 29, 2007(describing a woman Howarth interviewed).

the apparent absence of degradation in the eyes of an Indian woman, particularly when caste is taken into account. Polluting work like glass crushing or carrying construction rubbish is typically assigned to members of the Dalit caste (formerly known as untouchables). From a Western viewpoint, however, the conditions of surrogacy in India may appear very degrading indeed. A widely quoted report on a clinic in Gujarat claimed that the women were effectively imprisoned for nine months, only permitted to leave the premises for hospital checkups, and confined to an upper-floor room lined with eight to ten single iron bedsteads, with barely enough room to walk between them.[41]

Degradation is a far more subjective concept than the objective Marxist criterion of exploitation in terms of disparity of value, yet it does seem necessary to count it into the mix in order to explain responses like that of the Indian "surrogate" mother. Where the difference between the price of the baby paid by the commissioning couple and the wages paid to the "surrogate" is as great as it can be in India,[42] exploitation is obvious to the eye of the beholder, yet because the conditions of her labor are less degrading than her literal daily grind, the Indian "surrogate" denies that she is being exploited.

As Heather Widdows argues, however, it is extremely exploitative, even coercive, to take advantage of someone's lack of other choices for keeping body and soul together.[43] It is important to retain the elements of power, coercion, and subordination in any definition of exploitation. A definition of exploitation that focuses only on disparity of remuneration overlooks those phenomena. Particularly for feminists, and where women's eggs are concerned, this point is crucial. Carole Pateman continues to insist, as she has done since publishing *The Sexual Contract* in 1988, that exploitation can

[41] Amrita Pande, *Commercial Surrogacy in India: Manufacturing a Perfect Mother-Worker*, 35 SIGNS: J. WOMEN IN CULTURE & SOC'Y 965 (2010). I have put the term "surrogate" in quotation marks throughout this chapter because it implies that the woman who gives birth is not the real mother, which is contrary to the common law position.

[42] The film *Made in India* depicts a situation in which the American commissioning couple are told that the Indian "surrogate" is receiving $7,000, in addition to the fee they are paying to the agency, while she tells the filmmakers that she is only receiving $2,000.

[43] Heather Widdows, Ethics and Global Governance: The Poverty of Choice, Professorial Inaugural Lecture at the University of Birmingham (Mar. 24, 2011) [hereinafter Widdows, Ethics and Global Governance].

only be considered in the context of gender subordination.[44] Subordination is the relationship that makes exploitation possible, she argues, a point that Marx tends to ignore by putting exploitation first in his analysis.

Too often, I would add, the concept of payment is used to close down the discussion before gender subordination and exploitation can be considered – on the naïve and simplistic grounds that if women have chosen to accept payment, then their choice must be regarded as free. In the global egg trade, gender subordination masquerades as free choice, and it is to the inadequacy of the language of choice that I shall now turn.

Choice, Autonomy, and Reproductive Freedom: The Idols of the Marketplace

In his *Novum Organum* the philosopher Francis Bacon introduced the metaphor of four idols, which represent fixations of the mind: concepts unthinkingly venerated beyond their due.[45] Until we purge our thought of such fixations, he argued, we cannot analyze conceptually or progress scientifically. Among his four idols – of the tribe, the cave, the theatre, and the marketplace – the idols of the marketplace represent concepts and words that have come to be endowed with a false significance because they facilitate easy exchange of ideas. Where the idols of the marketplace dominate, people substitute words for thought and feel that they have won an argument when they have used the sacred mantras to most telling effect. In this section I want to argue that in much modern bioethics, choice, autonomy, and reproductive freedom have degenerated into idols of the marketplace – both in Bacon's original sense and in the way that they are used to justify free markets in human tissue.

When philosophers, lawyers, and policy makers try to outflank each other by deploying supposedly knockdown arguments based on free choice, autonomy, and reproductive freedom, Bacon's idols of the marketplace are receiving their libations and sacrifices. There are many examples of this style of argument; here is one from Julian Savulescu: "To ban a market in organs is paradoxically to constrain what people can do with their own lives."[46] Constraining choice is intended to be utter anathema in this argument, so

[44] Carole Pateman & Charles Mills, Contract and Domination 201 (2007).
[45] Francis Bacon, The Advancement of Learning and New Atlantis (1974).
[46] Julian Savulescu, *Is the Sale of Body Parts Wrong?*, 16 J. Med. Ethics 117 (2003).

that there is nothing more to say – although it might be objected that even that prophet of liberty, John Stuart Mill, recognized that there have to be some constraints on what I as an individual am allowed to do, in order to prevent trespassing on others' right to manage their own lives. The narrowly individualistic conception of "reproductive freedom" is particularly blind to the rights of others, as if the human race reproduced by parthenogenesis.

Another example of the attempt to use choice as a knockdown argument can be found in the 2007 announcement from the UK Human Fertilisation and Embryology Authority (HFEA) that after a public consultation, it was reversing its previous position and allowing women to donate eggs for stem cell research. "Given that the medical risks for donating for research are no higher than for treatment, we have concluded that it is not for us to remove a woman's choice of how her donated eggs should be used."[47] Given that the consultation document had been titled *Donating Eggs for Research: Protecting Donors*, not *Donating Eggs for Research: Should It Be Permitted?*, the HFEA seemed to have made its own choice already. What was driving the demand for eggs was not lengthy queues of women demanding the right to donate for research as well as IVF: even after the announcement, women chose to stay away in droves.

Not only is the use of free choice as a knockdown argument philosophically and politically dubious: it also constrains free debate, ironically enough. As Heather Widdows puts it:

> As a result it becomes impossible to critique any practice if someone – anyone – has chosen it – as to do this is apparently to deny and undermine someone's autonomy. Not surprisingly ethicists have often given up on wider critiques and simply sought to ensure that choice is as informed and genuine as possible. It is this silencing and "trumping" which is so destructive in the choice model.... The consent model reduces all ethics to choice and silences and trumps other ethical concerns. This does not protect the individual, but leaves him or her vulnerable and open to exploitation.[48]

[47] *HFEA Statement on Donating Eggs for Research*, Feb. 21, 2007, *available at* http://www.hfea.gov.uk/471.html. The argument about comparative risks was disproved almost immediately after the announcement when a *Lancet* article offered convincing evidence that the best standard of IVF treatment should not need to involve doses of hormones at the levels routinely used to provide eggs for research. Esther Heijnen et al., *A Mild Treatment Strategy for in-Virto Fertilisation: A Randomised Non-Inferiority Trial*, 369 LANCET 743 (2007).

[48] Widdows, Ethics and Global Governance, *supra* note 43.

Of course, the emphasis on respecting individual choice was foundational to liberalism: as Mill enunciated it in *On Liberty* and *On the Subjection of Women,* it was an instrument for social justice, extending full moral agency to oppressed and subordinated groups.[49] But a narrowly individualistic interpretation of freedom to choose ignores the social context within which choices are made and can be turned to justifying *in*justice. The philosopher Zahra Meghani argues that we must consider individual choices in the context of global neoliberalism and its policies: privatization, deregulation, and commodification.[50] Rather than relying on an apolitical, one-size-fits-all argument like "choice," we have to understand local political and economic realities. When the "choice" argument is used to claim that the disadvantaged groups have accepted their lot freely – for example, when it is used to justify kidney sales by poor vendors in Third World countries – it becomes an instrument of subordination. Only recently have ethnographers and political analysts begun to challenge that argument by producing evidence showing that kidney sellers in Pakistan and elsewhere feel they had little choice, under pressure from creditors and feudal landlords. Now the sellers bitterly regret their forced action; one says that he sees himself as only half a man, while almost all insist they would never advise anyone else to do what they have done.[51] The authors of this study accuse Western analysts who view these sales as freely made choices of parochial cynicism.

The differentiated and sensitive analysis that Meghani recommends should not be confined the local political and economic realities in the Third World, of course.

In the United States egg sales are rising rapidly, so much so that some commentators identify the current situation as a buyer's market.[52] Are more women exercising their free choice? Might they not be they selling their eggs because women are more likely than men to bear the brunt of public service job cuts, because student debt is rising, or because egg sale

[49] John Stuart Mill, On Liberty (1859); John Stuart Mill, *On the Subjection of Women, in* The Collected Works of John Stuart Mill (F.E.L. Priestley ed., 1963–1984).

[50] A. Robust, *Particularist Assessment of Medical Tourism,* 11 Developing World Bioethics 16 (2010).

[51] Farhat Moazam et al., *Conversations with Kidney Sellers in Pakistan: An Ethnographic Study,* 39 Hastings Ctr. Rep. 29 (2009).

[52] Marcy Darnovsky, *Eggs, Wombs and the Economy: Hard Times Fuel a Buyer's Market,* Biopolitical News, Dec. 8, 2008, http://www.biopoliticaltimes.org/article.php?id=4427.

is one of their few remaining options in the global economic downturn? Only a doctrinaire or naïve libertarian would opt for the free choice explanation alone. Egg brokerage agencies themselves identify the economic recession as the prime cause of increased applications from would-be sellers.[53]

The source of the emphasis on autonomy and choice in bioethical discourse is usually thought to be Kant, with his conception of individuals as autonomous members of the "kingdom of ends." But while autonomy has attained the status of *primus inter pares* among the widely followed "four principles" of medical ethics,[54] Kant himself specifically states that it does not apply to trading body tissue. To treat the body as a fungible object is to treat the provider not as a member of the kingdom of ends, but merely as a means – even if the person voluntarily consents to treat her own body in this fashion.[55] While autonomy is routinely invoked to justify organ sales, the theorist from whom reliance on autonomy is derived himself denies that autonomy can rightfully apply to that case. The original carefully enunciated and bounded concept has degenerated into a sloppily loose explanation that no longer resembles its originator's version: in fact, it contradicts it. So this is a prime instance of the idols of the marketplace.

As Cynthia Cohen rightly remarks,[56] Kant was reacting against the Hobbesian tradition in which dignity is identified with price and a person's value is set by the market. "The value or worth of a man," Hobbes writes, "is as of all other things, his Price: that is to say, so much as would be given for the use of his Power.... As in other things, so in men, not the seller, but the buyer determines the Price."[57] Kant objects to this formulation because different people have different values on the market, a condition that undermines the equality of respect demanded by a correct interpretation of autonomy. The sale of a kidney thus differs from its donation, in which all "sellers" have the same "price," that is, no price. Egg markets value certain

[53] Crimaldi, *supra* note 33.

[54] Tom Beauchamp & James Childress, Principles of Biomedical Ethics (6th ed. 2009).

[55] Maria Marzano-Parisoli, Penser le Corps (2002).

[56] Cynthia B. Cohen, *Public Policy and the Sale of Human Organs,* 12 Kennedy Inst. Ethics J. 47 (2002). *See also* Nicole Gerrand, *The Misuse of Kant in the Debate about a Market in Human Body Parts,* J. Applied Phil. 59 (1999).

[57] Thomas Hobbes, Leviathan 15 (1968).

traits above others – for example, intelligence, musicality, height, and, of course, race – and thereby fail the criterion of respecting the persons who bear those traits equally.

Kant never intended his conception of autonomy to be reduced to the simplistic formulation that whatever I choose to do merits respect because I have chosen to do it. Autonomy deserves respect because individuals merit respect as rational members of the kingdom of ends. When they behave irrationally or fail to recognize others as ends rather than as mere means, those others, as equally rational members of that kingdom, are not obliged to respect their decisions as autonomous. Freedom is not the right to do whatever we please, but to determine our actions in accordance with the categorical imperative, with duties that are unconditionally binding on all.[58] To the extent that we have rights, they derive from the manner in which others follow those duties.

The Kantian conception of autonomy is a very long way from the debased and obviously fallacious formulations that underpin much of the dominant view of choice, freedom, and autonomy. These common preconceptions can be summarized without too much caricature in these two blatantly false assertions:

1) Whatever we do, we have chosen to do.
2) Whatever choices we make deserve respect.

But given that these statements are fallacious to the point of fatuousness, how have they come to be the idols of the bioethical marketplace? How have the ideas of choice, autonomy, and reproductive freedom taken on the status of an ideology or even a religion?

To some degree the elevation of these idols was well intentioned. It was praiseworthy to want to extend patient autonomy and choice in the old-style hierarchical medical environment, just as Mill was right in his desire to extend agency and rights to subordinated groups such as women. But as the corporate dominance of medicine and research gathered pace, liberal bioethicists, like progressives in other areas, lost the plot. As Marcy Darnovsky has written, when liberalism refuses to take a moral stance and excludes ethics from public policy in the name of tolerance, as it began to

[58] Ruud ter Meulen, *Care for Dependent Elderly Persons and Respect for Autonomy, in* CAMBRIDGE MED. ETHICS WORKBOOK 134 (Donna Dickenson et al. eds., 2010).

do in the 1960s and still does, it loses the ability to offer resistance to the corporate state and market forces.[59]

In the United States the dominance of the idols of the marketplace can best be understood in terms of abortion politics. (It is much more difficult to see why the idols are also so dominant in the United Kingdom, particularly because they are so strongly espoused by influential theorists like Julian Savulescu and John Harris who view themselves as utilitarians, although traditional Benthamite utilitarianism arose in opposition to Kantian deontology and viewed rights as "nonsense on stilts.") Not only did U.S. progressives and fundamentalists alike assume that the only issue in bioethics was the status of the embryo: those who opposed limitations on the right to abortion made a tactical decision to frame their argument in terms of privacy rights and free choice. Of course, there is a certain circularity here: progressives chose to present their arguments in terms of free choice because choice was already ensconced in its temple niche as a powerful and supposedly benign idol.

It then became difficult for proponents of abortion rights to separate out women's autonomy right to control their bodies in that instance from the wider context of reproductive choices, including the "right" to sell eggs or to become a contract mother. Abortion politics has played into the exemption of gametes from the general prohibition on organ sales in the National Organ Transplant Act 1984, because the notion that the state should control reproductive decisions of any kind is perceived as the thin end of the wedge by abortion rights advocates.[60]

As Lisa Ikemoto has written, in the decades since *Roe v. Wade*, the commercialization of assisted reproductive technologies has perverted the argument from choice.

> The linkage between choice, autonomy and equality was reworked into an understanding of reproductive choice as an aspect of free-market individualism.... Choice underwent its own nuclear transplant. Bodily integrity,

[59] Marcy Darnovsky, *"Moral Questions of an Altogether Different Kind": Progressive Politics in the Biotech Age*, 4 HARV. L. &POL'Y REV. 99 (2010).

[60] Alexander Capron, contribution to panel on Global Challenges and Opportunities, The Tarrytown Meetings (Center for Genetics and Society), July 25, 2011. At the same meeting, Judy Norsigian of the Boston women's collective Our Bodies Ourselves likewise expressed disquiet about the difficulties IVF and egg sale have posed for their commitment to letting women choose for themselves, once informed of the facts.

decisional autonomy and equality were replaced with free-market individualism and ownership.[61]

Women's rights advocates are now becoming increasingly troubled by the way in which they have been coopted into worshipping the idols of choice, autonomy, and reproductive freedom. The new reproductive technologies have genuinely extended opportunities for previously infertile people who can afford them, but the unthinking use of the rhetoric of choice "has enabled the fertility industry to develop unfettered and leaves us ethically vulnerable,"[62] in the words of Francine Coeytaux of the Pro-Choice Alliance for Responsible Research. Yet it is often said that we have no practical alternative – that we have no choice about the predominance of choice, as it were. As the example of France has already suggested, I think that is unnecessarily supine. In the final section of this chapter, I will briefly develop some elements of an alternative policy that allows us to topple the idols of the marketplace.

Conclusion: Beyond, but Back to, Altruism

One-way altruism is better known as exploitation, as I have already argued. There is certainly merit in denunciations of a system that allows private firms to make profits on the backs of unpaid donors, that fails to serve ethnic minorities equitably,[63] and that assumes that women should be more altruistic than men.[64] As I have also argued, however, the direction of the argument could go in two directions from there: eliminating the pretense of altruism by converting entirely to a for-profit system applying to both sellers and buyers, or retaining the altruism and eliminating the pretense by requiring *all* parties to be altruistic. We could move "beyond altruism" as mere rhetoric if we take the first course, abandoning it altogether, or

[61] Lisa Ikemoto, *Eggs as Capital: Egg Procurement in the Fertility Industry and the Stem Cell Research Enterprise*, 34 SIGNS: J. WOMEN IN CULTURE & SOC'Y 763, 768, 779 (2009).

[62] Francine Coeytaux, *Choice in the Biotech Age: The Need for a New Ethical Framework*, *available at* www.thetarrytownmeetings.org (accessed July 21, 2011); *see also* Francine Coeytaux et al., *Assisted Reproduction and Choice in the Biotech Age: Recommendations for a Way Forward*, 83 CONTRACEPTION 1 (2011).

[63] GOODWIN, BLACK MARKETS, *supra* note 6

[64] D. Zimmerman et al., *Gender Disparity in Living Renal Transplant Donation*, 36 AM. J. KIDNEY DISEASE 534 (2000).

beyond "altruism" as a sort of brand label and back to *genuine* altruism – by purging egg and organ provision of illicit commodification and exploitation, masquerading under the guise of free choice and reproductive liberty.

That second choice may sound unrealistic – although France has decided to retain similar policies – but it is actually more unrealistic to expect that an entirely for-profit system can work. There is too great a disparity between sellers' and buyers' market positions. Where buyers want maximal quantities of eggs and sellers lack information about risks, there will almost inevitably be abuses, like the case in which a young woman nearly died after seventy ova were taken from her in one cycle.[65] It is quite incredible that in an age when evidence-based medicine is the universal mantra, we know so little about the long-term risks of hyperstimulation, cancer, or infertility to healthy young women from egg provision. The few studies that exist have concentrated on infertile women, who might have a differential rate of response to stimulation.[66] The independent Donor Sibling Registry gives a figure of 30 percent incidence of ovarian hyperstimulation, whereas the conventional figure is 2 percent. It is certainly arguable that women are not giving fully informed consent, in the absence of consistent and robust evidence.

To some extent proposals for an egg "donor" registry, first mooted as a worldwide body in 2001[67] and now being pursued on a more limited basis in California, would improve the problem of information imbalance. California state bill AV1317 mandates government warnings to egg "donors"; however, the bill's concomitant proposals for a registry failed for budgetary reasons, despite backing from both "prochoice" and antiabortion camps. Yet the IVF industry appears to have accepted that it cannot oppose the notion of a registry altogether, although it would probably prefer that the administration of such a body be in its own hands, rather than vested in a university research center or the Centers for Disease Control.[68]

[65] Allen Jacobs et al., *Seventy Ova*, 31 Hastings Ctr. Rep. 12 (2001).

[66] W. Kramer et al., *U.S. Oocyte Donors: A Retrospective Study of Medical and Psychological Issues*, 24 Human Reproduction 3144 (2009).

[67] C. Caligara et al., *The Effect of Repeated Controlled Ovarian Stimulation on Donors*, 16 Human Reproduction 2320 (2001).

[68] Tina Stevens, Contribution to Panel on Eggs and Sperm, Yours Mine and Theirs: Controversies and Concrete Strategies for Addressing Them, The Tarrytown Meetings, July 26, 2011.

A registry for eggs would allow women and medical professionals alike to know the genuine risks of egg provision; once those risks were more generally known, there might well be pressure to regulate egg sale much more strictly or even perhaps to disallow it altogether. Here there is a parallel in biobanking, which was unregulated at its inception in the 1940s, generating revenues of more than $100 million by 1994, but that was subjected to congressional investigation and regulation once medical concerns about HIV infection sparked a public outcry.[69] Biobank operations, like the trade in human eggs, were being conducted on a global scale: the House subcommittee investigating the need for regulation received a copy of a telefax from the Baltic Tissue Bank of St. Petersburg, which "advertised the availability for sale of a butcher's list of donated tissues, prices attached."[70] Yet regulation was not written off as impossible merely because the industry was both long-established and global. Could the same thing happen with the global egg trade? It is not a matter of "can't regulate," even where global trade in tissue is going on: as the biobank example shows, it is a matter of changing "won't regulate" to "will regulate, albeit under pressure."

The European Commission Tissue Directive (2004) bans payment for ova used in IVF. In December 2011, however, the UK Human Fertilisation and Embryology Authority announced that licensed embryo and gamete donation centers "may compensate egg donors a fixed sum of up to £750 per cycle of donation." Additionally, donors can be compensated "an excess amount" in cases where expenses (i.e. for travel, accommodations, child care) go above the amount the UK's fixed-sum allows per cycle. Even in the United States, which has been much less willing to regulate the egg trade than most other countries, there are straws in the wind. In 2007, for example, a state bill was introduced in the Maryland legislature to make paying for eggs a misdemeanor, punishable by up to ninety days in jail, a fine of up to $10,000, or both.[71] At the federal level, there should be a radical reexamination of the National Organ Transplant Act (1984) and the U.S. Anatomical Gift Act (1987), particularly the provision exempting

[69] Marc O. Williams, *The Regulation of Human Tissue in the United States: A Regulatory and Legislative Analysis*, 52 Food & Drug L. J. 409 (1997).

[70] *Id.* at 412 (quoting from congressional records).

[71] Nanette R. Elster, *Egg Donation for Research and Reproduction: The Compensation Conundrum, in* Baby Markets: Money and the New Politics of Creating Families 226 (Michele Bratcher Goodwin ed., 2010).

gametes as "renewable tissue" from the general ban on payment for tissue. Sperm is renewable, eggs are not, and the fact that the legislators seem not to have noticed is just another instance of that phenomenon I call "the lady vanishes."

Although it may seem a bit speculative, there can be said to be an incipient groundswell in bioethics against the simplistic "choice" model, and in politics against the dominance of the market. In bioethics, the charitable trust model developed by David Winickoff[72] and others exemplifies a practical way to enhance both altruism and tissue donors' control over the final uses of their contribution. In society at large, the economic crisis of 2008 and its ongoing ramifications have made a lot of people a lot less sanguine about markets. Why are bioethicists and biolawyers not among them?

In this final section I have only had time to illustrate a few of the many counterexamples to the facile theses that altruism is dead and that the market is the only feasible mechanism for allocating human tissue, particularly eggs. It is not really my task to design a completely altruistic system: all I really have to do in order to undermine the simplistic argument that there is no alternative to the market is to show that there *are* alternatives to letting the market dominate the provision of eggs. Like the "all swans are white" thesis in Karl Popper, the TINA argument (There Is No Alternative) is disproved by the sighting of a single black swan.

The question is why so many scholars and policy makers have accepted that argument that there is no alternative to markets in eggs. I have argued in this chapter that their acceptance is predicated in substantial part on a radical misreading of which term is emotive – exploitation or choice? – and which is a necessary critique. One is a subtle and nuanced concept with an honorable ancestry in political theory; the other is an advertising slogan. I am sure the reader can guess which I think is which.

[72] Andrea Boggio, *Charitable Trusts and Human Research Genetic Databases: The Way Forward?*, 1 GENOMICS, SOC'Y & POL'Y 41 (2005); J. Otten et al., *The Charitable Trust as a Model for Genomic Banks*, 350 NEW. ENG. J. MED. 85 (2004); J. Winickoff & D. Winickoff, *The Charitable Trust as a Model for Genomic Biobanks*, 349 NEW ENG. J. MED. 1180 (2003); D. Winickoff, From Benefit-Sharing to Power-Sharing, paper delivered at Governing Biobanks—What are the Challenges? At Oxford, June 25, 2008.

3 How to Create Markets in Contestable Commodities

Richard A. Epstein

Beyond Widgets

Standard economic theory has a strong preference for proving the efficiency of competitive markets by analyzing the market for widgets. It is a fair question to ask exactly what a widget is in the context of this theory, to which the appropriate answer is that it is a close relative of the gidget, the second notable good in neoclassical economic theory. As befits the low regard that the dismal science holds in literary circles, the term "widget" was introduced in a play by George S. Kaufman and Marc Connelly, *Beggar on Horseback*, in a dismissive sense, to refer to "some mechanical product without artistic or spiritual value,"[1] their own writings, for example. But this useful term has been fully co-opted by the economics profession for a useful function, namely, "to indicate a hypothetical 'any-product.'"[2] As will become clear, the word "widget" functions well when identification of a particular product is irrelevant to the exposition of a particular theoretical point.

The interplay of these two definitions is a central theme of this chapter: does a theory that works for the routine apply in settings with more distinctive qualities of artistic, or moral, significance? But for the moment, it is a fair question to ask why any economic theory would organize around a

[1] Wikipedia, *Widget (economics)*, http://en.wikipedia.org/wiki/Widget_(economics) (last accessed Dec. 26, 2012)

[2] *Id.*

This paper is an expanded version of the keynote address that I gave at the Contested Commodities Conference held at the University of Chicago on April 4, 2008. My thanks to Jeana Bisnar, NYU Law School, Class of 2010, for her usual expert research assistance.

mythical commodity, when no biologist would choose to study the animal kingdom by looking to unicorns or mermaids. There is, I think, no good defense for the quixotic biologist. But there is a powerful and respectable explanation as to why widgets and gidgets alike have served economic inquiry well: they allow for generalization in economic theory.

The major task of a positive theory of economics is to offer a description of the way in which self-interested people will behave given scarcity under conditions of uncertainty. A challenge that broad is one that can easily go astray. One sensible technique is to narrow down the inquiry to a more limited field to generate strong results that might not be replicable elsewhere. The decision to address the operation of only competitive markets is one such dramatic restriction, and the term "widget" helps establish the domain of the inquiry, by showing the level of generality that emphasizes market structure and not the physical characteristics of any particular good. The general economic account of competition presupposes that the problem of social order has been handled, so that the parties to an exchange – any exchange – know that the legal system will protect their goods and services from expropriation by third persons. It also assumes that there are numerous parties on both sides of the market, so that potential buyers and potential sellers each have a wide range of trading options. In addition, the basic discussion of competitive markets often assumes, first, that parties have full information about the relevant goods and, second, that the legal system supplies perfect enforcement of basic exchange obligations. These are perhaps austere assumptions, but by the same token useful ones.

Often, the one assumption that renders the other assumptions plausible – widgets and gidgets to the rescue – is that markets deal in *fungible* goods, which implies that one good in the class is every bit as good as another. In some cases these standard commodities are found in nature, but that state of affairs is less common than one might suppose. Instead, from the earliest times, reverse engineering was the rule. Recognized contracts such as *mutuum* – a transfer of some fungible commodity to one person in exchange for a promise to return a like good later on[3] – are only intelligible if we know that two things are alike in all relevant senses; otherwise the parity between the two parties, except for the element of time, is lost. More generally, in practice, everyone shares the basic intuition that markets, and

[3] *See* Barry Nicholas, An Introduction to Roman Law 167–68 (1962).

for that matter cartels, in fungible commodities are more easily organized than those in commodities in irregular or idiosyncratic goods. Accordingly, interested parties take active steps to fashion the needed standardization.[4] Various industry groups and trade associations will take it upon themselves to organize various grades or classes of goods in order to facilitate trade. There are, for example, multiple types of crude oil, each of which trades for a different price.[5] Similar classifications can be found for most agricultural commodities.[6]

There is ample justification for this reverse engineering. Create the standard commodities, and it becomes easy to have numerous parties on both sides of the market. Under those circumstances, the classical theory predicts that buyers and sellers will reach an efficient equilibrium in which all gainful exchanges take place, and all improvident ones do not. Once a market is in competitive equilibrium, it is no longer possible to make one person better off without making another person worse off. In addition, these markets have desirable dynamic properties in that changes in either supply or demand will lead to adjustments of both price and quantity. Whatever the moral qualms that people have about some markets, it is difficult to summon up either indignation or skepticism about markets that operate in this form.

Indeed, far from engendering either indignation or skepticism, these well-functioning markets are tremendously interesting to the insiders but remarkably dull to the rest of the world. People are generally attracted to markets in which there are shortages and intrigues, in which political influence can derail gainful exchanges, or where complex trading situations allow sharks to take advantage of the justifiable confusion of vulnerable persons. For starters, nothing beats the intrigue in rent-controlled markets, where each change of possession is filled with Sturm und Drang. Dying

[4] For a defense of this proposition, see Richard A. Epstein, *The Neoclassical Economics of Consumer Contracts*, 92 MINN. L. REV. 803 (2008).

[5] Crude oil is available in many varieties and qualities, depending on its specific gravity and sulfur content, which depend on where it has been pumped from. If no other information is given, an oil price appearing in UK and other European media reports will probably refer to the price of a barrel of Brent blend crude oil from the North Sea sold at London's International Petroleum Exchange (IPE). *Oil Markets Explained*, BBC NEWS, Oct. 18, 2007, http://news.bbc.co.uk/2/hi/business/904748.stm.

[6] *See, e.g.*, *Agriculture Marketing Service*, U.S. DEP'T AGRIC. http://www.ams.usda.gov/AMSv1.0/ (follow Grading, Certification and Verification).

tenants seek to pass on the unit to their second cousins. Departing tenants will sell keys to the apartment five times over. Irate landlords will turn off the heat to drive tenants out of their units – all because prices are kept artificially low. Ah, for a whiff of deregulation. Likewise the manifold difficulties in ethanol markets with their grotesque combination of tariff walls and domestic subsidies tell the same sorry story.[7] Regulation creates all sorts of strategic options that crowd out sensible, voluntary exchanges. It is not conceivable to think of any advanced society that could rid itself of residential leases or farm production. But lest people attack the ills of a competitive market, they should think long and hard about the painful outcomes in regulated markets – a result that holds whether we deal with good widgets or bad ones.

Organized Markets and Contestable Commodities

These observations about markets in general set the stage for the problem of this book. No longer can we assume that we are dealing with widgets and gidgets tradable in competitive markets. Rather, to use an old term, the modern concern with these *contestable* (or fringe) markets is whether exchanges (but typically not gifts, in light of the fascination with altruism) should be allowed to operate at all for these contested commodities in question. These contestable markets typically arise with respect to human beings and human organs and include practices such as the selling or adopting of babies and kidneys, livers, hearts, blood, and eggs (but usually not sperm). In these various contexts, the constant cries of "commodification" are not meant to show how market institutions introduced the standardization that makes voluntary exchange possible, as it historically has.[8] Rather, the new use of the term "commodification" has exactly the opposite valence. It is intended to explain why those supposed efforts at standardization and voluntary exchange, especially for valuable consideration, run against the moral grain, so that the transactions should be

[7] For a glimpse at some irk and ire, see Matthew Bandyk, *Subsidies and High Crop Prices*, U.S. NEWS & WORLD REP., Jan. 24, 2008, http://usnews.com/articles/business/economy/2008/01/24/subsidies-and-high-crop-prices.html.

[8] *See, e.g.*., MARGARET JANE RADIN, CONTESTED COMMODITIES (1996). For an example of an attack on commodification, see generally Elizabeth Anderson, Is *Women's Labor a Commodity?*, 19 PHIL. & PUB. AFF.71 (1990).

prohibited altogether, as they are, for example under the National Organ Transplant Act, or NOTA.[9]

In many cases, it is hard to pinpoint the reasons that evoke this harsh new epithet. In some cases, the fear is that persons in a vulnerable class are subject to exploitation by others. But that explanation does not quite cover the ground, because there are less intrusive ways to deal with the problem of undue influence. In extreme cases, an incompetent person can be given a guardian who is both bound and entitled to make decisions on his or her behalf. In cases of impaired capacity, the risk of undue influence can be met by ensuring that the vulnerable party receives independent advice before entering into any nonstandard transaction, such as the purchase and sale of a large plot of land.[10] It is instructive to note that for standard transactions in competitive markets, this approach is never taken, on the ground that even persons with limited capacity are protected by buying and selling goods at the market price. In other situations, the term "commodification" has what I regard as a more sinister use – to insulate certain transactions, such as those in labor and commodities, from the application of the antitrust law, as is done for labor organizations under the Clayton Act.[11] One might think that if labor were not a commodity, it could not be sold at all, like other goods that are called *res extra commercium.* But in this situation the phrase has a different significance. It may be not only sold, but also at monopoly power – which hardly counts as a social improvement. Yet in other cases it appears that the commodification objection to various types of transactions rests on the ground that they are somehow inimical to the essential nature of human beings or create a sense that undermines the dignity of individuals by treating them, or their body parts, as objects that can be bought and sold like a loaf of bread or a used car.[12]

[9] National Organ Transplant Act § 301(a), 42 U.S.C. § 274e(a) (2006). The relevant provisions of NOTA read: § 274e. Prohibition of organ purchases (a) Prohibition. It shall be unlawful for any person to knowingly acquire, receive, or otherwise transfer any human organ for valuable consideration for use in human transplantation if the transfer affects interstate commerce. 42 U.S.C. § 274e(a) (2006).

[10] *See* Jackson v. Seymour, 71 S.E.2d 181 (Va. 1952) (holding a sister's sale of land to her brother under pecuniary distress for grossly inadequate consideration resulted in constructive fraud, justifying rescission).

[11] Clayton Act § 6, Pub. L. No. 63-212, 38 Stat. 730 (1914) (codified at 15 U.S.C. § 17 (2000)) ("The labor of a human being is not a commodity or article of service").

[12] For a recent example, see Margaret Somerville, *At Heart, It's Slavery by Another Name,* GLOBE & MAIL, Aug, 13, 2008, http://www.theglobeandmail.com/servlet/

In undertaking this overview of contestable commodities, it is important to begin by dispelling some of the confusion about the behavior of individuals in organized markets. Much of the opposition to the liberalization of the rules that restrict voluntary exchange in these sensitive areas stems from a deep confusion regarding how any market in these contestable commodities would in fact work if it were freed of government constraints that limited either the subject matter of the transaction – I resist the use of the word "commodity" – the prices, or any other consideration that is or is not supplied in these transactions. The normative case for allowing these markets to flourish is improved by correcting the exaggerated accounts of how they are likely to perform.

Let us start with the idea of a market. There is, unfortunately, an incautious tendency to say that markets are in operation whenever voluntary transactions take place between buyers and sellers. That view captures something of the basic situation, but it is surely incomplete, even if not entirely unflattering. The key point is that voluntary exchanges do promote mutual gains between the parties, and in most instances they create neglected but critical positive externalities by improving the position of strangers to the transaction. But this one feature of voluntariness, standing alone, does not distinguish a market from a "casual" sale made between two neighbors, which are often governed by different rules.[13] Why does this difference matter? The simple point is this: casual sales are not always well thought out. There is no opportunity for the rules that govern these transactions to be corrected through constant massage in the light of previous errors. There is no chance for professionals to move into these markets so as to bridge the gap between uninformed buyers and sellers who are otherwise anonymous to each other. It would be, I think, enormously forbidding to require people to go naked into voluntary transactions, given their manifest lack of knowledge. Organize a market, and there is not just the single exchange that is involved: there is a network of transactions, and a plethora of third-person support personnel, from advisers to brokers, to life coaches, who can fill the gaps in information. It is in this regard critical to remember the vital difference between having enough knowledge to do something right by one's self

story/RTGAM.20080813.wcoorgan13/BNStory/specialComment/home?cid=al_gam_mostemal. The title says it all.

[13] *See, e.g.*, Restatement (Second) of Torts § 402A cmt.f (1965).

and knowing enough to seek advice from third persons before you go forward with any transaction. The whole point of markets is that they backstop individual exchanges with all sorts of supportive institutions.

Impersonal and Mechanical Markets?

Unfortunately, this key point is sometimes missed. Thus, in her chapter, Debora Spar reaches sound conclusions on the role of markets in dealing with reproductive practices. But she makes her task more difficult than it ought to be when she boldly claims that markets have nothing to say about reproductive freedom. "Markets are about money and prices, about putting buyers and sellers together in a neutral and impersonal environment. Markets do not care about reproductive rights, or indeed about any rights at all."[14] Later on she hammers the point home by noting the "normative void that lies at the center of commerce" and further asserts that "markets are entirely impersonal and mechanical constructs."[15]

From these odd observations Spar draws what is the right conclusion. Strong contracts enforced by the state are good ways in which to protect reproductive rights. But, unfortunately, she throws many unnecessary obstacles in our path by insisting on that moral void at the heart of these mechanical and imperfect markets. On one level, her mistake is the familiar one of anthropomorphism, or attributing to markets the characteristics of either individual human beings or machines when neither description is accurate. As noted earlier, a market arises when people get together on a regular basis to enter into some standard class of transaction. The market does not have any mental states of mind, even the elusive states of mind associated with corporations or governments, which act, of course, through their officers. Rather, the "decision" of the market represents in some sense the accumulation of separate decisions to buy and to sell made by the participants acting individually, not by some entity acting collectively through its designated agents.

There is more, however, to her instructive error than this single point. There is no doubt that many markets do operate in the anonymous form

[14] Debora L. Spar, *Free Markets, Free Choice?—A Market Approach to Reproductive Rights*, this volume.

[15] *Id.*

that Spar indicates. To go back to our earlier distinction, markets will tend to work in rapid and impersonal fashion when standardized commodities are bought and sold. No one wants to commune with his or her teller in withdrawing money from a bank, which is why ATMs do even better in these impersonal transactions. Any individual question that a bank teller might ask a customer as to why the money is needed would be rightly regarded as snooping. Fortunately, ATM machines do not ask any questions at all, even if they do after a fashion say welcome and hello. For these and other mass transactions, the impersonality of the market is not some necessary inherent attribute. It is, rather, a feature that discrete market actors design into their individual systems on the ground floor as a conscious social judgment as to how people ought to proceed in certain defined contexts. From the earliest times, these relationships are established under a norm that governs all transactions by strict and exact obligation.[16] The ATM will not dispense cash if there is insufficient money in the account. There are no excuses that are allowed, and no good faith adjustments to ongoing relationships.

Yet the entire universe of voluntary transactions does not consist of rapid, standardized, and anonymous transactions governed by these strict rules. Standard contract theory has developed a useful and enduring distinction between relational contracts such as partnerships, and spot transactions. The former include "franchise arrangements, long-term employment, professional partnerships, labor/management relations and, quintessentially, marriage."[17] The latter include individual purchases from unrelated parties, with little or no expectation of repeat business, such as purchasing a local brew in a town the buyer is passing through.[18] The difference was apparent from Roman times to the present. The less discretion there is in a transaction, the more possible it is to develop a complete contingent state contract: hence the ATM machine. The more discretion there is in a transaction, the more likely it is that the relationship will be open-ended and governed by some norm of good faith, as is typical with partnership-style situations,

[16] For the Roman variations, see the rules on stipulations, including guarantees, set out in GAIUS INST. 3.92–127. Note in particular the various formal rules on guarantors.

[17] Paul J. Gudel, *Relational Contract Theory and the Concept of Exchange*, 46 BUFF. L. REV. 763, 764 (1998).

[18] *Id.* For more on the importance of relational contract theories from their originator, see IAN R. MACNEIL, THE NEW SOCIAL CONTRACT: AN INQUIRY INTO MODERN CONTRACTUAL RELATIONS (1980).

where it is often impossible to set out in advance the precise duties between two parties and, given the closeness of their connection, inadvisable to do so. These relationships therefore have fallen since Roman times under the heading of bona fide contracts.[19] Once the partnership shares are set out in proportions, the particular obligations of each party are determined by personal considerations that are highly specific and bear no relationship to the impersonal and neutral environment that is sometimes associated with contracts. But this does not mean that the rules are vacuous. The best test for a good faith partnership relationship is whether one party accords the welfare of the second the same weight that he does his own. This expectation is reasonable because the partners are not selected at random but have chosen each other precisely because they have a level of trust in each other that most people do not have in any random person. Moreover, in many cases it is possible to give a sharp mathematical meaning to what is at stake. The most common manifestation is that each party shares pro rata in all gains and losses, regardless of which one controls the transaction. The Roman example of this was a partnership *omnium bonorum*, covering all goods, in which the two partners are supposed to share and share alike. Nonetheless the risk of opportunism remains, as when one party resigns precipitously in order to obtain an inheritance for himself that would otherwise have to be shared. The legal rule gives a share of that inheritance to the innocent partner. In addition, if it turns out that the innocent partner gets a similar inheritance, he can keep it himself.[20] The rule for bad faith partners is heads I lose; tails you win. The expected value of the breach is therefore always negative.

In this world, sales transactions are sufficiently varied that they cannot be easily pigeonholed into one category or another. Much depends, at a minimum, on the nature of the good sold and the parties to the transaction. For standardized commodities (again), discretion is not part of the game; checkout clerks do not have the power to negotiate price with customers or to reject those goods presented for sale on the grounds that they are ill-suited for the potential buyer. The goal here is to speed transactions along, if only

[19] *See* Gaius Inst. 3.137: "Likewise, in contracts of this description the parties are reciprocally liable, because each is liable to the other to perform what is proper and just; while, on the other hand, in the case of verbal obligations one party stipulates and the other promises." For a brief description, see Barry Nicholas, *supra* note 3.

[20] *See* Gaius Inst. 3.151. The last point is not explicit in this text but is clearly implied.

to preserve the sanity of the people standing next on the queue. In these contexts, the function of sales personnel is wholly ministerial, for people rarely like to discuss their deepest aspirations with strangers.

Once, however, we move to nonstandardized goods of greater value, we see the rise of the sales representative, whose job it is to match and, if need be, customize goods to the particular tastes and needs of a particular purchaser. These agents could be employed on matters as routine as the purchase of a suit or as complex as the design of a computer system for high-end users. In these contexts, the metaphor of the mechanical market is a total misnomer. The one point that is clear is that the more discretion that the deal requires, the more highly paid and skilled the sales rep will be. But no matter where they rank in the grand hierarchy, no sales reps can do well unless they first master the fine art of the schmooze, or how to elicit some sense of customer preferences so as to make the best fit of goods and needs. For the actual business of buying and selling, it is totally false to assume that markets operate in mechanical and impersonal ways. For example, the buyer in the transaction is much more likely to get the goods of his or her choice more quickly when the seller is able to figure out his or her preference set. Good communication and high levels of trust are needed for this relationship to work.

There is no way we can operate without these special arrangements, today or any other time. The elements of trust, discretion, and reputation explain these markets, which indicate why it is hard for outsiders, without tutelage or sponsorship, to break in. They also explain why family connections often overlap business ones, and why ethnic or racial groupings are used as a kind of informal bond to keep them together, especially in small businesses that depend more on trust than on formal audits and bureaucratic controls. Paradoxically, the same concern with trust and natural affinities explains why the transition to larger business entities often fails – the parties cannot bleed the family and racial preferences out of the new setting when enlisting strangers into the business. What starts out as family or ethnic cooperation ends up as indefensible nepotism that makes the interests of outsiders ever more precarious. But keep the point in perspective. Even with all their special baggage, small family and ethnic businesses are voluntary exchanges for mutual gain. However, it would be odd to describe the transactions involving trust as dealings in commodities, unless a commodity is defined to be anything of value, regardless of whether it has standardized features.

It should not be assumed that these small groups will become extinct in a larger market economy. No way; for there is much to like about these transactions. No matter how complex the larger social order, smaller units in it will depend on these tight firms for some portion of their productive activity, and that is why the relentless advance of modernity has not led to their extinction. But these transactions have serious limitations in the organization of larger social institutions.[21] Close personal relationships limit the size of these firms and these markets. The smallish numbers tend to create pockets of monopoly profits that are difficult to bleed out by free entry. Transactions are slow and cumbersome, and the social devices that are needed to back them up are expensive to operate, and also limited by the kinds of people that can broker them. So there is no way, for example, that one could operate a modern system of banking with ATMs and credit cards on this model of the personal market. Quite the opposite, the only way that we can get standardized transactions in monetizable units is through impersonal arrangements that allow for rapid transactions at low cost. Any individual variation cannot be tolerated. Efforts to exclude applicants from a credit card system are self-defeating because if the card's bill is paid, who cares about ethnic connections or taste in food. The point is that the complex equilibrium in any market has both personal and impersonal kinds of activities working side by side. The genius of a system of markets is that it sorts between the two forms of association. By letting people follow their own instincts it does not have to prefer one kind of arrangement over the other. Instead it is able to adapt the rules of contract law to facilitate the differences.

Business Relations for Contestable Commodities

We have now laid the groundwork for dealing with the proper social response to contestable commodities. The key point in this discussion is that, once armed with an accurate theory of market relationships, we must

[21] For a detailed account of the shortcomings of systems relying exclusively on personal connections, see Nirav D. Shah, *From Exchange to Subsistence: Corruption and the Fragility of Transitional Legal Systems* (on file with author).

undertake the descriptive work before we deal with the normative questions. Nothing is more common for persons who are against exchange relationships in contestable commodities than to project the standard legal and social arrangements that work for real, that is, fungible, goods onto the world of these so-called commodities. As a legal matter, they implicitly assume that the strict rules applicable to financial transactions carry over without a beat, missing the entire good faith side of the equation. Socially, their depiction of how these businesses are conducted becomes so repellant that one wonders whether anyone could defend their use. The individuals who attack commodification think that the poor behavior that is observed in illegal markets will carry over to legal ones. Yet economic theory predicts the opposite: legalization allows both new entrants and third parties into the market, thus making transactions far more transparent than they are in illegal markets. Let me give a few examples of the basic point.

Medical Care

In many circles there is a widespread concern about medical privacy, especially with respect to psychiatric care. No one likes to share intimate information with persons who have no use for it, and the reluctance is even greater when it is thought that disclosure of the information can be used to the detriment of the person to whom the disclosures pertain. The basic norm for all medical care information is that once received it will not be broadcast to the rest of the world, but will in general be held in confidence by those who receive it for limited use. This norm exists independently of any form of regulation, and certainly without the extensive regulations of HIPAA, the Health Insurance Portability and Accountability Act,[22] which has ushered in an incredible array of absurd regulations imposing restrictions in the name of privacy that no sane person would care to note. Such gems include keeping individuals' names off hospital doors, so that people looking for their own family members keep peering into rooms where they are most definitely not wanted.[23]

[22] 5 U.S.C. § 552(b)(6).

[23] For a recent discussion, see Richard A. Epstein & David A. Hyman, *Controlling the Cost of Medical Care: A Dose of Deregulation,* at 24, *available at* http://papers.ssrn.com/sol3/papers.cfm?abstract_id=1158547 (critiquing the Frequently Asked Questions posed on the HIPAA Web site, available at http://www.hhs.gov/hipaafaq/).

But there are other cases, more relevant to this discussion, where the market has moved beyond the regulatory framework. And psychiatric care is near or at the top on anyone's. So the market adapts. Extensive efforts are made to sort out these medical relationships, including steps to ensure that no patient knows the identity of any other patient.[24] It is in one door and out the other. People do not mill around a waiting room as with other forms of medical practice. Firms understand the point as well, for they often allow individuals to receive counseling on psychiatric, sexual, weight, or marital problems from persons who are not located in the workplace, where the information gathered is never put into personnel files, where it could be used against the employee. Firms have learned that it is better to provide the care than let the condition remain untreated. Nor should we think that these sensitive meetings take place in bars, gyms, or nightclubs. The purveyors of these services are intent on making their clients both secure and comfortable in order to improve the effectiveness of the treatment or therapy.

The conclusion is clear. The sensitive issues raised in all these relationships are met with voluntary responses that are sensitive to the dignity demands of patients. The point is telling because so much of medical ethics treats autonomy, or the right to make decisions dealing with one's health and welfare, as the primary good.[25] That good corresponds to the rule of

[24] For a pre-HIPAA approach to addressing the physical and pragmatic limitations of patient confidentiality, as well as a discussion of its import as part of the treatment process, see Perry B. Spiegel ,*Confidentiality Endangered under Some Circumstances without Special Management*, 27 PSYCHOTHERAPY: THEORY, RES., PRAC., TRAINING 636 (1990), *available at* http://psycnet.apa.org/index.cfm?fa=main.showContent&view=fulltext&format=HTML&id=1991-16747-001 (addressing the "exceptional effort" that should be made to manage "physical factors" such as "scheduling, and office location and layout"). For a list of painfully minute voluntary practices, posted by a Division of the American Psychological Association, see Samuel Knapp, *Accidental Breaches of Confidentiality*, AM. PSYCHOL. ASS'N DIV. 31 SPTA NEWSLETTER ARTICLE CO-OP, *available at*ttp://www.apadiv31.org/Coop/AccidentalBreachesOfConfidentiality.pdf (addressing private entrances, soundproofing, and staggered scheduling of patients who potentially know one another, among other things).

[25] *See* Steven Pinker, *The Stupidity of Dignity*, NEW REPUBLIC, May 28, 2008, at 28, *available at* http://www.tnr.com/currentissue/story.html?id=d8731cf4-e87b-4d88b7e7-f5059cd0bfbd (discussing the questionable role of "dignity" in bioethics and its relationship to autonomy, which Pinker regards as "the bedrock of bioethical research and practice"). Pinker's review is of HUMAN DIGNITY AND BIOETHICS: ESSAYS COMMISSIONED BY THE PRESIDENT'S COUNCIL ON BIOETHICS, President's Council on Bioethics (2008), *available at* http://bioethics.georgetown.edu/pcbe/reports/human_dignity/human_dignity_and_bioethics.pdf.

self-rule on receiving treatment, and has the kind of cold, impersonal feel that Spar identifies with markets. But the flip side is that within this framework, treating patients with dignity and respect in their vulnerable conditions is a key mode of doing business, which is why the respect for dignity is an essential element of the physician-patient relationship, preferred by both autonomous parties. Context matters. No one would confuse these sensitive dealings with those of travel agents or car salesmen, where the expectations are so different. The voluntary sorting in these markets is complete. There is a real question whether any state-run agencies could do as well in these contexts, given their budgetary constraints.

Adoption Agencies

The same story plays out with respect to adoptions in the gray market. Here the anticommodification norm is one that prohibits the adopting parents to pay cash or other considerations to the natural mother (let alone the father) who surrenders the child for adoption.[26] When these adoptions are run through state agencies, there is a strong tendency to go by the book, so that such matters as age of the adopting couple, income, and separate bedrooms for children are the orders of the day.[27] But the pattern of private adoptions is different. The first point is that intermediates help with the matching function in these cases. Their use reduces the likelihood that the birth mother and the adoptive parents will not hit it off. Those intermediates can give clear indication of the kinds of information that the birth mother wants to acquire about the adoptive couple and the adoptive couple about the birth parents. Each has concerns about the fitness and health of the child. The intermediates can address the concerns on both sides of the relationship by assuring both sides of the reliability of their opposite number. In addition, it is commonplace in private markets for adoptive couples to produce resumes, even videos, of their family life, which are shown to the birth mother to persuade her they will be good parents. Sometimes one

[26] *See, e.g.*, ARIZ. REV. STAT. ANN. § 13-3625 (2008); KAN. STAT. ANN. § 59-2121 (2007); MINN. STAT. § 259.55 subdiv.2 (2008); N.Y. SOC. SERV. LAW § 374 (6) (McKinney 2007).

[27] A primary tool is the "home study," which includes a home visit and both health and income statements, among other things, and is required in some variation by the laws of every state. Child Welfare Information Gateway, *The Adoption Home Study Process: Factsheet for Families* U.S. DEP'T HEALTH & HUMAN SERV. (2004), *available at* http://www.childwelfare.gov/pubs/f_homstu.cfm.

or more interviews are held to see that the parties click on key issues like religion, sexual orientation, and the like. There are virtually no reported incidents of scandal that arise from these settings.

And so why the concern with baby selling? In the *Baby M* case, the point was put as follows:

> The evils inherent in baby-bartering are loathsome for a myriad of reasons. The child is sold without regard for whether the purchasers will be suitable parents. The natural mother does not receive the benefit of counseling and guidance to assist her in making a decision that may affect her for a lifetime. In fact, the monetary incentive to sell her child may, depending on her financial circumstances, make her decision less voluntary. Furthermore, the adoptive parents may not be fully informed of the natural parent's medical history. Baby-selling potentially results in the exploitation of all parties involved. Conversely, adoption statutes seek to further humanitarian goals, foremost among them the best interests of the child.[28]

This account seems overwrought in light of the procedures that are used in dealing with private adoptions. Why could they not be used in all cases? Indeed, it is hard to unpack all the errors that are compressed into this single ill-considered paragraph. For starters, all we know from gray market adoptions is that the birth mother is deeply concerned about the well-being of the child, for otherwise these inquiries would never be made. The stated procedural concerns with counseling and guidance of the birth mother, as well as full disclosure to the adopting parents of the medical history, are the sorts of things that are routinely provided. At most, there is some need for simple disclosures. There is surely no case for the ban. Nor are there grounds to say that the decision is not voluntary, especially in light of the procedures that are generally followed. Were that the case, then the birth mother would be equally coerced in the context of a decision to surrender a child to adoption through a state agency. And the claim that the statutes further humanitarian goals that private adoptions do not is utterly devoid of any empirical foundation. Indeed, it is completely incredible that the private procedures should "exploit all parties involved." Who would push hard to adopt procedures that lead to joint ruin? Dangers of abuse there surely are, but that only takes the discussion back to the procedural safeguards that are easily implemented with or without regulation.

[28] *In re* Baby M., 537 A.2d 1227, 1241–42 (N.J. 1988) [hereinafter *Baby M* Case] (citations omitted).

Indeed the only case in which there was an extended controversy was the *Baby M* case, which arose for one reason and for one reason only. There were no strong contractual protections to make it impossible for the surrogate birth mother to back out of the contract and keep the child. At the end of the day, the surrogate birth mother was awarded visitation rights and the biological father was granted custody over the child,[29] which created immense logistical problems. In situations where the contracts are enforced, there are few if any reported problems that arise out of these arrangements. "Where surrogacy is legal, as in California, it appears to thrive."[30] Yet the New Jersey court was replete with commodification reasons why that transaction should not be enforced, by making comparisons to baby-selling arrangements that it did not quite understand. In these cases, too, there are obvious reasons why the relationship between the buyers and sellers, if those terms be used, will not be mechanical and impersonal. The acquiring parents have a deep interest in the health of the child, which means that they have a strong interest in selecting healthy women to bear the children and in monitoring their conduct during the relationship. Likewise the birth mother has a strong interest in the well-being of a family that takes care of her child.

These points are important because they explain why this market works well even though it has to operate within the constraints of laws prohibiting baby selling (as the transfer of parental rights is often misnamed).[31] In the first place, the rules in question do not prohibit the adopting parents from covering expenses, which is an inducement to enter into the deal no matter how it is described or justified. Second, the major consideration for the birth mother is the assurance that the baby will be well cared for, so there is, inevitably, compensation paid on the account of the parent in the form of the hefty expenditures used to raise the child. For the upper-middle-class families that dominate these markets, this could easily run into the hundreds of thousands of dollars through college, and, increasingly, beyond. Thus, the limits on cash contributions matter relatively little. These cases

[29] *Id.* at 1259.

[30] Carol Sanger, *Developing Markets in Baby-Making: In the Matter of Baby M*, 30 HARV. J. L. & GENDER 67, 96 (2007) (citation omitted), *reprinted in* CONTRACT STORIES 127 (Douglas Baird ed., 2007).

[31] For my discussion of some of these issues, see RICHARD A. EPSTEIN, MORTAL PERIL: OUR INALIENABLE RIGHT TO HEALTH CARE 228–35 (1997).

are not like the kidney cases where the want of valuable consideration rules out, except in the organ swap cases, any valuable consideration in return. This market may not be ideal, but it is certainly functioning.

All of this does not necessarily imply that surrogacy arrangements are ideal, for they are subject to a set of inherent limitations that no social arrangements can overcome. The adoptive mother cannot carry the child to term, for example. So some women prefer to carry eggs obtained from other women; doing so enables them to experience pregnancy and to avoid the awkward transfer of the baby after birth. Those egg markets raise separate problems of their own, given the strong preference to collect eggs from gifted women in their early twenties.[32] Once again restrictions on personal behavior have to be imposed by the recipients, which require a good deal of counseling, tact, and persuasion to implement successfully. But here too the market is active – the prices of eggs tend to be falling. There are serious medical risks to deal with, but little sign that the contracts that are now in place fail to deal with the various emotional and personal issues that commonly arise.

Organ Transplantation

One area where the arguments about commodification in all its forms are made is organ transplantation, where the National Organ Transplant Act (NOTA)[33] prohibits all transactions for voluntary consideration. Two chapters in this book address the arguments about commodification and organs. Both Michele Goodwin and Jamila Jefferson note that this ban is not directed solely toward arrangements that are boorish or insensitive. It is directed to any case that includes cash or other "valuable consideration,"[34] a term that excludes various kinds of moral inducements, but includes things other than cash that have a monetary value. The most common objections are that organ sales will lead to the commodification of the human body, a

[32] *See* Bernadine Healy, *The High Cost of Eggs: Donors at Risk*, U.S. NEWS & WORLD REP., Jan. 13, 2003, at 44, http://health.usnews.com/usnews/health/articles/030113/13donor.b.htm; Jim Hopkins, *Egg-Donor Business Booms on Campuses*, USATODAY.COM, Mar. 15, 2006, http://www.usatoday.com/money/industries/health/2006-03-15egg-donors-usat_x.htm.

[33] 42 U.S.C. § 274e(a) (2006).

[34] *Id.*

diminished respect for the voluntariness of consent, a compromise of individual autonomy, and a reduced level of emotional support within families.[35] Similar and other arguments are offered in the previous chapter by Donna Dickenson. Still other writers think that legalization reflects "the folly of the privileged, not the reality of the poor."[36] Yet again, the question is whether these fears are borne out by the experiences we already have. On this issue, the first objection to the ban is its overbreadth. Narrower restrictions could easily deal with the dangers of the poor, whose organs are generally not in demand because of their lower expected quality. Nor is there any reason to think that people will be routinely mistreated in some impersonal and heartless fashion, as all the available evidence cuts the other way. There are now extensive efforts to collect kidneys from live and cadaveric organs. The solicitations are often quite delicate, and it is commonly understood that a poor approach could shipwreck what might otherwise be a successful donation. Although there are breakdowns in these solicitations, on balance people are aware of the delicacy of the situation and seek to take steps in order to prevent such breakdowns.

Similarly, it is now lawful to exchange in so-called organ swaps that involve four instead of two people. The simplest case involves two couples, where, say, the husband of one has an organ that is compatible with the wife of the second, but not that of his own wife. The same is true for the other couple. Working an exchange of organs is best understood as a combination of a gift and a swap, which has been held legal in an opinion letter written to the General Counsel of Health and Human Services,[37] which has now been codified in the Charlie W. Norwood Living Donation Act.[38] These transactions involve delicate situations that are regularly overcome. There is no reason that the same cannot be applied to cases of organ sales. The legitimate concerns about donor suitability arise currently in any case involving gratuitous live transactions, and the protocols that are used

[35] Walter Graham (executive director of UNOS) to Francis L. Delmonico (president of UNOS), Apr. 6, 2006.

[36] Mark D. Fox, *The Price Is Wrong: The Moral Cost of Living Donor Inducements*, 6 AM. J.TRANSPLANTATION 2529 (2006).

[37] *See Legality of Alternative Organ Donation Practices* under 42 U.S.C. § 274e, 31 OP. OFF. LEGAL COUNSEL (2007), *available at* http://www.usdoj.gov/olc/2007/organtransplant.pdf.

[38] Charlie W. Norwood Living Organ Donation Act § 2, 42 U.S.C. § 274(e)(c)(4) (describing paired donations).

in those cases could be carried over to cases where cash or other valuable consideration is allowed.

In addition, it is critical to note that once this market goes above ground, the social horribles will disappear. People will be able to get counseling and advice, which no one will supply in an illegal market. Third persons can broker these transactions, as now takes place in other markets. Indeed, many of the proposals for a "regulated organ" market that offer to put restrictions on these kinds of intermediaries are likely to make these markets less responsive to human needs than the current arrangements.[39] If brokers and headhunters are commonplace in real estate and employment markets, why bar them here?

The Return of Neoclassical Economics

There is no reason to think that in any contestable market, private individuals will not respond to the necessities of the situation if they are allowed to do so. An entire class of objections to deregulation is therefore misguided. Now that I have discussed the limitations of Debora Spar's account of markets, let me return to it once again, only this time to address its strengths. My objection to her account of the impersonal nature of markets only explains how individuals will react to different classes of transactions once they are legal. But her analysis of markets is dead-on for two other issues critical to the successful operation of any and all markets. The first one, which arose in connection with *Baby M,* is what happens when contracts are not enforced. On this point the answer is the same across the board, for simple exchanges and relational contracts. Weaker enforcement leads to reduced reliance on voluntary exchange and, for cases that matter, the substitution of more costly mechanisms to secure mutual compliance. It is worth noting that in the organ swaps that are now legal, there is no real contractual enforcement, because no court will order specific performance of a promise to remove a kidney. So an alternative assurance device has developed. Everyone goes

[39] *See, e.g.,* ARTHUR J. MATAS, POLICY ANALYSIS – A REGULATED SYSTEM OF COMPENSATION FOR LIVING KIDNEY DONATION: RATIONALE AND CONCERN (2007) ; Arthur J. Matas, *Why We Should Develop a Regulated System of Kidney Sales: A Call for Action!* 1 CLINICAL J. AM. SOC'Y OF NEPHROLOGY 1129 (2006).For my response to these points, see Richard A. Epstein, *Altruism and Valuable Consideration in Organ Transplantation, in*WHEN ALTRUISM ISN'T ENOUGH (Sally Satel ed., 2008).

under anesthesia at the same time, so that there is perfect simultaneity in what is termed an "altruistic" transaction. But in some cases where damages and/or specific performance is available, they could be used to improve the situation. In addition, legalization makes it possible for third persons to fill a variety of intermediate roles, supplying a wide range of services: a list of potential organ sellers and organ buyers, for example.

More importantly, Spar is right when she invokes the general norm that the higher the price, the greater the supply. This point has been doubted with organs, but the evidence from Iran shows that even in that highly imperfect regulated market featuring a government monopoly at fixed prices the supply of organs for sale increases, and the queues for organs diminish.[40] Thus the central theorem of economics is orthogonal to the differences between spot contracts and relational contracts. In both cases, as the price increases, the supply will increase. Once again, the descriptive power of the simplest version of neoclassical economics predicts huge shortages when price is kept, with modest exceptions for various expenses, at zero. Indeed, even if we assume a modest level of altruism - defined here as a willingness of some people to supply goods at a negative price[41] - the shortages remain acute, as is precisely what we observe. The clear moral of this entire episode with organs is that we need to keep both the social understandings of individual transactions *and* the basic theorems of neoclassical economics before us. The former allow us to explain how these transactions will proceed if anyone is allowed to go forward on mutually advantageous terms. The latter explains why increases in price will result, not in a change of how business is done, but in the level of organs supplied. In most cases we muddle through fairly well. But in organs, where the zero price constraint is a death sentence for thousands of people each year, we see the true banality of the concern with commodification. Misplaced moral qualms about markets do not come cheap: they lead to the unnecessary death and suffering each year of thousands of human beings who could be saved by people

[40] *See* Benjamin E. Hippen, *Organ Sales and Moral Travails: Lessons from the Living Kidney Vendor Program in Iran*, CATO INSTITUTE POLICY ANALYSIS No. 614, Mar. 20, 2008, *available at* http://www.legalbluebook.com/Rules.aspx?ContentSectionAssetID=410#(c) (detailing the plan, warts and all).

[41] For a detailed explication of this notion, see Richard A. Epstein, *The Human and Economic Dimensions of Altruism: The Case of Organ Transplantation* (Univ. Chi. Law & Econ., Olin Working Paper No. 385 2008).

with less lofty sensibilities and greater common sense. Here, as in so many other areas, technology has outstripped moral philosophy. It is time to end the contests over the so-called contestable commodities. The right question to ask in these vital areas is not whether markets should be formed, but how they should be formed.

PART II

The Blind Side of Altruism

Abuse, Coercion, and Fraud

4 Compelled Body Part Donations from Children

Michele Goodwin

I. Introduction

Parents may be free to become martyrs themselves. But it does not follow they are free, in identical circumstances, to make martyrs of their children before they have reached the age of full and legal discretion when they can make that choice for themselves.[1]

In thinking about altruism's limits, I want to consider the politics of organ donation, particularly from the perspective of children. Compelled organ and tissue donation from children is a passively accepted norm. As such, a debate as to whether and under what circumstances children may serve as medical donors is largely nonexistent. The lack of scholarship in this domain might indicate that the whim of parents in organ retrieval from children is too complicated and morally bounded to unravel easily. Further, compelled tissue and organ donation are spheres largely overlooked in state and federal regulation. Thus, at a glance, the case law involving the use of children in organ and tissue transplants indicates judicial deference and social ambivalence. Yet, risks are at stake, including the danger of devaluing the autonomy, privacy, and integrity of children.

This chapter considers the contemporary reach of "rescue doctrine," or the Good Samaritan rule. It scrutinizes whether and under what circumstances parents' rationalization for compelling organ and tissue donation from their children is ever proper or legitimate. In other words, when and under what circumstances can parents impose that duty – to rescue – on

[1] Prince v. Massachusetts, 321 U.S. 158, 170 (1944) (holding that parental authority is not absolute and that the state may permissibly regulate and control the conduct of children if doing so is in the best interest of a child's welfare).

their children to save the life of another person? This chapter critiques what I refer to in prior scholarship as "reproductive altruism," meaning creating a child as a lifesaving resource for a dying child.

Yet, I am not fully satisfied by this terminology. Indeed, this term, "reproductive altruism," might be an inadequate descriptor, but the aim is to speak more precisely to what happens on the ground, which is not direct altruism, but imposed, manufactured, or compelled altruism. Sophisticated reproductive technologies afford parents the means to create organ and tissue donors, but legislation and jurisprudence in the United States have yet to address these modern scenarios.

This chapter offers insights, drawing from Kazuo Ishiguro's compelling work, *Never Let Me Go*,[2] I explore how judicial considerations might be framed and what values are most essential to preserve in establishing a framework for conscripted living donations, particularly from children. Indeed, this chapter explains why we should care about compelled organ transplantation from children. One of the more obvious concerns is that reproductive altruism undermines foundational principles of altruism, including autonomy and informed consent. These principles govern federal and state guidelines for organ and tissue donation. As important, the right to refuse in medical treatments and experiments is a nondebatable point made clear by Nuremberg. Importantly, how and whether to save a dying child's life is likely the most difficult decision for parents of terminally ill children. Whether the law should intervene in these life and death situations or whether legislators have anything to say in the regulation of these sensitive medical decision exposes the ethical, economic, and legal tensions.

Ishiguro's novel is an insightful journey of a world imagined, but unstudied, as of yet, by academics. With his languid prose, a very sad dystopia awaits us. The irony, of course, is that his fictionalized future represents more of a contemporary legal realism where children are produced or created specifically to serve as "donors" and to provide "gifts" to others. Ishiguro questions the broader usage of preimplantation genetic diagnosis and in vitro fertilization through innuendo; the children here are "clones" created in test tubes. He plays with the knowledge that "they know, but don't know,"[3] meaning that the children simply adapt to the life given them.

[2] Kazuo Ishiguro, Never Let Me Go (2005).

[3] *Id.* at 266–68.

In the novel, these children are born either to enhance medical understanding or to serve as "donors" and "carers" until they die. The haunting tale teases the reader along because the children – despite their macabre predetermined purpose – are quite normal; they are the children born through advancements in biotechnology. That they are born specifically to serve as "altruistic" organ donors is an incidental matter. This is Ishiguro's point. Much as the controversial, yet illuminating research on happiness suggests,[4] bound people adapt and children are resilient. The children know and understand Ishiguro's world, where their sacrifices are socially, legally, and psychologically normalized. Yet, his prose corrupts the reader into a type of complicity with the concept of compelled donation from children because that reality is normalized in his novel. No longer is it a question as to whether creating individuals to save the lives of others is ever justifiable; in Ishiguro's novel our satisfaction with if not absolute reliance on the cures that result from biotechnological advancements has made donors and carers necessities and a responsibility that the state willingly assumes (as the clones are effectively wards of the state).

Much as an adopted child ponders over her connections to a biological parent, so do these children secretly seek and search for their "possibles" (the individuals who provided their DNA and genetic material).[5] They look for their possibles among the faces of people in pornographic magazines, figuring – as Richard Titmuss[6] conjectured decades ago – only individuals among the skid row population would be desperate and destitute enough to participate in a cloning program. Thus, Ishiguro insinuates that one possible (and dramatically horrific) outcome associated with incentives for organs might be that only the poor and socially disconnected will participate and such programs will necessarily violate general moral and ethical principles.

Ishiguro's novel provides a provocative backdrop for a legal study of compelled donation; his veiled references to slavery touch upon Richard Titmuss's[7] plea against incentives for blood and organ donation. Yet, as the

[4] Richard H. Thaler & Cass R. Sunstein, Nudge: Improving Decisions About Health, Wealth, and Happiness (2008)

[5] Ishiguro, *supra* note 2, at 139.

[6] Richard Titmuss, The Gift Relationship: From Human Body to Social Policy 245 (1971).

[7] *Id.* Titmuss warned against the promotion and implementation of incentives for blood and organ donation, claiming that incentives denigrate personhood and would ultimately undermine the supply pool by attracting the "skidrow."

author suggests, an organ shortage coupled with overwhelming demand will necessarily lead to complicated and oft-times undesirable options. The proper question will be, What options pose the least harm, risk, coercion, and fraud, and also provide the greatest social utility. In other words, where is utility most gained? As Neil Komesar observes in his foundational work on comparative institutional analysis, all choices – when law and resources strain – are necessarily burdened.[8] The problem, however, is that societies become wedded to systems and legislatures to laws – even bad ones – and change is regarded as an insurmountable obstacle.

The use of children as organ suppliers is but one of the problematic externalities of an organ procurement system that relies *exclusively* on altruism. Federal regulations strictly prescribe the altruistic conditions of organ procurement. For example, there cannot be any "valuable" consideration for an organ. The U.S. transplantation system is decidedly anti-incentive and anti-market and many bioethicists embrace this aspect of domestic organ transplantation, arguing that it promotes fairness, equity, and human dignity, while avoiding the corruption and indignity of commodification. And yet, state and federal governments ignore forced use of children as organ and tissue donors. On one hand, the laws are overinclusive. On the other hand, the federal and state regulations governing organ transplantation are underinclusive as the protection of children is a missing link.

A. Understanding Demand-Side Dynamics

When is it reasonable to ask a child to donate her kidney, liver lobe, or lung to save a sibling? Is it ever reasonable to impose a rescue duty on a child? Fifty years ago, these questions served to whet the imaginations of philosophers and ethicists, yet such queries offered limited if any practical consequence. Children and relatives simply died from terminal illnesses now treatable by organ replacements. Thus, even if in abundant supply, children were not needed for spare parts. Nor were technological advancements at a stage of sufficient sophistication to facilitate the broad-scale use of children as organ and tissue donors. In the United States as well as the rest of the world, grieving families prepared for death, not organ transplant

[8] *See, e.g.*, NEIL KOMESAR, LAW'S LIMITS: RULE OF LAW AND THE SUPPLY AND DEMAND OF RIGHTS 3 (2001).

waiting lists, bone marrow registries, or in vitro fertilization (specifically for the purpose of creating a donor child).

Beyond the value of a provocative thought experiment, technological incapacity served to shield children from any serious or meaningful consideration as rescuers of dying siblings or relatives. Equally, transplantation involved significant risk and expense. The dramatically low odds of surviving a transplant in the absence of effective immunological rejection medications cautioned against transplants. These factors combined made the prospect of child organ donors more illusory than real.

However, biotechnology now affords cures for terminal illnesses heretofore only imagined. For example, leukemia causes more deaths in children than any other disease. It is also the most commonly treated disease with bone marrow transplants (BMT).[9] In severe cases of leukemia, not only will the autoimmune system of the child deteriorate, but an organ transplant might also be recommended. In contrast to that bygone era, physicians and parents now urge and seek the involvement of siblings to aid their dying brothers or sisters. Such decision making may be medically sound, but morally and legally fraught. These matters are complicated by concerns for individual autonomy, privacy, and bodily integrity of the "well" child.

For example, nearly thirty years ago, approximately four hundred fifty BMTs were performed on children annually.[10] By 1997, the number had more than quadrupled to more than two thousand BMTs per year.[11] This steep incline can be attributed to a few factors, including greater access to the technology and increased medical insurance coverage for the treatments. As well, researchers now know that BMT effectively treats more illnesses than previously understood. There are more than fifty genetically inherited blood disorders that may lead to deficiency in the blood, immune, or metabolic system in a child. For these diseases, and especially

[9] *Bone Marrow Transplantation and Peripheral Blood Stem Cell Transplantation*, NAT' L CANCER INST., http://www.cancer.gov/cancertopics/factsheet/Therapy/bone-marrow-transplant (accessed Feb. 11, 2007); *Glossary at a Glance*, NAT' L KIDNEY FOUND., http://www.kidney.org/news/newsroom/fs_new/gloss@glance.cfm (accessed Feb. 11, 2007).

[10] Deane L. Wolcott et al., *Psychological Adjustment of Adult Bone Marrow Transplant Donors Whose Recipient Survives*, 41 TRANSPLANTATION 484 (1986).

[11] *See* Corinna Kaarlela, Press Release, University of California San Francisco, After Child Donates Bone Marrow to a Sibling, Self-Esteem Often Fares Worse than That of Non-Donor Brothers and Sisters (Aug. 8, 1997).

leukemia, bone marrow transplantation is the best known treatment and cure available to patients. Yet, despite its relative efficacy, the technology is not without significant complications and drawbacks for the donor and the recipient. Frequently, these drawbacks are described from the perspective of the patient needing the transplant, thereby overlooking the common burdens equally experienced by the child who surrenders her bone marrow.

Significantly high dosages of chemotherapy and radiotherapy remain the preferred treatment to suppress the child's immune system in order to prevent bone marrow rejection. The graft will fail if the injected bone marrow cells are rejected by the recipient. In the alternative, the graft might attempt to destroy the recipient's immune system, causing a severe medical emergency know as graft-versus-host disease (GVHD). Approximately 50 percent of all patients who receive bone marrow transplants will develop GVHD.[12] If it occurs within the first one hundred days after the transplant, dermatitis, enteritis, and hepatitis are well known side effects. Conditions associated with GVHD that occur more than one hundred days after the transplant can result in an autoimmune syndrome that destroys organs. Chemotherapy reduces the likelihood of such occurrences and for that reason is used to treat these conditions as they arise. Yet, chemotherapy and radiotherapy expose patients to problematic externalities as these treatments are known to cause organ damage in both the short and long terms. Infections are common side effects of BMT procedures. The infections may be difficult to treat given the preexisting vulnerable health care status of the patient.

To reduce the likelihood of complications such as those described, physicians emphasize the importance of close donor matches.[13] Some critics, including Dr. Clive Callender, assert that there is overreliance on close matches in light of alternative medical therapies. In reality, close donor matches, particularly from siblings, are less medically risky and convenient;

[12] *Protein Level Predicts Who Will Develop Deadly Complication after Bone Marrow Transplant*, LAB BUS. WK., Mar. 19, 2006, at 294 (discussing a recent University of Michigan study).

[13] Note, however, that some physicians and researchers reject the notion that exact matching should be the only prescribed course of research to address BMT related treatment protocols. *See Use of Alternative Donor Transplants in Children with Early Ph+ ALL Encouraged*, LAB BUS. WK., Mar. 12, 2006, at 63.

sibling donations reduce costs and other burdens for the recipient, parents, and physicians. Siblings account for more than half of living donors - they are easily accessible, available, and need not be tracked down. The pressure to donate is so strong that it may veer into the coercive. Importantly, there is no negotiation process for the child who surrenders her bone marrow or organ.

Consider a case reported in a midwestern newspaper in March 2006, involving an Oklahoma family - the Freemans - who intended to use their five-year-old daughter to supply bone marrow for a sibling to be born later that year.[14] The Freemans acknowledged the likelihood that with each child they conceived, the possibility of the children inheriting a terminal genetic disease. Yet, with this knowledge the couple continued to grow their family. Why?

According to Kristina Dudley, "the Freemans [were] hoping for a smoother medical ride with their fourth child.... However, the chances of his immune system growing stronger and faster appeared better because of his ... big sister, Brittany."[15] In other words, Brittany's parents - the Freemans - planned for Brittany to serve as a bone marrow donor if their children's health failed. The Freemans were not alone; their soon-to-be-born son's physicians supported the compelled donation plan. Despite the child's misgivings about being a donor, Mrs. Freeman expressed relief that Brittany was a match, "but at the same time, she's only 5 years old. I definitely wish there was another way. It's a bittersweet situation."[16] When Brittany "asked if she could wait a few years before she had to take part in a transplant," the Freemans demurred. Mrs. Freeman recalls, "We said that's not possible. Now she's glad she can help."[17]

More recently in France, a Turkish family underwent sophisticated reproductive therapies to create a child donor who will provide stem cells for their existing children who were born with a rare genetic disease.[18] A court

[14] Kristina Dudley, *Family Ready to Battle Immunodeficiency Again*, TULSA WORLD (Okla.), Mar. 8, 2006, at 3.

[15] *Id.*

[16] *Id.*

[17] *Id.*

[18] Joseph Bamat, *France's First 'Saviour Sibling' Stirs Ethical Debate about Biotechnology*, FRANCE 24, Feb. 8, 2011, http://www.france24.com/en/20110208-france-first-saviour-baby-donor-biotechnology-stem-cell-research-clamart-umut-fryman (last updated Feb. 9, 2011).

cleared the way for this procedure,[19] following legal precedent previously established in England.[20] To be sure, these decisions expose significant ethical, moral, legal, and medical tensions. Autonomy is a complicated concept in such cases – whose autonomy should prevail? Substantively, the autonomy of the intended donor must take priority. However, by law, children are deemed "incompetent," thereby unable to make independent medical and legal decisions in most circumstances. Therefore, courts and doctors defer to parents. Yet, in these cases, parents and doctors may have conflicting interests; parents wish to save the lives of their dying children, and so do the doctors. Most often, the doctor treating the sick sibling becomes the de facto physician for the donor, adding to the conflicting interest. When realistically framed in this way, the vulnerability of donor siblings comes into sharper view.

The clear benefit of compelled sibling donation is that it saves the lives of dying family members. However, at what cost? Avoiding transplant waiting lists lessens the stress and psychological burdens for all parties involved except the compelled donor children. Donor siblings are readily available for probing, testing, and supplying supplemental doses of blood, lymphocytes, granulocytes, and bone marrow. And yet, donor children are exposed to (if they do not experience) myriad medical and psychological setbacks, which proportionately may pale in comparison to their sibling's preoperative suffering but are real nonetheless. BMT and organ transplant operations require general anesthesia, which although routinely used in serious medical surgeries, nonetheless carries significant risks, including death. According to the National Marrow Donor Program, more common problems include fatigue, faintness, headaches, soreness, inability to walk properly, difficulty climbing stairs, pain at the

[19] The use of reproductive technologies to ensure that an unborn child does not have the same disease as his sibling and to ensure s/he is a match for an existing sick child is regulated by Agence de la Biomédecine, which issues licenses for the procedures on a case-by-case basis. *See Le Figaro: The First "Drug Baby" Umut Talha – an Ethical Challenge*, Eye Dr De Lengocky Blog (Feb. 8, 2011), http://eyedrd.org/2011/02/le-figaro-first-drug-baby-umut-talha.html.

[20] In April 2005, the House of Lords ruled that the use of preimplantation genetic diagnosis to create a child whose umbilical cord stem cells could cure a sibling's blood disorder was permissible. *"Savior Siblings," Made to Order*, Zenit, May 5, 2005, http://www.zenit.org/article-17587?l=english.

intravenous spot, sore throat, pain sitting, pain at the collection site, nausea, and vomiting.[21]

Indeed, donor children's health status as the non-ill children may uniquely work against them in underappreciated ways. Child donors live in the shadows of siblings with serious, life-threatening medical conditions. Donors are far less sympathetic patients when compared to their dying siblings. In fact, these child "rescuers" are commonly overlooked as patients, never fully conquering the social and psychological transition from healthy children to nontherapeutic patients. There is an implicit bias that regards donor children's "healthiness" as a permanent invincibility. Undervalued, then, are their vulnerability, contemporaneous and future physical and mental health risks, and right to be free of nontherapeutic medical treatments. Also undervalued and perhaps less contemplated are the potential future conflicts with their siblings.

Oddly, reproductive altruism is difficult to reconcile with a rather robust U.S. jurisprudence that rejects rescue doctrine. U.S. common law jurisprudence imposes no duty or obligation on an individual to rescue another unless he caused the peril. And while critics contend that the no duty rule promotes ambivalence, nonfeasance, passivity, and anticooperative behavior, there are forceful rationales for the rule. Indeed, common law jurisprudence is intentional and not blind to the moral appeal of rescue.[22] In *Union Pacific Railroad Co. v. Cappier*, Justice Smith explains:

> For withholding relief from the suffering, for failure to respond to the calls of worthy charity, or for faltering in the bestowment of brotherly love on the unfortunate, penalties are found not in the laws of men, but in that higher law, the violation of which is condemned by the voice of conscience, whose sentence of punishment for the recreant act is swift and sure. In the law of contracts it is now well understood that a promise founded on a moral obligation will not be enforced in the courts.[23]

In *Union Pacific*, the question before the Court was whether the company had a duty to render timely, competent aid to Irvin Ezelle, a trespasser, struck by a passing railway car as he illegally crossed train tracks. The Kansas

[21] *See Donation FAQS*, Nat'l Marrow Donor Program, http://www.marrow.org/DONOR/marrow_donation_advanced.html (accessed Mar. 10, 2006).

[22] *See* Union Pac. Ry. Co. v. Cappier, 72 P. 281, 282–83 (Kan. 1903).

[23] *Id.* at 282–83.

Supreme Court answered in the negative, although it acknowledged that a general moral duty may exist in such circumstances. Relevantly, the Court declined to extend legal protection or award civil damages for such a moral duty. According to Justice Smith, only the "omission or negligent discharge of legal duties" should "come within the sphere of judicial cognizance."[24] In other words, absent a statutory duty to aid or third party injury resulting from direct negligence, U.S. law will not hold a company liable should they fail to render aid. The Court's holding should not be misread to apply exclusively to corporate entities. To the contrary, the common law no duty to rescue rule protects individuals against being forced to rescue or endanger themselves to aid another. As clear-cut as this landmark case and subsequent jurisprudence may be, the legal principles that undergird it are inconsistently applied in medical therapy cases involving children.

Thus, despite a firm jurisprudence clarifying that neither moral duties nor Good Samaritan principals give rise to legal duties and obligations in the United States, courts consistently defer to the interests of parents in sibling organ and tissue donation cases. The law is terribly inconsistent. On one hand, a company is spared the obligation to provide assistance or aid to a passerby. On the other, children as young as two years old may be compelled to submit to nontherapeutic medical surgeries to benefit a sibling or other family member. To understand better how courts justify the latter, Part II turns to examining the narrow jurisprudence involving child tissue and organ donations.

II. Psychological Benefit: Legal and Social Constructions

Despite the degree to which this metaphor pervades transplantation practice, our studies have demonstrated that "gift-giving" or altruism is not necessarily the primary motivation when families decide to donate. Families often donate for nonaltruistic reasons, for example a desire to see their loved one live on in the recipient.[25]

There exists a presumption now embedded in law that characterizes living donations from children to their siblings as providing a "psychological benefit" for the child donor. This concept was first instantiated in law in a 1969

[24] *Id.* at 282.

[25] Laura A. Siminoff & Kata Chillag, *The Fallacy of the "Gift of Life"*, 29 HASTINGS CTR. REP. 34, 40 (1999).

Kentucky Court of Appeals case, *Strunk v. Strunk*,[26] the first written opinion to address sibling donation. The case provides a provocative foundation for sibling donation doctrine. On the one hand, it establishes happiness and psychological benefit to the prospective donor as salient, determinative factors in authorizing a transplant. On the other hand, psychological benefit can credibly be read as a proxy for acquiescing to parental desire as the question posed by courts is whether the healthy sibling would be sad if the unhealthy sibling died.

At issue in *Strunk* was whether the court possessed proper legal authority to permit a kidney to be removed from "an incompetent ward of the state" on a parent's petition for the purpose of transplantation into his sibling.[27] The court answered in the affirmative, urging that the surgery was "necessary."[28] The appeals court opined that principles laid out over the centuries in the United States as well as abroad were sufficiently broad "not only to cover property but also to cover all matters touching on the well-being of [Strunk]."[29]

However, the facts in *Strunk* are particularly relevant as they help to explain why the court took great pains to save the life of the dying son over the objections of the donor's *guardian ad litem*. Equally, the record illumes the problematic eugenics legacy that undergirds and precedes the *Strunk* case, namely, a jurisprudence that emphasized social fitness and the perception that heredity determined moral, physical, and intellectual character. Eugenical thought, which became entrenched in U.S. law through the Supreme Court's ruling in *Buck v. Bell*,[30] carved out legal exceptions to equal protection and declared that the intellectually unfit deserved lesser standards of privacy, autonomy, and due process.

[26] Strunk v. Strunk, 445 S.W.2d 145, 146 (Ky. Ct. App. 1969). Three unreported Massachusetts decisions addressed whether parental authority to consent to similar medical procedures involving twins was permissible. These cases, however, were not reported and thus were not readily accessible to judges and law clerks in other jurisdictions. The justices hearing *Strunk* might have been less aware of these cases. *See* Masden v. Harrison, No. 6865 1 (Eq. Mass. Sup. Jud.Ct. June 12, 1957); Hushey v. Harrison, No. 6866 6 (Eq. Mass. Sup. Jud. Ct. Aug. 30, 1957); Foster v. Harrison, No. 6867 4 (Eq. Mass. Sup. Jud. Ct. Nov. 20, 1957).

[27] *Strunk*, 445 S.W.2d at 145.

[28] *Id.* at 146.

[29] *Id.* at 148.

[30] Buck v. Bell, 274 U.S. 200 (1927).

In reaching its holding, the *Strunk* court significantly alluded to eugenical thought and values, deploying terms like "feeble-minded" and "disabled" to describe the incompetent donor.[31] The mother, Ava Strunk, petitioned the court for the removal of one of Jerry Strunk's kidneys for implantation in his brother, Tommy.[32] As the court inspected, the two brothers shared little in common: Jerry, a twenty-seven-year-old man possessing the limited cognitive capacity of a six-year-old with an IQ of 35, and confined to a state-funded institution, and Tommy, a twenty-eight-year-old employed student enrolled at the University of Cincinnati.[33] Yet, the majority found Jerry's happiness to be linked to Tom's survival,[34] and although Jerry's *guardian ad litem* urged against the operation, the court was not persuaded.[35] The court presumed that "emotionally and psychologically[,] ... [Jerry's] well-being would be jeopardized more severely by the loss of his brother than by the removal of a kidney."[36] Notably, this was the wrong inquiry to pursue. That Jerry was mentally incompetent, with an IQ of 35, may have been more probative for the court than the close bond between the brothers that the justices allude to but fail to substantiate with any clear evidence.

Strunk launched a precedent, which introduces happiness and psychological benefit in courts' analyses of child sibling donation. Indeed, psychological benefit becomes the relevant test for the court. Effectively, so long as it can be established that the donor child would be happier if his sibling survives, courts authorize these compulsory "donations." Yet, courts pursue these inquiries about happiness and psychological good without ancillary empirical study, consultation with more nuanced psychological literature, projections about the donors' future perspectives, or expert testimony from former child donors. Quite simply, the *Strunk* court explored less probative, elementary questions: Would Jerry be sad if his elder sibling died? Would Jerry be happy if Tommy lived? Relevantly, such questions are immaterial to assessing constitutional risks and harms associated with compulsory, nontherapeutic surgery, including protecting autonomy, privacy, and due process. In this case, the donor's cognitive capacities played

[31] *Strunk*, 445 S.W.2d at 146.
[32] *Id.*
[33] *Id.* at 147.
[34] *Id.*
[35] *Id.*
[36] *Id.* at 146.

a pivotal role in the court's ruling and subsequent judicial application in sibling donor law.

Consider the 1970s predicament of cousins in *McFall v. Shimp*,[37] a noteworthy case because it addresses matters similar to those at issue in *Strunk:* the demand for a transplant, only one viable source of supply, and a dying relative. The key litigant in *McFall*, Robert McFall, suffered from a rare bone marrow disease, aplastic anemia; his death was imminent absent a bone marrow transplant from a suitable donor.[38] He sought an injunction against the only person known as a suitable donor, his cousin Robert Shimp, demanding that the latter undergo a procedure to remove bone marrow for implantation into his body.[39] When the cousin refused to become a donor, McFall sought judicial relief to compel the donation. The important legal question before the court was whether the law had any role in their personal controversy: *whether the law could compel bone marrow donation between two competent adults.* Wisely, Judge Flaherty refused to issue the injunction.

The judicial opinion is unambiguous: a dying person is not endowed with a special right to invade another's body even if to save his own life.[40] The court made clear that altruism cannot be compelled, and donation cannot really be a gift if it is mandated. Courts are not in the position to "change every concept and principle upon which our society is founded."[41] According to Judge Flaherty:

> The common law has consistently held to a rule which provides that one human being is under no legal compulsion to give aid or to take action to save another human being or to rescue. A great deal has been written regarding this rule which, on the surface, appears to be revolting in a moral sense. Introspection, however, will demonstrate that the rule is founded upon the very essence of our free society.[42]

In preserving "no duty" rules, societies are bound to witness harms and moral challenges; Robert McFall died one month after the court issued its opinion.

[37] McFall v. Shimp, 10 Pa. D. & C.3d 90 (1978).

[38] *Id.*

[39] Dennis Williams, *Bad Samaritan*, Newsweek, Aug. 7, 1978, at 35.

[40] *McFall*, 10 Pa. D. & C.3d at 91.

[41] *Id.*

[42] *Id.*

What lessons can be learned from the two cases discussed? Importantly, the ruling in *Strunk* was a slippery slope; the case was not limited to "mentally deficient persons," but rather to persons who were incompetent to make those complicated transplant decisions independently, especially minors. The ruling expanded judicial authority to permit compulsory organ harvesting, which – in the case of minors – consistently coincides with and affirms parental appeals. In failing to predict the robust technological developments that would facilitate better diagnosis of diseases and make organ transplantation more accessible, the court was shortsighted.[43] Within a few years of *Strunk*, jurisdictions across the country in Virginia,[44] Texas,[45] and Connecticut[46] adopted its expanding jurisprudence. The *Little v. Little*[47] case permitted a mother (one week after declaring her teen daughter incompetent) to order her daughter's kidney removed so that the organ could be provided to the girl's brother. The court concluded that the fourteen-year-old, although declared incompetent, could nevertheless benefit psychologically from surrendering her organ to a sibling.[48]

Subsequent jurisprudence expanded the *Strunk* ruling to include mentally competent child living donors.[49] In *Hart v. Brown*,[50] Connecticut parents of seven-year-old twins sought a declaratory judgment to permit the removal of one daughter's kidney for implantation in the other. The intended recipient's physician refused to perform the necessary surgeries,

[43] *See* Emily Denham Morris, Note, *The Organ Trail: Express versus Presumed Consent as Paths to Blaze in Solving a Critical Shortage*, 90 Ky. L.J. 1125, 1149 (2001) (asserting that "one problem with most of the regulations passed and common law rules set out by courts regarding organ and tissue donation has been short-sightedness when dealing with future technological advances. Courts do not have crystal balls that can predict the future" of technological advancements).

[44] *See* Hurdle v. Currier, 5 Va. Cir. 509, 513 (1977) (opining that under the circumstances parents possessed the legal authority to require minor daughter to surrender her kidney to her sibling).

[45] *See* Little v. Little, 576 S.W.2d 493, 500 (Tex. Civ. App. 1979) (opining that mother has the legal authority to substitute judgment for fourteen-year-old daughter for purposes of consenting to kidney "donation").

[46] *See* Hart v. Brown, 289 A.2d 386, 391 (Conn. Super. Ct. 1972) (holding that parents have authority to require a seven-year-old daughter to surrender her organ for donation to twin sibling).

[47] *Little*, 576 S.W.2d at 493.

[48] *Id.* at 500.

[49] *See id.* (holding that nothing in Texas law forbade the court's granting authority to a mother to have her daughter's kidney removed to aid her brother).

[50] *Hart*, 289 A.2d at 386.

and the hospital was unwilling to permit the use of its facilities unless the court declared the parents legally able to consent on behalf of their daughter to organ removal for procurement to her sister.[51] Consistent with the judicial approach in *Strunk*, the Connecticut Superior Court found that Kathleen's participation in the organ donation process would be "most beneficial" to her.[52] The court reasoned that Kathleen would be happy if her family was happy.[53]

Strunk's instructive posture paved the way for the *Hart* court as it too reached beyond the original intent of substituted judgment theory by expanding its scope to children.[54] Yet, is "immense benefit" the appropriate standard of review? The longevity of happiness in a child or a family is difficult to predict. Families separate, divorce, and may be later reconstituted with different people. Placing responsibility on a child to promote that type of happiness through uninformed, nonconsensual, and invasive surgeries stretches the boundaries of pragmatic decision making. It may be the case that circumstances present an opportunity for family members, particularly children, to help in extraordinary ways, but the courts' analyses in these cases have yet to establish the pragmatic limitations and reconcile those with moral principles and preexisting legal rules.[55]

Ex post *Strunk* and its progeny, a few conclusions can be drawn about compulsory organ and tissue harvesting from children. Notwithstanding *Curran v. Bosze*[56] (a case involving nonmarried separated parents, with conflicting views on donation), the first and most obvious conclusion is that children do not possess the "right to refuse" an organ or tissue harvest. Second, even if children have a recognizable *interest* to refuse organ harvesting, that interest is subordinate to the *rights* of parents and courts to substitute their judgment. Third, courts are reluctant to interfere with parental authority and decision making, thereby effectively reducing, or altogether eliminating, the function of the courts in grappling with these complex issues. The outcomes in these instances will be obvious and the

[51] *Id.* at 387.
[52] *Id.* at 389.
[53] *Id.*
[54] *Id.* at 387–88.
[55] *See* Michael T. Morley, Note, *Proxy Consent to Organ Donation by Incompetents*, 111 YALE L.J. 1215, 1240–43 (2002) (arguing that guilt often influences organ donating decisions).
[56] 141 Ill.2d 473 (Ill. 1990).

proceedings pro forma; unless there is conflict between the parents, their decision to compel organ donation will carry. Fourth, the *Strunk* progeny demonstrates the plasticity of the law as related to minors (and incompetent persons). Courts have ostensibly created an exception to the rescue doctrine for children. The legislative and judicial failure to recognize the contradictions is manifold.

III: Altruism and the Vernacular Problem

As described in Part II, so long as courts predict that children will benefit psychologically from the compulsory donation, the transplants are deemed permissible. This deeply entrenched jurisprudence exposes the problem of vernacular in organ transplantation that extends beyond terminology. Indeed, language is a powerful tool in the transplantation industry, and to the extent that children become the subjects of organ donation – as givers and receivers – the language of the "gift" may obscure conflicts of interests, violations of medical norms, manipulation, coercion, parental pressure, and abuse. To this end, legal scholars and medical professionals insufficiently scrutinize the concept of altruism. The problem lies in an entrenched deductive reasoning that frames altruism as always morally defensible, possessing higher-order values and no corruption.

Yet, on inspection, horrible abuses are facilitated in the name of altruism; as Dr. Naomi Duke reminds us in Chapter 3, slavery was one construction of altruism, forcing blacks into free labor; children serving in armies, whereby youth are coerced into "volunteering" for the sake of "saving" their tribes, governments, or communities, is another; and numerous other examples can be offered. The important lesson is that such sacrifices for the common good exact an enormous social price. The moral value of those types of sacrifices is not easily quantifiable, not because they are *invaluable*, but because the costs may be socially and legally incalculable or morally unjustifiable.

Compelled organ donation from living children is but one additional problematic by-product of the "gift" or "altruism" model, and a collateral component of assisted reproductive technology and preimplantation genetic diagnosis in that these technologies provide the means for creating donor babies. Typically, involuntary service of one kind (i.e., army service) or another (paying taxes for a police force) is predicated on a theory of social contract. This theory suggests that individual sacrifice inures benefits to the whole. This reasoning holds up, generally, but may be fallible in universal application. Organ transplantation is one such domain.

The social contract assumes equal bargaining and acquisition power, and in our present *altruistic* organ and tissue donation systems we perhaps presume the same.[57] However, this view of altruism in the transplantation and broader body parts industry does not probe whether all individuals are situated similarly, even within families, particularly children and the mentally incompetent.[58] Most theories of altruism, including Rawls's utilitarian views on social justice and fairness, are premised on democratic societies that adhere to nondiscriminatory principles. But such altruistic theories, even if appealing, do not consider law and status as we know them in our society. So they tend to overlook preexisting imbalances in society and the compromised status of those traditionally marginalized or discriminated against, such as children, whose authority is subordinate to that of their parents.[59] Understanding the nuances of status and language is critical to the study of organ transplantation, particularly donation.

For example, in the realm of human transplantation, organs are often referred to as "gifts" and "miracles."[60] Indeed, therein exists a significant problem of vernacular and perception. Living donation cases, particularly those involving children, are deeply nuanced and may be influenced by

[57] *See* THOMAS NAGEL, THE POSSIBILITY OF ALTRUISM 3, 19, 82, 88, 100, 144 (1970); Eric A. Posner, *Altruism, Status, and Trust in the Law of Gifts and Gratuitous Promises*, 1997 WIS. L. REV. 567, 585 (1997) (stating that "altruistic gifts make the beneficiary better off, because the beneficiary prefers the gift to nothing; and they make the donor better off because the donor derives utility from the donee's increase in utility"); *see also* GEORGE P. FLETCHER, LOYALTY: AN ESSAY ON THE MORALITY OF RELATIONSHIPS 18–19 (993).

[58] *See, e.g.*, Martha E. Ertman, *What's Wrong with a Parenthood Market? A New and Improved Theory of Commodification*, 82 N.C. L. REV. 1, 19 (2003) (declaring that sperm donor anonymity "is crucial because family law often links biology to parental rights and responsibilities").

[59] *See, e.g.*, Michele Goodwin, *Deconstructing Legislative Consent Law: Organ Taking, Racial Profiling & Distributive Justice*, 6 VA. J.L. & TECH. 2 (2001) (critiquing the moral and legal legitimacy of presumed consent statutes that allow for the nonconsensual removal of tissues from cadavers and their disparate impact on communities of color).

[60] *See Organ Donation: Miracles Come from Tragedy*, WICHITA FALLS MED. MAG., http://www.medmag.org/miracle.html (providing testimonials about Gloria Key Harrison, whose death and subsequent donations benefited fifty people) (accessed Oct. 31, 2006).

myriad factors, including guilt, pressure, coercion, and shame. Transactions involving child donors further expose the problematic linguistics of altruism; compelled organ donation from children is the most basic form of objectification. For this reason, in an important research study, Siminoff and Chillag assert that the "gift" concept does not work.[61] Indeed, in many instances, gifting is not entirely altruistic, but strategic planning (i.e., donations to museums, charities, and schools).

However, the limited legal and medical vernacular for describing the processes of organ transfer disserves its participants, including its victims. Courts reinforce the limited vernacular of the transplantation industry.[62] In *Georgia Lions Eye Bank v. Lavant*, for example, the Supreme Court of Georgia dismissed parents' claims that the harvesting of their deceased son's corneas occurred without their consent.[63] The court applied the term "donation" to the nonconsensual retrieval. According to the court, the state statute that authorized nonconsensual cornea retrieval promoted justice and did not violate individual rights because it benefited others. The language of "benefit" and "gifting" to others pervades child transplant cases.

IV. Conclusion

When altruism is the exclusive legal forum for organ and tissue procurement, demand creates pressure within the limited pool, causing tissue and organ solicitation to spread into black markets and seep into less desirable altruistic subsystems.[64] Parents, patients, relatives, and friends confront burdened choices. The legal alternatives are limited when altruism is the only legally permissible form of organ and tissue procurement. The jurisprudence involving compelled donations from children[65] of siblings dying

[61] *See* Siminoff & Chillag, *supra* note 25.

[62] *See* Georgia Lions Eye Bank v. Lavant, 335 S.E.2d 127, 128–29 (Ga. 1985) (noting, "certainly, the General Assembly has it within its power, in the interest of the public welfare to authorize this procedure, which yearly benefits hundreds of Georgians").

[63] *Id.*

[64] *See* John Lawrence Hill, *Exploitation*, 79 CORNELL L. REV. 631, 645 (1994) (suggesting that the most controversial alternatives in organ transplantation would be to create markets wherein living donations are solicited).

[65] *See* Cara Cheyette, Note, *Organ Harvests from the Legally Incompetent: An Argument Against Compelled Altruism*, 41 B.C. L. REV. 465, 469 (2000) (cautioning against the use of incompetent persons as organ donors, declaring "organ harvests from children and mentally disabled adults should be categorically prohibited.... Using the most

from terminal illnesses presages future dynamics where the biological lines of family may be less determinative, and therefore more fluid.[66] The biology of family may be replaced by "family relationship," which would seem logical given the sometimes legally and socially arbitrary or ambiguous nature and definition of family.[67] Blended households, step-siblings, adopted siblings, siblings born of ovum or sperm transactions, surrogate siblings, negotiated siblings (children of same sex parents, born with the aid of an involved friend), and foster siblings all represent adaptations of the traditional nuclear family "child" model.[68]

Indeed, the social contract functions only when mutual bargaining power and beneficial reciprocity exist. The benefits need not be equal, but should be of some tangible value to both parties. It also seems important that individuals be allowed to express their generosity and humanity in ways that at times may burden their liberties, including bodily integrity and privacy, in the aid of another. Thus, it would be unwise to proscribe prophylactically all living donations, including from children. Instead, courts must instantiate a balancing test beyond what is now established.

First, it must be clearly understood that compelled living donations from children and incompetent persons are the least desired forms of procurement. Donations from persons legally incompetent cannot easily fit under the umbrella of altruism; the heightened probability for compromising their humanity and dignity makes it so. Alternatives must be considered for desperate parents and siblings beyond the reach of the most vulnerable members of their families. In the past, federally mandated altruistic procurement for bone marrow constrained alternatives. In a recent Ninth Circuit case, *Flynn v. Holder*,[69] this legacy was lifted as the court ruled that

vulnerable members of society to shield us from the pain of a loved one's illness or imminent death is unfair").

66 *Id.* at 505–06.

67 Note, *Looking for a Family Resemblance: The Limits of the Functional Approach to the Legal Definition of Family*, 104 Harv. L. Rev. 1640 (1991) (offering a different legal view of what family means in the United States, calling it a rapidly changing "anachronism").

68 *See* Larry V. Starcher, *Supreme Court Page: The Family of 2003*, W. Va. Law., Nov. 2003, at 8 (pointing out that "we have now moved into the twenty-first century, and the percentage of American children living in 'traditional' married nuclear families is well below a majority.... Single parents are raising 30% of our nation's children. In some urban areas, 30 to 60% of children are being raised by neither biological parent").

69 No. 10-55643, 2012 WL 1001300 (9th Cir. Mar. 27, 2012).

bone marrow donors could be legally compensated, a ruling that will likely increase the pool of potential donors, thereby expanding parental options. However, this ruling extended only to bone marrow donations, leaving organ procurement laws intact.

Second, minors younger than thirteen years old should be prohibited from participating in living donation procedures. An age barrier would be no different from standards regulating day-to-day activities from work and driving to the purchasing of alcohol and cigarettes. Children less than thirteen substantially lack the capacity to appreciate the nuances of these transactions, including potential future health risks. This may also be true for teenagers; however, it is more likely that teenagers will be more literate, knowledgeable, educable, and aware than seven-year-olds. Their understanding of the transplantation process will be more substantive than symbolic, allowing meaningful dialogues about risks and benefits of tissue and organ harvesting.

Third, a *guardian ad litem* should always be appointed in child donor cases. Fourth, psychological screenings for the children involved as well as the adults in their lives should be required to assess how well the parties understand the risks, benefits, and long-term consequences of their actions. Fifth, an independent physician must be appointed for the prospective donor to prevent conflicts of interest. Finally, a statement should be issued to the court from the donor explaining why she desires to participate as an organ or tissue donor. Limiting the participation of children may reduce the pool of viable organs, and other solutions must be sought. However, limiting the pool of child organ and tissue donors will necessitate and, one hopes, force a reconsideration of the altruistically based procurement regime.

5 Quid pro Quo Altruism

Jamila Jefferson-Jones

The Mississippi governor, Haley Barbour, granted clemency to Jamie and Gladys Scott on December 29, 2010. This decision indefinitely suspended their double life sentences and freed them after sixteen years in prison for armed robbery. The price of their liberty: Gladys's kidney. In keeping with the explicit terms of the National Organ Transplant Act (NOTA),[1] this stipulation for release was permissible, because no money was exchanged; some might argue that it was "altruistic." The legal and political irony in this cannot be overstated.

In other words, depending on one's frame of reference, Barbour's discharge condition did not violate U.S. federal law requiring that all organ donations be "altruistic." But the release and the conditions on which it was based highlight a perniciousness that can be cloaked under the wings of altruism. For example, in his official statement regarding the release of the Scott sisters, Governor Barbour said, "Gladys Scott's release is conditioned on her donating one of her kidneys to her sister, a procedure which should be scheduled with urgency."[2] Taken at its value, there was a liberty interest at stake in this case, and that would seemingly violate NOTA's provisions banning organ exchanges based on "valuable consideration." However, there was no federal investigation into Barbour's clemency condition, nor

[1] 42 U.S.C. §§ 273–74.

[2] Gov. Barbour's Statement Regarding Release of Scott Sisters, Dec. 29, 2010, *available at* www.governorbarbour.com /news/2010/dec/12.29.10scottsistersrelease.html (accessed Feb. 4, 2012).

This chapter developed from my broader thinking on the topic, including The Exchange of Inmate Organs for Liberty: Diminishing the "Yuck Factor" in the Bioethics Repugnance Debate, 16 J. Gender Race & Just. (2012).

any sanctions or reprisals from the secretary of health, who oversees the NOTA provisions.

Barbour's critics had much to say, but not much about Barbour's altruism or that of Gladys. One could hardly argue that altruism is not involved with donating a kidney. And commentators have noted over time that when governors grant clemency something altruistic is taking place; maybe we could call it a "political altruism." However, the "altruistic" terms on which these women's releases were granted are nonetheless disturbing. They are what some commentators refer to as "yucky." This chapter seeks to unpack that "yuck" factor and examine the internecine conflict between altruism and incentives in organ transplantation. This chapter analyzes both on a nuanced scale, articulating why altruistic measures may at times be "yucky" and at the same time challenging the notion that incentives in organ transplantation are necessarily always repugnant.

To explain, the same "yucky" or repugnant sentiment that follows Gladys Scott's forced kidney-liberty exchange is deployed by those who oppose systems that would allow living donors to receive incentives in exchange for "donating" organs. These critics usually couch their opposition in terms of forgoing commodification in favor of preserving human dignity.[3] However, critics of living-donor organ sales, such as Francis Delmonico, have developed their arguments well beyond "yuck" or unreasoned repugnance. They contend that under such systems healthy poor people who lack the information necessary to give informed consent will be coerced by the ailing rich into selling their organs.[4] They further urge that these organ vendors will ultimately be disadvantaged physically and financially.[5] Among the hazards they claim are the loss (or partial loss) of an organ, respecting which they may not have received adequate medical care, and the desperation that may have caused them to misrepresent

[3] *See, e.g.*, Cynthia B. Cohen, *Public Policy and the Sale of Human Organs*, 12 Kennedy Inst. Ethics J. 1, 48 (2002) (arguing that the payment of organ donors would constitute a "deni[al] of embodied human dignity ... and would violate a fundamental conviction...: that we should not treat human beings ... as commodities"); Francis L. Delmonico et al., *Ethical Incentives—Not Payment—for Organ Donation*, 346 New Eng. J. Med. 25 (2002).

[4] Delmonico et al., *supra* note 3, at 28.

[5] *See* M. Goyal et al., *Economic and Health Consequences of Selling a Kidney in India*, 288 J. Am. Med. Ass'n 1591(2002) (concluding that those who sold their organs in Chennai, India, were ultimately disadvantaged by continued poverty coupled with poor health).

their eligibility to donate in order to reap the perceived financial benefits of donating.[6]

This chapter uses the Barbour/Scott organ quid pro quo as its primary case study to contemplate whether NOTA's prohibition against the trading of organs for "valuable consideration" should include an exception that would allow state and federal prison inmates to donate organs in exchange for release or credit toward release. Such a stance surely raises questions about quid pro quo exchanges and retribution, including whether the state would be coercing the forfeiture of body parts as punishment or in exchange for freedom. That said, an exception to NOTA's valuable consideration prohibition might serve to modernize our current altruistic organ donation policy into one that may allow for future flexibility in responding to needs of both potential donors and donees.

This particular case study is used because it ties together competing normative interests and dynamics in the human biological exchange sphere. It engages race, social justice, politics, and medical necessity. Other examples could also be used to describe and analyze the welfare interest at stake in human exchange (ova, sperm, and renting wombs) or organ transplantation. Or, other cases could be analyzed that factor in the imprecise and often ambiguous definitions that attach to altruism, such as the case involving using children as organ donors. The Scott case serves well in this project and is particularly salient because it involves a population in urgent need of organ transplant policy reform, federalism issues, and an important thought experiment: the use of prisoners as organ donors.

Part I discusses the legality of the clemency condition imposed on Gladys Scott's release. Part II critiques the Scott sisters/Haley Barbour narrative, unpacking how Governor Barbour settled on the kidney donation clemency condition and why the terms became acceptable to the Scott sisters, their attorneys, and the civil rights community. Finally, in Part III, the chapter proposes a kidney swap framework wherein inmates may be eligible to exchange organs for liberty without triggering the repugnance or "yuck factor" response.

[6] *See* Gabriel M. Danovitch & Alan B. Leichtman, *Kidney Vending: The "Trojan Horse" of Organ Transplantation*, 1 Clinical J. Am. Soc'y of Nephrology 133 (2006).

I. NOTA and the Legality of Governor Barbour's Kidney Clemency Condition

A. The Relevant Demographics of the Kidney Shortage

The stakes are high in organ procurement and transplantation. About 116,500 people were registered on the U.S. organ transplant waiting list at the end of 2012. Of those, nearly two-thirds - approximately 94,475 - are waiting for a kidney. However, only approximately 16,000 kidney transplants are performed each year. What we know from Richard Epstein's chapter is that thousands will die this year and next, just as in the past, because too few organs enter the transplant system. Only one-third of the kidneys eventually transplanted will be from living donors, despite the higher overall quality of living-donor kidneys, which survive in a recipient on average for twice as long as deceased-donor kidneys.

The shortage of kidney donors - both living and deceased - results in lengthy wait times for kidney transplants. More than half of the patients on the kidney transplant waiting list have been on the list for two years or more. More than a third of kidney transplant candidates have been waiting for three or more years. Even worse, those considered too old or too sick will be shaved from the list. Therefore, even though four thousand people per year die of end stage renal disease (ESRD) while waiting for a kidney,[7] we know that figure does not fully capture the true extent of the human toll as the government removes candidates who will soon die from the list. They are unaccounted for.

The statistics for black ESRD patients are even more alarming than the overall national data. Blacks, who represent only 13 percent of the U.S. population, are disproportionately represented as 30 percent of those on the kidney waiting list. The extent of the problem is striking. The numbers of black patients who have been hoping for a kidney for two years or more and three years or more are 37 percent and 38 percent, respectively. Black patients on the kidney waiting list also die at a rate averaging approximately

[7] Based upon Organ Procurement Transplantation Network (OPTN) data as of January 6, 2012. OPTN, http://www.optn.transplant.hrsa.gov/data (accessed Jan. 15, 2012). The data herein regarding those on the kidney transplant waiting list do not include the 2,100 individuals who are waiting for a kidney along with another organ.

fifteen hundred people per year – a number that represents 38 percent of all kidney waiting list deaths.[8]

Drilling down further into the dynamics that attend the Barbour-Scott clemency deal, the number of Mississippians anticipating an organ transplant is quite small relative to the rest of the nation: 168 individuals. These patients are almost exclusively in need of kidneys. Of the 168 waiting list patients in Mississippi, 145 are waiting for kidneys; the remaining 23 are waiting for a heart transplant. Black Mississippians are even more disproportionately represented on that state's kidney transplant waiting list than nationally, as 80 percent of the ESRD patients on Mississippi's kidney waiting list are black. Blacks, however, make up only 37 percent of Mississippi's total population. Given these statistics, it is hardly surprising that three-quarters of those who died in Mississippi in the last year while awaiting a kidney transplant were black.[9]

B. NOTA's Prohibition of Incentivized Organ Exchanges

Despite the nationwide kidney shortage, federal transplant policy has clung steadfastly to altruistic giving in organ donation, thus resisting compensating donors or their families in any way. For example, Section 301 of NOTA, entitled "Prohibition of Organ Purchases," makes illegal the "transfer [of] any human organ for valuable consideration for use in human transplantation" and imposes a fine of up to $50,000 and five years in prison upon one who knowingly violates that prohibition.[10] Consistently and vocally, proponents of Section 301 critique any threat to modify NOTA's valuable consideration prohibition as that might result in the commodification of human organs. They note its repugnancy. Yet, altruism often escapes a more probing examination from these camps.

Indeed, what appears to be grounded in altruism may be more illusory than real as payments are involved at many levels of the "altruistic" organ transplantation system. Section 301 lists kidneys as among its defined "human organs"[11] but does not positively define what constitutes "valuable

[8] *Id.*

[9] *Id.*

[10] 42 U.S.C. § 274e, and (a–b).

[11] *Id.* at § 274e(c)(1) ("The term 'human organ' means the human (including fetal) kidney, liver, heart, lung, pancreas, bone marrow, cornea, eye, bone, and skin or any subpart

consideration." Instead, the term is defined in the negative. Thus, "'valuable consideration' does not include the reasonable payments associated with the removal, transportation, implantation, processing, preservation, quality control, and storage of a human organ."[12] This permits hospitals, doctors, organ procurement agencies, and other medical industry providers to receive payment for their services. Donors, on the other hand, are allowed to recoup certain losses, as "valuable consideration" also does not include the "expenses of travel, housing, and lost wages incurred by the donor."[13]

Despite the lack of a concrete definition of "valuable consideration" under Section 301, it has been widely accepted that not only are direct cash payments to donors prohibited, but a wide range of donor incentives are also violative of NOTA. Therefore, when scholars such as Michele Goodwin and Richard Epstein and policy makers have proposed various incentive regimes aimed at increasing the number of organ donors, those proposals have usually been made with an eye toward amending Section 301 to expand the list of that which does not amount to valuable consideration. These proposed incentives have included college scholarships, housing, and the payment of household bills.[14] Even federal lawmakers have tried unsuccessfully to provide living organ donors with tax credits, life insurance policies, and guaranteed unpaid medical leave in exchange for their donations.[15] State legislative efforts have largely mirrored those of their

thereof and any other human organ (or any subpart thereof, including that derived from a fetus) specified by the Secretary of Health and Human Services by regulation"); *see also* 42 C.F.R. § 121.13 ("'Human organ,' as covered by section 301 of the National Organ Transplant Act, as amended, means the human (including fetal) kidney, liver, heart, lung, pancreas, bone marrow, cornea, eye, bone, skin, and intestine, including the esophagus, stomach, small and/or large intestine, or any portion of the gastrointestinal tract").

[12] 42 U.S.C. § 274e(c)(2).

[13] *Id.*; *see also* the Charlie W. Norwood Living Donation Act, Pub. L. No. 110-44 (2007) (clarifying that paired donations—those in which the intended recipient of an organ donation receives a donation from another donor when she is not biologically compatible with her intended donor—do not constitute the transfer of a human organ for valuable consideration).

[14] *See* Michele Goodwin, Black Markets: The Supply and Demand of Human Body Parts (2006); Jake Linford, *The Kidney Donor Scholarship Act: How College Scholarships Can Provide Financial Incentives for Kidney Donation While Preserving Altruistic Meaning*, 2 St. Louis U. J. Health & Pol'y (2009).

[15] Chad A. Thompson, *Organ Transplantation in the United States: A Brief Legislative History*, *in* When Altruism Isn't Enough: The Case for Compensating Kidney

federal counterparts both in their tactics and in their overall failure to mitigate organ shortages.[16]

In part, what drives the failure of these policies is a blind adherence to altruism. A vision of altruism as a pure, unblemished, unburdened mode of "giving" or "bestowing" is complicated and not fully informed. On one hand, this view of altruism prevents its proponents from recognizing payments for services as "nonaltruistic" or at least compromised altruism. On the other hand, it is important to note that quite worthy platforms to save lives have withered on the vines, while the proponents of altruism attack those models for their honest and transparent incentive-based approaches.

II. Interest Convergence: Political Expedience, Altruism, and Kidney Clemency

In order to understand fully how altruism and incentives worked in the Barbour/Scott case, it is important to unpack the overlapping and competing narratives. In these narratives real-life considerations unfold, just as they would in many or any other context involving clemency for donating an organ. In each instance, there will be convicts serving "time" for doing a "bad" thing, a governor who must evaluate whether the instant case deserves his pardon, and a society that evaluates whether the actions are morally, legally, and socially justified. In this case all those narratives come to bear in striking ways that cannot be divorced from gender, race, and political aspirations.

A. Not So Altruistic: Narrative Collision and Interest Convergence

For more than a decade, while behind bars, the Scott sisters steadfastly maintained their innocence. Eventually their incarceration gained

DONORS 131, 141–43 (Sally Satel ed., 2008). *But see* the Organ Donor Leave Act, Pub. L. No. 106-56 (1999) (providing federal employees with seven days' paid leave for donating bone marrow and thirty days of paid leave for donating organs).

[16] *See* Thompson, *supra* note 15, at 140. One notable exception is South Carolina's failed effort at instituting an inmate organ-for-liberty exchange discussed herein. However, unlike Mississippi's Barbour, the proponents of the measure in South Carolina recognized the danger that such an exchange may have run afoul of NOTA.

national attention, including from the Innocence Project, a national legal-aid clinic dedicated to exonerating the wrongly convicted. Gladys's and Jamie's plight, however, did not attract the national media spotlight until January 2010, when doctors confirmed that Jamie's kidneys were failing.[17] This revelation, coupled with pressure from the Scott family, the National Association for the Advancement of Colored People (NAACP), and others, prompted Governor Barbour - then a possible presidential candidate - to issue an order in December 2010 to free the Scott sisters in January 2011.

There is, however, an argument that neither the pressure from inside Mississippi (from the Scott family and the local NAACP) nor exogenous forces outside Mississippi (the national NAACP, marchers, bloggers, or the national media) would have swayed Governor Barbour had it not been for his own national political aspirations. Thus, in some quarters, Governor Barbour's release of the Scott sisters was seen as a mere political ploy[18] or *hardly altruistic.* Jamie and Gladys's mother, Evelyn Rasco, shared that sentiment: "To me [Barbour's decision to grant clemency] was a political decision. It's not that he actually had any sympathy for my daughters or cared about them."[19]

The double life sentences imposed on Jamie and Gladys Scott came under fire by civil rights activists and the Scott sisters' national media advocates as examples of disparate racial treatment in sentencing.[20] Backing up such claims are studies and a compelling body of scholarly works, including by Song Richardson, that evidence blacks routinely receive harsher sentences

[17] *See* Timothy Williams, *Jailed Sisters are Released for Kidney Transplant,* N.Y. TIMES, Jan. 8, 2011, *available at* 2011 WLNR 445674.

[18] *See Recent Remarks Raise Suspicion Over Gov.'s Motive,* JACKSON CLARION-LEDGER, Dec. 31, 2010, *available at* 2010 WLNR 25707088 (reporting that "social networking sites ... lit up with speculations that [releasing the Scott Sisters] ... was a political ruse to ... shore up a presidential campaign").

[19] *Scott Sisters Free Today,* JACKSON CLARION-LEDGER, Jan. 7, 2011, *available at* 2011 WLNR 395769.

[20] *See, e.g.,* Leonard Pitts, Op-Ed., *Justice, Mississippi Style,* BUFFALO NEWS, Nov. 23, 2010, *available at* 2010 WLNR 23361245 ("If you are poor or black, the justice systemhas long had this terrible tendency to throw you away like garbage. If you doubt it, ... try to imagine some rich white girl doing double life for an $11 robbery. You can't"). The rare circumstances of a judge's reading the life sentence instruction in a robbery relatively lacking in violence is discussed in more detail in Section C of this Part II.

than do whites and that, as compared to whites, blacks are far more likely to be disadvantaged in the criminal justice system, including the decision to incarcerate at all.[21]

In explaining how such civil rights injustices are remedied, Professor Derrick Bell wrote that the "the interest of blacks in achieving racial equality will be accommodated only when it converges with the interests of whites."[22] This provocative principle serves as the foundation for his "interest convergence" theory. The Scott sisters' story is illustrative of a brief moment of interest convergence.[23] This brief moment, rather than representing interest convergence on the macrolevel, as in the instance cited by Bell – that of the Supreme Court's decision in *Brown v. Board of Education*[24] – was instead interest convergence on the microlevel in that it affected the interests of just a few: Jamie and Gladys Scott and Governor Haley Barbour. Although merely reflective of "micro-interest convergence," the timing of Barbour's release of Jamie and Gladys Scott gives additional credence to Bell's assertion that "racial justice – or its appearance – may, from time to time, be counted among the interests deemed important by ... society's policymakers."[25] As demonstrated later, Haley Barbour needed very much to appear racially tolerant and capable of leading a diverse nation at just the same time that Jamie Scott needed to be released for a lifesaving renal transplant. This convergence of the particular interests of Haley Barbour and the Scott sisters provides a key to answering the question of how Governor Barbour settled upon the kidney donation clemency condition and how a condition that would normally engender a "yuck factor" response came to be acceptable to the Scott sisters, their attorneys, and the civil rights community.

[21] Tushar Kansal, *Racial Disparity in Sentencing: A Review of the Literature* 4 (2005), *available at* http://www.sentencingproject.org/doc/publications/rd_sentencing_review.pdf (accessed Feb. 9, 2012).

[22] Derrick A. Bell Jr., Comment, *Brown v. Board of Education and the Interest-Convergence Dilemma*, 93 Harv. L. Rev. 518, 523 (1980).

[23] In explaining Derrick Bell's stance regarding interest convergence and the Supreme Court's Decision in *Brown v. Board of Education*, 347 U.S. 483 (1954), Richard Delgado and Jean Stefancic described 1954 as follows: "The interests of whites and blacks, for a brief moment, converged." Richard Delgado & Jean Stefancic, Critical Race Theory: An Introduction 19 (emphasis added).

[24] 347 U.S. 483 (1954).

[25] Bell, *supra* note 22, at 523.

B. The Scott Sisters' Story

On Christmas Eve 1993, Jamie and Gladys Scott, then twenty-one and nineteen, respectively, were convicted of masterminding an armed robbery. No one was injured during the commission of the crime, which netted eleven dollars. Prior to that time, neither sister had a criminal record.[26] Specifically, Jamie and Gladys were accused of luring two male acquaintances to a secluded area, where the men were then robbed by three teenage boys. The teens all claimed that Jamie and Gladys planned the robbery.[27] Jamie and Gladys tell a different story: that they caught a ride with their two acquaintances after their own car would not start but got out of the acquaintances' car because of unwanted advances and sexual harassment. They claim to have been unaware of the impending robbery by a group of boys that were targeting the men in the car.[28]

The teenage robbers did not implicate Jamie and Gladys in their initial statements to the police; however, the jury believed the prosecution's assertion that Jamie and Gladys orchestrated the robbery. As a result, each sister was convicted and sentenced to two consecutive terms of life in prison. Their three male accomplices, on the other hand, were spared lengthy jail sentences. Two of the three teens testified against the Scott sisters at trial. Those two teens served approximately three years in prison. The third boy recanted, testifying that authorities threatened that if he did not testify that Jamie and Gladys were behind the robbery, they would send him to Parchman prison, where they said he would surely be raped. He was released on parole in 2006.[29]

Officials never explained why such severe sentences against Jamie and Gladys were necessary to achieve the state's goal; nor did they clarify why the women's sentences were so disproportionate to those of the males involved in the crime. The only explanation for the disproportionate sentences is that of their mother, Evelyn Rasco, who surmised that the sentences were

[26] *See* Bob Herbert, *So Utterly Inhumane*, Op-Ed., N.Y. Times, Oct. 12, 2010, *available at* 2010 WLNR 20384708.

[27] *See* Gladys Scott, *I'm Not Bitter*, Jackson-Clarion Ledger, Apr. 6, 2011, *available at* 2011 WLNR 6727736.

[28] *See Victim: Sisters in on Holdup*, Jackson-Clarion Ledger, Jan. 9, 2011, *available at* 2011 WLNR 490945.

[29] *See* Herbert, *supra* note 26.

retribution exacted against her family for testimony that family members gave against a corrupt Scott County sheriff.[30] There is also some speculation that the sisters' sentences were graver than those of the teens who actually robbed the victims because the judge also believed Jamie and Gladys organized the crime.[31]

However, in Mississippi, only juries can impose a life sentence for a robbery.[32] The sisters' current attorney of record, Chokwe Lumumba (who did not represent them at trial), noted that "in the majority of robbery cases, even the ones that are somewhat nasty, they [state judges] don't read that instruction [authorizing the jury to impose a life sentence]."[33] Indeed, Ken Turner, the district attorney who prosecuted the case, admitted, "Normally, life sentences are only returned when it is a grisly case, and this case wasn't particularly grisly."[34] Nevertheless, he offers no explanation as to why the life sentence option was included in the jury instructions.[35] He does, however, admit that the life sentences meted out to the Scott sisters were atypical and agreed that reducing their sentences would have been "appropriate."[36] Eventually, Governor Haley Barbour agreed that the life sentences that Jamie and Gladys received were "unusually long."[37]

C. Haley Barbour, "The Boy from Yazoo City"

Haley Barbour is the most celebrated native son of Yazoo City – the principal town and seat of government of Yazoo County, Mississippi – on the southern edge of the state's Delta region. Historically, the Mississippi-Yazoo Delta is the land of fertile alluvial plains, generations of rich white planters,

30 *See* Pitts, *supra* note 20 (referencing Ms. Rasco's theory and her claim that the corrupt sheriff's successor vowed revenge).

31 *See* Williams, *supra* note 17.

32 *See* MISS. CODE ANN. § 97-3-79 ("Every person who shall . . . be guilty of robbery and, . . . shall be imprisoned for life in the state penitentiary *if the penalty is so fixed by the jury*; and in cases where the jury fails to fix the penalty at imprisonment for life . . . the court shall fix the penalty at . . . any term less than three (3) years.") (emphasis added).

33 Herbert, *supra* note 26.

34 *Sisters Doing Life for Robbery Get Project's Attention*, JACKSON CLARION-LEDGER, Aug. 4, 2003, *available at* 2003 WLNR 18082572.

35 *See* Herbert, *supra* note 26.

36 *Victim: Sisters in on Holdup*, *supra* note 28.

37 *Scott Sisters to be Freed*, JACKSON CLARION-LEDGER, Dec. 30, 2010, *available at* 2010 WLNR 25703608.

and the poor descendants of African slaves. More than any other region of Mississippi, it is steeped in Mississippi's antebellum past, and more than any other recent Mississippi politician, Haley Barbour is steeped in the culture and lore of the Delta. Haley Barbour is not just a son of the Delta, but a scion of Mississippi politics. His great-great-great-great-grandfather, Walter Leake, was the first U.S. senator from Mississippi, after it gained statehood in 1817, and served as its third governor from 1822 to 1825. His paternal grandfather was a judge. His older brother was elected mayor of Yazoo City while Barbour was in college. Barbour even claims to be a descendant of the Choctaw chief Greenwood Leflore, who served in the Mississippi state senate in the mid-1800s.

In fall 2010, Barbour was the president of the Republican Governors' Association and a successful former Republican National Committee chairman. As such, he was widely regarded as a likely contender for the GOP presidential nomination. However, some National Republican leaders and political observers became concerned that Barbour, a white conservative from Mississippi, might be "too southern" for the national stage – implying that either his actual racial politics or others' perceptions of the historic racial climate in Mississippi might hinder any national candidacy.[38] By winter 2010, Barbour proved the pundits right. He was quoted in December in the conservative magazine the *Weekly Standard* as saying of the civil rights era: "I just don't remember it as being that bad."[39] In the same interview, he went on to praise the members of the segregationist White Citizens' Council as peacekeepers who should be credited with the uneventful desegregation of the schools in his hometown of Yazoo City.[40] Barbour later released a statement calling segregation and the Citizens' Council "indefensible."[41] His original statement, however, was the beginning of the end

[38] *See What Are Barbour's Chances?*, JACKSON CLARION-LEDGER, Feb. 27, 2011, *available at* 2011 WLNR 3860399; *see also Scott Sisters to be Freed, supra* note 37 ("As a white Southern Republican considering a challenge against the nation's first black president, Barbour's race relations are likely to be under the microscope").

[39] Andrew Ferguson, *The Boy from Yazoo City: Hayley Barbour Mississippi's Favorite Son*, 16 WKLY. STANDARD no. 15, Dec. 27, 2010.

[40] *See* Governor Barbour's Statement Regarding *Weekly Standard* Article, Dec. 21, 2010, *available at* http://www.governorbarbour.com/news/2010/dec/12.21.10govbarbour-weeklystandard.html (accessed Feb. 4, 2012).

[41] *Id.*

of Barbour's moment in the spotlight as a potential GOP contender. As 2011 approached, he attempted to rehabilitate his reputation on civil rights issues and racial equality by announcing a celebration of the fiftieth anniversary of the Freedom Rides,[42] calling for a civil rights museum in the state capital of Jackson,[43] and finally agreeing to free the Scott sisters.[44]

How do Barbour's political aspirations map onto the Jamie and Gladys Scott narrative? Jamie and Gladys Scott originally petitioned for a pardon from the governor; however, what they ultimately received was an indefinite suspension of their sentences, the functional equivalent of parole. They are, therefore required to report monthly to a parole officer, secure judicial permission before traveling, refrain from associating with those with criminal records, and pay a monthly fee of $52 each for the cost of their supervision. After their release from prison, the Scott sisters again petitioned Governor Barbour for a full pardon.

Indeed, in early April 2011, Barbour not only denied their petition, but, through his spokesperson, sent the message that any future petitions from the Scott sisters would be denied. The sisters' supporters vowed to make their pardon an issue should Barbour attempt to run for the presidency. By April's end, however, Barbour announced that he would not seek his party's nomination for the office of president, and as he was term-limited as governor, no longer *needed* to improve his local or national image. What might have appeared at first to be the highest form of altruism from a sitting governor in the end turned out to be driven by deep personal and political interests. Importantly, political and personal interests may significantly influence the instances when state lawmakers choose to be altruistic. Barring political expediency, the Scott sisters had nothing to offer Barbour. Their interests were no longer convergent. Barbour remained true to his word and did not include the Scott sisters in his end-of-term pardons,

[42] This announcement was made on the 2011 Martin Luther King Jr. holiday. *See Gov. Barbour Formally Announces Celebration of Freedom Riders*, Jan. 17, 2011, *available at* http://www.governorbarbour.com/news/2011/jan/1_17freedomridersanniversary.html (accessed Feb. 4, 2012).

[43] *See Text of Governor Barbour's State of the State Address*, Jan. 11, 2011, *available at* http://www.governorbarbour.com/news/2011/jan/1.11.11%20Gov.%20Barbour's%20State%20of%20the%20State%20Address%20TEXT.pdf (accessed Feb. 4, 2012); *see also What Are Barbour's Chances?*, *supra* note 38 (citing these events as Barbour's attempts to "reach ... across the racial divide").

[44] *See What Are Barbour's Chances?*, *supra* note 38.

which included rapists, murderers, drunk drivers, and others who committed heinous crimes. He pardoned two hundred convicted felons, more than two dozen of whom had been convicted of homicide.[45]

III. A Proposed Program for Inmate Organ Donations

A. Interest Convergence in the Inmate Organ Donation Context

Professor Bell's model of interest convergence can be applied beyond the racial equality context to other scenarios where the interests of the relatively powerless and those of the relatively powerful align to create a moment of opportunity for the disadvantaged person or group of persons to advance their cause. The interest convergence in the Scott/Barbour case - Jamie's dire medical need with Barbour's political aspirations - serves to heighten repugnance in some quarters. However, placing aside Barbour's complicated interests and the troubling quid pro quo, by adapting Bell's interest convergence model to the interests of inmates as they converge with those of the individuals awaiting transplants, one can argue that such convergence lends support to the creation of an inmate organ donation program. Part III turns to examining who benefits from and who might be harmed by an inmate organ donation program

NOTA's proponents argue that preventing the trading of organs for valuable consideration protects the most vulnerable members of society - among them the poor and minorities - from becoming mere organ farms for the ailing wealthy. Other proponents claim that NOTA's prohibition is consistent with our country's long-standing tradition of altruistic organ donations. NOTA, however, was not initially conceived as antiincentive.[46] In fact, NOTA's main proponent, Representative Al Gore Jr. of Tennessee, initially considered the use of incentives and only backed away from the idea after congressional hearings exposed heightened fears of exploitation fostered by *private* organ markets.[47] However, with an overwhelming number of

[45] *See* Holbrook Mohr & Emily Wagster Pettus, *Outgoing Governor Pardons Nearly 200, Including Killers*, Seattle Times, Jan. 11, 2012, *available at* 2012 WLNR 710434.

[46] *See* Thompson, *supra* note 15, at 134 ("Early [Congressional] hearings [on NOTA] held little opposition to incentives for organ donation.").

[47] *See id.* at 134–35.

patients lingering and dying on the transplant waiting list, a policy of strict altruistic organ donations is outmoded. Moreover, altruism is deeply contextualized – so much so that limited instances within the altruistic context actually amount to the blindest, purest forms of giving. Some people force their children to donate, others might donate only because they work with the person who needs the organ, and yet others, including family members, might otherwise *not* donate but do so because of a preexisting relationship. When closely examined, what passes for altruism may not be so very selfless at all. For these reasons, a narrow and tightly regulated market, as an exception to NOTA, may prove extremely beneficial to both prisoners and patients.

In 2007, the South Carolina legislature introduced Senate Bill 480 (hereinafter, SB 480), which provided a six-month sentence reduction for inmates who consented to donate their kidneys. SB 480 was never enacted (in part because of concern about the legislation's violating Section 301).[48] Indeed, commentators and critics pointed out that "[c]ertainly [a reduction in prison time] … must be considered 'valuable consideration' for purposes of NOTA," and, thus, SB 480, had it passed, would have violated Section 301.[49] Had its proponents been successful in passing this legislation, South Carolina would have been the first state to reduce prison sentences for organ donors.

B. Blood-Time and the Case against Coercion

Biological procurement from prisoners is nothing new in the United States. Sixty years ago, beginning in the 1950s, a number of states enacted statutes that created what came to be known as "blood-time" programs under which inmates who donated blood were awarded good-time credit, thereby reducing their prison sentences.[50] Three states, Alabama, Oklahoma, and

[48] *See* Jenny Jarvie, *Inmates Could Trade an Organ for an Early Out*, L.A. TIMES, Mar. 9, 2007, *available at* 2007 WLNR 4464503.

[49] Emily C. Lee, *Trading Kidneys for Prison Time: When Two Contradictory Legal Traditions Intersect, Which One Has the Right-of-Way?*, 43 U.S.F.L. REV. 507, 549 (2009); *see also* Christopher M. Burkle, *The Mississippi Decision Exchanging Parole for Kidney Donation: Is This the Beginning of Change for Altruistic-Based Human Organ Donation Policy in the United States?*, 86 MAYO CLIN. PROC. 417, 417 (2011) (agreeing with and citing Lee, *Trading Kidneys*).

[50] *See, e.g.*, ALA. CODE § 14-9-3 (2002) (providing that every prisoner who donates at least one unit of blood to the American Red Cross shall be entitled to a thirty-day reduction

Virginia, maintain blood-time programs. Other states' programs were discontinued in the 1980s as blood supplies became tainted by human immunodeficiency virus- (HIV)-infected plasma. Despite advances in blood screening technology, the discontinued state prison blood-time programs have not been reinstituted.

However, it must be noted that during the period in which such programs were in place, rarely if ever did the concerns about prisoner donations mirror the arguments against organ donation-based sentence reduction programs. Rather, the plasma programs were discontinued for purely medical reasons and, in some cases, reinstated as donation programs without the time credit component and with other limitations designed to ensure that only the healthiest inmates are eligible to donate.

Clearly, there are distinctions between organ- and plasma-based sentence reduction programs. Blood is not a prohibited "human organ" under NOTA.[51] Despite its not being classified as a "human organ," analogizing blood-time programs with a proposed "organ-time" program may be useful. This bit of history reminds us that there is a precedent within states and their criminal justice systems to engage in pareto superior exchanges, whereby prisoners reduce their sentences by giving back to the broader community through donation. Critics of incentives rightfully distinguish blood from organs, noting that blood, unlike the organs enumerated in NOTA, is regenerative (bone marrow excepted). The standard, however, should not be regeneration, but the criminal justice system's ability to orchestrate a scheme under which an incentivized organ exchange will not be deemed coercive.

of his sentence, such deduction to be applied one time per twelve-month period); CAL. PENAL CODE § 4352 (repealed 1968) (giving a five-day sentence reduction per pint of blood donated by a prisoner, up to four times per year); MASS. GEN. LAWS ch. 127 § 129A (repealed 1989) (providing for sentence reductions for blood donations), MICH. COMP. LAWS ANN. § 791.233a (repealed 1982) (allowing that when determining a prisoner's fitness for release on parole, the parole board may consider the prisoner's blood donations); 57 OKLA. STAT. § 65 (providing that an inmate serving in any county jail shall be entitled to receive three days' credit for each pint of blood that he donates during his first thirty days in jail and five days' credit for every pint donated in any sixty-day period thereafter); R.I. GEN. LAWS § 42-56-25 (repealed 1988) (giving sentence reductions for blood donations in certain situations), VA. CODE ANN. § 53.1-191 (allowing the parole board of the state of Virginia, with the consent of the governor, to give good-time credit to a person who donates blood to a fellow inmate and "in unusual circumstances" providing that "a prisoner may receive credit for donating blood . . . to blood banks").

51 *See* 42 U.S.C. § 274e(c)(1).

Traditionally, coercion involves the threat that an unfavorable change in circumstances will occur if the coerced does not take the action desired by the coercer.[52] Thus, without a conditional threat, coercion cannot be said to exist. In the case of an inmate donation program, the state would not threaten to (or actually) punish an inmate if he chooses not to donate. Rather, the state would offer to change the circumstances of those who did choose to participate favorably. Thus, rather than a conditional threat, the program would consist of a conditional offer and would, therefore, not meet the definition of coercion. A prisoner who did not participate would be no worse off in the length of her sentence or the circumstance of her confinement than before the offer to participate was made.

The important questions in framing a prison-organ donor program relate to reducing the likelihood of fraud, coercion, and exploitation. However, perception also matters; programs that are perceived by their very nature as a form of exacting retribution will fail. Donation, in lieu of confinement, therefore, should not be offered as part of a plea arrangement, as part of a sentence, or as *the* condition of release, as in Gladys Scott's case. Rather, the inmate must be free to choose or reject donation, such choice being made after careful, studied consideration.

There remains the question whether, if not coercive, a reduced prison or jail sentence in exchange for an organ represents an "undue inducement" – one in which the thing offered (liberty) is so attractive that a prisoner's ability to make an autonomous, rational decision would be overridden to such a degree that she would disregard her better judgment and donate an organ to obtain that liberty. The danger of undue inducement, like that of coercion, can be overcome by creating an environment in which the proposed inmate donor can gather facts sufficient to develop informed consent to donate.

C. A Proposal for an Exchange of Inmate Organs for Liberty

An inmate organ donation program should consist of five components: (1) screening, (2) donor education, (3) donation and release, (4) postoperative care and follow-up, and (5) continued outreach and education. Additionally, such a program should include provisions for judicial oversight. Finally, the

[52] *See Coercion*, Stanford Encyclopedia of Phil., *available at* http://plato.stanford.edu/entries/coercion/ (accessed Feb. 9, 2012).

program should be structured so as not to place inmates in a position where eschewing the donation program can worsen their circumstances.

1. Screening

Inmates who express an interest in donating an organ should undergo screening to determine their eligibility for the program. Screening will assess the candidate's suitability for the program from both a penological and a medical standpoint. Jurisdictions adopting an inmate donation program may want to limit the program by type of conviction, length of sentence (or remaining length), or other factors. Medical screening is imperative; it allows for weaning out inmates with communicable diseases, medical conditions contraindicating donation, and other conditions unsuitable for transplant. Medically unsuitable candidates would be rejected as program candidates. To mitigate rejection and further promote the education goals of organ donation, any inmate who agrees to undergo screening and participate in the educational process (as described later) may receive modest credit toward release.

The screening process may achieve other transplantation goals. For example, even if a candidate backs out of organ exchanging after screening, such a regimen would also serve to expand donor registries, including the bone marrow registry. Even post release, former inmates may be identified as a match for a particular candidate and may choose to make a donation at that time. In the case of bone marrow, it is likely that an inmate who registers at the time of screening may not until some point in the future be called upon to donate.

2. Donor Education

During the time in which medical screening takes place, potential inmate donors will undergo some months of patient education. This process allows for advising inmates about the risks and benefits of organ and human tissue donation. The goals of an organ donation education program in prisons are twofold: (1) to promote and ensure informed consent; and (2) to attenuate the timeline between acceptance into the program and actual donation. The purpose of lengthening the time between agreement and donation is to lessen any pressure that an inmate may feel to donate immediately by actually removing the option of immediate donation. The attenuated timeline reduces pressure and therefore desperation and thus a longer education timeline will also provide ample opportunity for potential donors to opt out of the program. Again, an inmate would receive credit toward release for time spent in the education phase of the program. Some interested candidates may be rejected for medical reasons before completing the education phase. As discussed previously, they would be entitled to credit toward release for the part of the education phase that they had completed.

3. Donation and Release

Upon completing the months-long screening and donor education process, a candidate shall appear before a judge in order to be cleared to donate and to be released from prison. Such a hearing will be designed to confirm informed consent and the absence of coercion. Donation will take place in a public or private hospital under the care of the same transplant surgeons who care for noninmate donors. The state and the recipient's insurer will be responsible for medical costs. On completion of surgery, the donors will no longer be deemed to be in state custody.

4. Postoperative Care and Follow-Up

As part of the program, a donating former inmate will be entitled to postoperative care in the hospital and to follow-up care after discharge. Such follow-up care shall take the place of normal parole or probation obligations and will last as long as necessary for full recuperation, as determined by the former inmate's doctors.

5. Continued Outreach and Education

The final phase of the program should be optional for the former inmate. In this phase, the prison participant will be provided additional education and have the opportunity to participate in community outreach programs aimed at increasing organ donors. It is anticipated that participating states will devise measures to provide training to inmates choosing continued participation.

IV. Conclusion

What happens if the Scott sisters' story is replicated – if it is multiplied across prison populations? Were programs put into place that allowed prison inmates to trade their kidneys (or portions of their lungs, livers, or pancreases) in exchange for a reduced sentence, it follows that transplantation can be multiplied exponentially. True, the Scott sisters' case resembles a classically repugnant exchange in which coercion, coupled with political expediency, played a major role. Their case provides a cautionary note. Yet, it also provides an inspired idea. Prison-based organ transplant leniency exchange programs will likely save lives while avoiding coercion, fraud, and pressure.

6 Situated Bodies in Medicine and Research: Altruism versus Compelled Sacrifice

Naomi N. Duke

I. Introduction

When considering the ethics of using the human body in medical research and education, historical and contemporary rules and tools for engagement, such as the Nuremberg Code,[1] the Declaration of Helsinki,[2] the Belmont Report,[3] and the Code of Federal Regulations,[4] immediately come to mind. These four guiding documents do not represent an exhaustive list of instruments that guide the use of the body in scientific and medical investigation and treatment. However, these ethical guidelines and the periods corresponding to their creation and endorsement often frame breeches of ethical behavior as products of a particular time, such that procedures performed before the codification of rules of conduct may be relegated to a status of diminished accountability or perhaps reframed as acceptable processes and outcomes in the quest for knowledge.

In the chapter that follows, the reader is invited to set aside the timelines and social milieus anchoring the ethical guidelines introduced earlier. Instead, I invite you to consider a loftier subject - humanity - as the primary lens by which to evaluate past and present conduct involving scientific and medical research, training, and education. Inherent in the challenge

[1] *The Nuremberg Code*, reprinted in 313 Brit. Med. J. 1448 (1996).

[2] World Med. Ass'n Gen. Assembly, *Declaration of Helsinki* (2008) [*hereinafter Declaration of Helsinki*], *available at* http://www.wmna.net/en/30publications/10policies/b3/17c.pdf.

[3] Nat'l Comm'n for the Prot. of Human Subjects of Biomedical & Behavior Research, *The Belmont Report* (1979) [hereinafter *Belmont Report*], 44 Fed. Reg. 23,192 (Apr. 18, 1979), *available at* http://www.hhs.gov/ohrp/archive/documents/19790418.pdf.

[4] Protection of Human Subjects, 45 C.F.R. pt. 46 (2009).

is a reconsideration of the entrenched notion that ethical principles are uniquely rooted to or should be defined by particular periods in history. In other words, a by-product of anchoring bioethical principles to medicine's moral failings during particular periods further associates prevailing privileges and prejudices with a blip in time. Such a perspective considers medicine's moral failings as episodic rather than systemic. It will tend to focus on one set of "bad" medical actors - those who are caught - while ignoring others.

Consider the case of early twentieth-century eugenics. The Nuremburg Code, which substantively anchors modern-day bioethics, was a direct response to the horrors experienced by victims of Nazi Germany. Yet, there were other important, coinciding medical horrors taking place, including eugenics, in other parts of the world, namely, the United States. Indeed, Germans borrowed their eugenics platform from the model law enacted in more than two dozen U.S. states.[5] Eugenics laws were enacted as early as 1907 in the United States. The problem, then, is the microexamination of what is "owed" to humanity.

By focusing on humanity, the concept of personhood[6] may be judged by its relationship to intersecting qualities defining human nature: the presence of consciousness, the ability of self-awareness and self-reflection, the capacity to perceive and experience complexity in positive and negative sensations and emotions, and the need for authentic relationships, resulting in a very different filter in which to assess behavior in the scientific and medical realms.[7] Here, inherent in this construct of personhood is an ethical status recognizing the sanctity of the individual, an identity, and a sense of self that is represented by a physical being.

This is particularly relevant as African Americans were conscripted as the altruistic bodies in the United States. The perversity of slavery is rooted

[5] Daniel J. Kevles, *From Eugenics to Patents: Genetics, Law, and Human Rights*, 75 ANNALS OF HUMAN GENETICS 326, 327 (2011).

[6] The construct for personhood presented here extends beyond that assigned by rights and duties formally recognized in a body of law, as the law may be impacted by prejudice introduced by the majority, and change in the law often lags that of advances in the study of the human condition and ethics.

[7] See HARRIET WASHINGTON, MEDICAL APARTHEID: THE DARK HISTORY OF MEDICAL EXPERIMENTATION ON BLACK AMERICANS FROM COLONIAL TIMES TO THE PRESENT(2006), for comprehensive historical and contemporary reference to the mistreatment of black bodies in the context of medical education and research, military training, and the scientific industry.

in a corrupted notion of the conscripted and solicitous body – the body that is forced, trained, and programmed to give. In denying the sanctity and the dignity of bodies of color, the conscription of these bodies as vessels of exploration was publicly, morally, and legally permissible in the name of advancing the nation's interest in population control, perfecting experimental protocol, understanding physiology and the body's response to external provocation, and developing medical treatments and technologies. Indeed, as African Americans became the body commons, their oppression became shrouded in altruistic language. Their involuntary servitude and oppression contributed to the "greater good."[8]

The historical reference to "situated bodies," such as African Americans during and after antebellum,[9] Native American subjects of radiation experiments,[10] and Jews mutilated and subjected to the horrors of Nazi medical experimentation,[11] remain instructive for contemporary times. The account of medical missteps, including the invasion of and injury perpetrated on vulnerable communities, adds to the urgency and importance of rethinking altruism.

This chapter begins by outlining the defining tenets of pure altruism, its theoretical promise, and its potential for corruptibility. The chapter illuminates the limitations of the concept, particularly in the realms of medical education, clinical research, translation of research at the bedside, and nontherapeutic procedures. Part II explains how altruism is often deployed in medicine and research. Part III builds from there to argue that altruism is corruptible and sometimes deployed to justify and reframe the subordination of individuals and populations of color. Part IV examines whether current protections – mostly rooted in medical ethics – effectively prevent or provide adequate disincentives to prevent abusive practices in the name of medical and scientific advancement. It begs the question, Are these guidelines enough? The chapter concludes with recommendations for

[8] *Id.* at 69.

[9] *See id.*

[10] See *Human Radiation Experiments: Hearing before the Committee. on Governmental Affairs, U.S. Senate*, 104th Cong. 180 (1996) (letter from Deputy Att'y Gen. Jamie Gorelick, Assistant Att'y Gen. Deval Patrick, Sec'y of Energy Hazel O'Leary, Sen. Ted Stevens, &Sen. John Glenn, to Att'y Gen. Janet Reno) (Mar. 6, 1996), for a comprehensive discussion of human radiation experiments.

[11] *See, e.g.*, VIVIEN SPITZ, DOCTORS FROM HELL: THE HORRIFIC ACCOUNT OF NAZI EXPERIMENTS ON HUMANS (2005).

moving forward, focusing on key principles and values, including respect for humanity, the restoration of voice, and prioritizing autonomy.

II. Altruism

Pure altruism places the welfare of others on equal footing with one's own. Philosophers suggest that the individual must have a sense of well-being and a sense of self in which there is a belief that he or she possesses something that may be of benefit to others.[12] Motivation and process are critical in defining an act as altruistic, and in this context, A's action (or generosity) is purely altruistic only if it originates prior to B's action (or generosity). Altruism is active; it requires voice and self-rule. Altruism may be socially situated, the product of a decision-making process in which the internal values of the person and external forces are implicated as influential. However, the individual must act as an independent, free agent. The intent guiding the altruist's behavior must be *other-directed* for altruism to be achieved. An altruistic act may also carry with it the possibility of lessening one's welfare, but the focus remains on advancing the welfare of another,[13] singularly or in a collective sense. Altruism is punctuated by human compassion and respect for persons.

History demonstrates that common constructions of altruism are not immune to corruption. Goodwin points to this in Chapter 4, including her observation that children may be compelled to provide organs for siblings and such actions are typically referenced as "altruistic" when in fact they may be the products of coercion. Indeed, altruism may serve as a "cover" or proxy for other actions, including manipulation, coercion, and abuse.[14] Its invocation to describe situations in which individual and group choice are constrained and circumscribed represents the artificiality that may burden altruism as a conceptual value and as a descriptor of human behavior. True choice is about power, the power to avail an individual of social, political,

[12] See, for example, C. Daniel Batson et al., *Empathy and Altruism*, *in* OXFORD HANDBOOK OF POLITICAL PSYCHOLOGY 417 (C.R. Snyder & Shane J. Lopez eds., 2nd ed. 2009), for a discussion of altruism.

[13] Kristen Renwick Monroe, *A Fat Lady in a Corset: Altruism and Social Theory*, 38 AM. J. POL. SCI. 861, 862–63 (1994).

[14] *See* Michele Goodwin, *My Sister's Keeper? – Law, Children, and Compelled Donation*, 29 W. NEW ENG. L. REV. 357, 378–79 (2007).

and legal protections and, within this context, to consider, evaluate, and offer or decline to offer oneself in service to others. Thus, attempts to redefine or reframe forced or blind participation in an act represent a distortion of the true meaning of altruism.

For this reason, reframing medical experimentation, training, and scientific inquiry conducted upon those who by law, custom, or social status could not offer consent cannot now be labeled altruism. Michele Goodwin offers an important historical reference to Dr. Marion Sims, a man widely considered to be the "father of gynecology."[15] Sims perfected the cesarean section, designed and patented tools used for gynecological examinations, and otherwise ushered in new hygienic and surgical protocols in obstetrics. Yet, Sims did not accomplish this alone. Key to the development of his surgical know-how and the advancement of gynecological medicine was the use of African American slave women. These women, most of whom endured involuntary experimental operations without the aid of anesthetics, lacked the legal capacity to consent and likely would not have consented if given the choice. In other words, the victims of Dr. Marion Sims's nefarious experimental surgeries intended to perfect gynecologic examinations for his white patients were not altruists. Nor were they free to resist his authority or exploitation because they were his slaves.

Altruism is not the defining process when the conduct of the body is determined by those other than the individual. When the body's exposition and sacrifice occur at the will or impulse of an external collective, neither is altruism evidenced nor can it be achieved. Indeed, "the surrender of one's body to medical experimentation is entirely outside the enforceable social contract."[16] Importantly, the integrity and character of the unknowing individual are not called into question by such circumstances, but the system situating the individual diminishes the individual's personhood.

III. Altruism, Medicine, and Scientific Research

Crucially, trust facilitates one's willingness to contribute to a larger cause or willingness to place oneself in jeopardy on behalf of someone else. Pure

[15] Michele Goodwin, Black Markets: The Supply and Demand of Body Parts 31 (2006).

[16] Hans Jonas, *Philosophical reflections on Experimenting with Human Subjects*, 98 Daedalus 219, 231 (1969).

altruism involves giving of oneself for the gain of others without an expectation of reciprocal benefit. In the distinct realms of scientific and medical research, altruism can only be established and present if the individual's integrity and personhood are preserved. These are essential components of altruism and must be achieved in order for an act to be truly voluntary, selfless, and committed to aid the other. In medicine, we must guard against exploitation emanating from explicit and implicit devaluations of the voice of the individual and for members of a group. Yet, what is so often unstated in analyses about altruism, particularly in medicine, is the importance of trust.

Undeniably, trust is sometimes elusive in medicine or taken for granted. Often, it is expected that patients should surrender it to their physicians without the latter acquiring trust by earning it.[17] However, there are good reasons for instantiating trust in a dialogue about altruism. The goals of research and medicine create or exacerbate conflicts of interests. Indeed, the inherent and opportunistic potential for exploitation of the individual (who may not be a patient or becomes a patient under coercive circumstance) is heightened in medical research, thus necessitating a check on participant motivations. Conflicts of interests in the medical-research relationship are difficult to ignore on inspection: research platforms driven by the need to publish, obligations to secure research dollars (i.e., conduct medical research involving human subjects), admonitions to teach and train, and the desire for financial gain and public recognition. Physician or medical researcher interests - and often the two are indistinguishable because a patient's physician may be a medical researcher - may not align with that of the patient. And while this is to be expected in some circumstances, contemporary medical research demands may incentivize conduct from medical researchers that deemphasizes the importance of sharing information, building and establishing trust, promoting patient autonomy, and preserving integrity and personhood.

Given the preceding, there are two important factors to consider: a) how medical science normalizes a more credible vision of altruism and b) rethinking and developing a more nuanced understanding of what

[17] See e.g., Michele Goodwin & Song Richardson, *Patient Negligence*, 72 Duke J.L. & Contemp. Probs. 223 (2010).

we cataloged in the past as altruism. The latter point is particularly pertinent, because precedent matters in medicine. In other words, medicine should guard against revising historical wrongs, such as coerced action as altruism. In her chilling, yet historically relevant book, *Medical Apartheid,* Harriet Washington unpacks systemic and continuous medical research abuse against people of color.[18] Notably, the experiments that Washington copiously documents are treated in hindsight as useful to medical research, commendable, and valuable contributions by the human subjects. But this type of account is lacking. In considering how and why medical abuses, including radiation studies, skin cancer studies on black prisoners (involving infecting them with diseased or compromised tissues), and others, could persist long after Nuremburg and the termination of the notorious Tuskegee Study (denying syphilitic black men medication to treat the disease), the relevance of historical accounting takes shape.[19]

Indeed, contemporary bioethics is helpful on this point as it demands a more sophisticated way of understanding altruism. According to bioethics doctrine, altruism necessarily requires autonomy, voluntariness, and justice to be operative. These principles are not newly associated with medicine; they predate many or overlap with the abuses described previously. This point is particularly relevant as it helps us to understand how mistakes in medicine can carry over or be reified. Understanding this history also demands a more complete examination of what altruism requires.

Collectively, autonomy, voluntariness, and social justice serve as the foundational principles of modern-day bioethics. However, it is worth articulating and understanding what these principles signify individually. For example, the autonomous individual has free will and the power of self-determination. Autonomy heralds a notion of control at the micro- and macrolevels. This sense of capacity drives individual choice, group identity, and a perception of value. Yet autonomous expression cannot be valued only for one group in society. Thus, women's autonomy cannot be subordinate to that of men – their husbands, fathers, brothers, or uncles – though

[18] WASHINGTON, *supra* note 7.
[19] *Id.*

that was historically true. Neither can the autonomy of people of color be less important than that of whites or regarded as less imperative in medical decision making and human subject research.

The individual's decision must be free of intentional and illegitimate causal influence.[20] Voluntariness is likened to self-control and autonomy, the ability to choose after taking into consideration all available and relevant bias-free information.[21] Thus, full disclosure, including communication of risks to the individual, proposed benefits and to whom, and potential interests in monetary gain, is required in voluntary actions. In medical and research contexts, ideally, the individual not only provides informed consent for participation, but also fully identifies with the ends of the project.[22] Voluntariness includes the right to withdraw from participation.[23] Recognition of a right to withdraw necessitates that participants know that they are involved in research from the beginning. From this flows the capacity to vacate or to refuse to participate. Indeed, the concept of voluntariness becomes moot when individuals are denied full control of their decision to participate in a medical experiment.

Likewise, altruism cannot be achieved when justice is not in operation. Justice is a distributional concept. It helps to locate the benefits and burdens associated with participation in a particular activity. Ideally, equilibrium should be achieved. In other words, we should be mindful about whose bodies we call upon in medical research and why, lest negative social impacts emerge. In medicine and scientific investigation, we must consider whether the populations used in clinical trials and medical experimentations reap the benefits of that research. Such issues are not confined to the domestic, but also implicate clinical trials in developing nations. Historically, people of color have been significantly disadvantaged and they have been the subject of research with limited, if any, realization of benefits accompanying gains in knowledge.[24]

[20] Paul S. Appelbaum et al., *Voluntariness of Consent to Research: A Conceptual Model*, 39 HASTINGS CTR. REP. 30, 33–34 (2009).

[21] Robert M. Nelson & Jon F. Merz, *Voluntariness of Consent for Research: An Empirical and Conceptual Review*, 40 MED. CARE V69, V74 (2002).

[22] Beverly Woodward, *Challenges to Human Subjects Protections in U.S. Medical Research*, 282 J. AM. MED. ASS'N 1947, 1950 (1999).

[23] Nelson & Merz, *supra* note 21, at V70.

[24] WASHINGTON, *supra* note 7, at 69.

IV. Race, Medicine, and Research: The Misuse of Altruism

Postracialism in U.S. discourse might suggest that attention to race in medicine perpetuates racial sensitivities and serves no meaningful purpose. Indeed, it could be perceived that connecting altruism with race and medicine is far too tenuous for purposeful academic inquiry. However, such perspectives fall short of acknowledging historic truths that track onto persistent, contemporary realities. On the one hand, autonomy, voluntariness, and justice provide a valuable backdrop to guard against manipulation, coercion, exploitation, and abuse in medical research. On the other hand, persistent social and racial stereotypes, ranging from the perceived intellectual inferiority of persons of color, to myths about their social habits, hygiene, and moral sensibilities serve to justify denying them personhood, agency, and often the respect and quality of care afforded whites. Key here is to understand that when personhood is unacknowledged or undermined for certain groups, their privacy and the value of their consent may be perceived as less meaningful or relevant.

Enslavement provides an extremely potent example. On the one hand, it is a rare centuries-long episode in the United States. On the other hand, some of the stereotypes employed to justify slavery are slow to dissipate fully from common view. Slavery exposes how groupthink facilitated abuses under the guise of scientific inquiry and medical intervention. During the antebellum period, medical experimentation exploiting African Americans was justified on weak intellectual argumentation: the belief that blacks belonged to a different species; that they harbored diseases that would threaten whites; that blacks, including their children, were immune to pain and anxiety; that they were prone to what now is termed sexual addiction; and that they possessed an innate self-destructiveness necessitating supervision.[25] These core assumptions provided a foundation for widespread abuse and unchecked violations of law against African American during the eugenics era and Jim Crow period. More relevantly, what might appear episodic emerges as a continuation of the black body's being used as an altruistic centerpiece of American medicine.

[25] *Id.* at 58, 73.

A. Tuskegee's Lessons

Tuskegee is perhaps one of the most visible references of medical malfeasance in the twentieth century. The Tuskegee Syphilis Study began as an observational study of untreated syphilis among an economically depressed group of African American men in Macon County, Alabama.[26] Hundreds of economically disadvantaged black men were recruited into the study, which was sponsored in part by the U.S. government. Researchers wanted to learn about the effects of untreated syphilis on the body. In order to acquire this knowledge, they needed recent corpses of syphilitic bodies.

For this reason, researchers misled the research subjects, deceived them about their treatment, denied them penicillin, watched as they infected their wives, observed as their children were born maimed from the disease, and continued the study for four decades. The study, which began in the 1930s, was terminated in 1972. None of the men was informed that the medications provided were no more potent than aspirin. None of the human subjects were provided antibiotics, such as penicillin, despite common medical knowledge that penicillin treated syphilis. However, valuable medical knowledge emerged from the study. Indeed, development of the sera resulting from the Tuskegee study led to the creation of more reliable tests for syphilis, such as the fluorescent treponemal antibody absorption test.[27]

The Tuskegee experiment was anchored in the pretext of altruism. Researchers at the nation's leading medical schools and government health officials colluded to deceive uneducated, trusting men. Most perniciously, researchers pressed these men to participate in the study. Medical officials preyed on the research subjects, using "altruism" to elicit participation. And in playing on their emotions, government officials sent annual letters, commending the research subjects on their participation.

However, context matters in volunteerism and altruism. Participation or volunteerism under false pretense is not altruism, just as altruism under duress cannot be explained as purely altruistic. This observation is not to suggest that the intuitions to be altruistic absent the coercion were never

[26] See JAMES H. JONES, BAD BLOOD: THE TUSKEGEE SYPHILIS EXPERIMENT (1993), for general review of the events surrounding the Tuskegee Syphilis Study.

[27] WASHINGTON, *supra* note 7, at 177–78.

present or potential. Rather, compelled volunteerism, particularly under false pretense, amounts to research abuse, whose product is adulterated.

B. Henrietta Lacks: HeLa Cells

Henrietta Lacks's medical exploitation at the Johns Hopkins University Hospital presents another historic landmark where race, science, and coercion collide. Lacks - a deceased African American woman - is the mother of scientific invention. Yet, the nonconsensual exploitation of her body and the subsequent profiteering present a cautionary tale. To foreground her story, she died indigent, without so much as a tombstone. Yet doctors, researchers, laboratories, hospitals, and corporations profit handsomely from her cell line.[28] Indeed, her cell line is likely the most valuable that ever existed. Yet, she and her family never consented to the harvesting of her cells, their use in research, the commercialization of the cell line, nor any of the thousands of uses of her biological material.[29] Is that altruism?

The science of cell-line cultures and the use of human cells for medical treatment are born from her long-lived cervical cancer cells, known as HeLa cells.[30] HeLa cells have been used to test vaccines and "today, the science of cell-line culture has enabled cultivation and therapy with stem cells, including red blood cells, white blood cells, and platelets."[31] The inclusion of Henrietta Lacks as a research participant and the failure of her physicians to obtain informed consent or even to disclose the use of her cells upon harvesting were facilitated by notions grounded in greed, expedience, gender subordination, and racism. For example, researchers may have believed that Lacks *owed* Johns Hopkins and its researchers for treating her at all. Indeed, during the 1950s, when she sought treatment at Hopkins, they segregated patients and did not treat poor African American women the same as their wealthy white female counterparts. As her *payment,* Lacks surrendered autonomy and by proxy the "say" in her body. And yet, her case was not unusual. Bodies of color were treated in separate areas of the hospital, rendered available and with limited privacy, thus vulnerable and often on pubic display.

[28] See REBECCA SKLOOT, THE IMMORTAL LIFE OF HENRIETTA LACKS 194 (2010).

[29] *See id.* for biography of Henrietta Lacks.

[30] *Id.* at 1.

[31] WASHINGTON, *supra* note 7, at 355.

It is important to understand how Lacks's status and experience become rewritten in history. The use of Henrietta Lacks as a source of cells to perfect experimental techniques is framed as a gift, a sacrifice marking a victory in the name of science. Evidence of this selective framing is seen in the writings of Howard Jones, the physician who performed the initial harvest of cells from Mrs. Lacks's tumor:

> But it was the best of times for science in that this very peculiar tumor gave rise to the Hela cell line, which has been available for the various studies.... Scientific progress and indeed progress of all kinds is often made at great cost, such as the sacrifice made by Henrietta Lacks.[32]

Contrast the admonitions of Howard Jones with the sentiment of a Lacks family member, "everybody always saying Henrietta Lacks donated those cells. She didn't donate nothing. They took them and didn't ask."[33]

C. Research Involving Children

The idea that children may be offered as *volunteers* in medical and scientific research settings is challenging to embrace as *altruism*, precisely because most medical research has the potential to cause harm.[34] At the outset, a central conflict arises with the knowledge that the minor cannot legally consent to participation in nonbeneficial research.[35] With risk attached to participation, such as bodily invasion, the presumption that a child would want to

[32] Howard W. Jones Jr., *Record of the First Physician to See Henrietta Lacks at the Johns Hopkins Hospital: History of the Beginning of the He La Cell Line*, 176 Am. J. Obstetrics & Gynecology S227, S228 (1997).

[33] Skloot, *supra* note 28, at 169 (recording conversation of Bobette Lacks, wife of Lawrence Lacks, the oldest son of Henrietta Lacks).

[34] An exception may be the situation in which a child suffers from an incurable illness; parents may consent to the use of an experimental treatment, knowing that the drug or other treatment may cause harm to their child. In that case, the parents are hoping for a breakthrough but may have an added motivation that participation of their child will contribute to progress made in finding a cure, so that no other child need suffer as their child has. See Michelle Oberman & Joel Frader, *Dying Children and Medical Research: Access to Clinical Trials as a Benefit and Burden*, 29 Am. J.L. & Med. 301, 308–17 (2003), for discussion of the legal and ethical challenges of parental and proxy consent, and physician fiduciary accountability in the context of childhood illness, failed conventional therapy, and enrollment in Phase I Clinical Trials.

[35] Leonard H. Glantz, *Research with Children*, 24 Am. J.L. & Med. 213, 230 (1998). Federal regulations require a combination of youth assent (when possible, in absence of developmental or disability limitations) and parent/guardian permission.

participate for the benefit of others is questionable.[36] For older children, the use of assent (affirmative agreement) may answer some concerns about voluntariness. However, the impact of parental influence and pressure cannot be ignored, especially when parental consent predates the youth's assent.

Most parents act in the best interests of their children. Usually, their actions are free of external, intentional, and illegitimate influence. Parents are expected to protect their children and most accomplish that goal. Medicine, however, presents challenges, both in cases where parents voluntarily hold their children up for research and where parents lack the power to keep their children from the reach of medical profiteers. Consider the latter: historical and contemporary evidence illuminates the use of children of color in experimental research and treatment.[37]

In published research, black children and those of "other" races are overrepresented in research compared to their census composition.[38] From a descriptive standpoint, black and Hispanic children are overrepresented in research involving potentially stigmatizing topics, such as child abuse and maltreatment, human immunodeficiency virus, psychiatric issues, and high-risk behaviors, compared with their participation in research in general.[39] There is also a slight predominance of representation for black children in clinical trials, as opposed to therapeutic research.[40] More recently, measles vaccine trials involving children living in the United States and abroad not only expose racial fault lines (such as the possible targeting of particularly vulnerable racial groups), but also reveal the frequent types of missteps when people of color are the research subjects. For example, these missteps include failing to obtain parental consent or obtaining parental consent under unethical pretense. Other violations include the failure to establish standard protections.[41] On inspection, such breaches are not

[36] *Id.* at 235.

[37] *See, e.g.*, Lainie Friedman Ross & Catherine Walsh, *Minority Children in Pediatric Research*, 29 AM. J. L. & MED. 319 (2003) (finding a "higher baseline participation" rate of minority children in certain types of research).

[38] *Id.* at 328. Hispanics – although this may reflect an undercount due to inconsistencies in reporting – and Asians are noted to be underrepresented on the basis of census proportions; Native American youth are represented at census-level proportion. *Id.* at 329, 331.

[39] Catherine Walsh & Lainie F. Ross, *Are Minority Children Under or Overrepresented in Pediatric Research?*, 112 PEDIATRICS 890, 894 (2003).

[40] Ross & Walsh, *supra* note 37.

[41] *See* Charles Marwick, *Questions Raised about Measles Vaccine Trial*, 276 J. AM. MED. ASS'N 1288 (1996).

wholly uncommon when research, race, and children collide. A controversial lead study provides a telling example.

A class-action lawsuit was filed in 2011 against the Kennedy Krieger Institute, an affiliate of Johns Hopkins. The lawsuit accused the organization of "knowingly exposing black children as young as a year old to lead poisoning in the 1990s as part of a study exploring the hazards of lead paint."[42] The study involved more than one hundred children, who lawyers claim were exposed to toxic levels of lead. The lawsuit emphasizes that researchers provided assurances that the houses the children were to live in (as part of the study) were "lead safe."[43] Despite the assurances, some of the children suffered symptoms of lead exposure, including what their lawyers claim to be permanent neurological injuries. Their lawsuit claims:

> children were enticed into living in lead-tainted housing and subjected to a research program which intentionally exposed them to lead poisoning in order for the extent of the contamination of these children's blood to be used by scientific researchers to assess the success of lead paint or lead dust abatement measures.... Nothing about the research was designed to treat the subject children for lead poisoning.[44]

One court compared the case to the Tuskegee Syphilis Study.[45]

Perhaps most chilling is the comment from one of the parents, David Armstrong. He took his son to doctors at Kennedy Krieger after discovering that his son had an elevated blood lead level. He had no idea that his son was being exposed to elevated levels of lead paint dust. Indeed, his son's lead levels increased nearly threefold during the study. For two years, blood was collected from his son, but researchers failed to alert him that his son's blood lead levels were rising and that it was likely the result of the study. According to Mr. Armstrong, his son was never offered medical treatments.[46] The father told the *New York Times*, "I thought they had cleaned everything and it would be a safe place.... They said it was 'lead safe.'"[47]

[42] Timothy Williams, *Racial Bias Seen in Study of Lead Dust and Children*, N.Y. TIMES, Sept. 15, 2011, at A11.

[43] *Id.*

[44] *Id.* (quoting the lawsuit).

[45] Grimes v. Kennedy Kreiger Inst., 782 A.2d 807, 816 (Md. 2001).

[46] Williams, *supra* note 42.

[47] *Id.*

V. Recurring Themes and Impacts: A Few Concluding Thoughts

Several themes emerge in historical and contemporary review of medical research when race is moved to the forefront rather than relegated to the shadows. For example, what becomes clear are the differential valuations of human lives: people of color in the United States, Jews in Hitler's Germany, and those in developing countries sometimes become the unwitting participants in pernicious medical research. Additionally, status emerges as an important theme. But for economic and racial marginalization, the groups described in this chapter might have been afforded the standard of medical-research care. However, status demarked the level of medical accountability and care afforded them. Law and its enforcement matter; however, there are no shortage of rules that disallow the conduct described in this chapter. These and other observations make clear that focus on the needs of the researcher or medical representatives at the expense of the safety and welfare of the participant cannot be justified as serving the common or greater good.

In reality, whose good really matters? In the cases described, "the most powerless group, which is also a racially distinct group *and* a captive group," suffers, while the "privileged group enjoys the benefits but shares neither the pain nor the risks."[48] This chapter, along with the companion chapters, disturbs the sacrosanct concept of altruism. Can altruism exist when either autonomy or the ability to grant consent properly is absent? I think not. Nor does substituted judgment provide a rigorous defense of the failure to obtain proper consent. Substituted judgment compromises informed consent, and the ability of individuals to exercise a right of refusal. It would be a mistake to ignore that motivations guiding the medicinal and research processes originate (in cases described herein) from individuals occupying a favored status in a larger sociopolitical structure. From that perch of power, it would not be unreasonable for one to conclude that laws and rules seem to matter only against the vulnerable rather than in their protection.

Researchers, educators, and innovators are charged with achieving a balance between the desire to pursue the quest for new knowledge and a duty to protect the rights and welfare of individual participants. Four

[48] WASHINGTON, *supra* note 7, at 69.

primary documents ground these regulations and ethical guidelines.[49] The Nuremburg Code[50] expresses fundamental moral principles for researchers, including patient autonomy and the rights of individuals to be placed above the goals of science and society, the importance of voluntary participation in the context of adequate information,[51] and a duty of concern for participant welfare in the research setting.[52] The Declaration of Helsinki extends the influence of the Nuremburg Code through its recognition of child assent, provision of guidelines for proxy consent, documentation of a distinction between medical research and medical care, acknowledgment of ethical obligations in publication, and mandate of independent ethical review committees in biomedical research.[53]

The Belmont Report, drafted by the National Commission for the Protection of Human Subjects of Biomedical and Behavioral Research, further defines boundaries between therapeutic practice and research and outlines three broad standards required for research with human participants: respect for persons (autonomy of choice), beneficence (maximizing benefit while minimizing harm), and justice (fairness in the distribution of burden and benefit).[54] The Belmont Principles position "persons … [as] social, moral, legal, and political entities with rights to whom obligations are due,"[55] such as informed consent procedures, the assessment of risks and benefits as a function of research design, and the selection of research participants.

Implied human protections are further extended through Title 45 Part 46 of the Code of Federal Regulations, the policy directing all federally funded research.[56] The regulations provide guidelines for the creation of Institutional Review Boards (IRBs), academic and community-located entities. IRBs are charged with several tasks, including reviewing research protocols and recommending modification where necessary, rejecting negligent and

[49] NAT'L INST. OF HEALTH, GUIDELINES FOR THE CONDUCT OF RESEARCH IN THE INTRAMURAL RESEARCH PROGRAM AT NIH (4th ed. 2007).

[50] See James F. Childress, *Nuremberg's Legacy: Some Ethical Reflections*, 43 PERSP. IN BIOLOGY & MED. 347, 349 (2000), for annotated reference to 10 Nuremberg principles.

[51] *Id.*

[52] *Id.*

[53] *Declaration of Helsinki, supra* note 2.

[54] *Belmont Report, supra* note 3.

[55] Eric J. Cassell, *The Principles of the Belmont Report Revisited: How Have Respect for Persons, Beneficence, and Justice Applied to Clinical Medicine?*, 30 HASTINGS CTR. REP. 12, 16 (2000).

[56] 45 C.F.R. pt. 46

reckless protocol, monitoring continuing projects, and reviewing adverse event reports.[57] The regulations also outline application for the standards of informed consent and qualifications for a minimal risk standard for research protocol.[58]

Notwithstanding the existence of numerous guidelines outlining principles of ethical conduct in medical research, clearly there have been breaches in their enforcement, particularly with people of color. Indeed, these protocols seem to matter less when people of color are the subjects. Yet, the potential for health and social benefits requires that individuals and communities of color continue to participate in research and activities aimed at furthering medical and scientific knowledge. How are we to resolve this tension?

Research involvement, including being visible and actively engaged in research design and protocols, offers the best chance to address resource allocation for the study and elimination of health disparities. Participation in medical research should include a promise of treatment that is efficacious for a broad population.[59] Research should be facilitated fairly and the distribution of benefits should reach everyone. Ideally, participation ensures access to experimental treatments for all to benefit from, especially in the absence of standard therapy (i.e., fairness in access).[60]

Reciprocity in obligation between researchers and participants must be a guiding principle. In fact, although pure altruism necessitates that the actor conduct himself or herself in the absence of an expectation of return, the integrity of an altruistic act is only validated in the absence of an exploitative and coercive environment. Thus, some individual protections are necessary. The social structural narrative must embrace an ethical imperative of

[57] June Gibbs Brown, Inspector General, *Institutional Review Boards: Their Role in Reviewing Approved Research*, DEP'T HEALTH & HUMAN SERV. (June 1998), *available at* http://oig.hhs.gov/oet/reports/oet-01-97-00190.pdf.

[58] In the context of informed consent, a waiver for exemption exists for research involving minimal risk where the rights and welfare of individuals will theoretically not be negatively impacted and it is believed it is impractical to obtain consent. The minimal risk standard requires that the probability of harms presented by research protocol not be above that incurred in daily life or activities or during routine physical and psychological examination. The standard's intended use is that of eliminating expedited review of a research protocol if more than minimal risk is involved.

[59] Ross & Walsh, *supra* note 37, at 323.

[60] *Id.*

equity and equal valuation of its persons. Researchers, clinicians, and educators must actively resist explicit and implicit motivations that advocate or rationalize the exploitation of groups based on status, whether by race, religion, or socioeconomic status. The scientific and medical establishments have an obligation of transparency.

Remedies for moving forward must advance autonomy and facilitate inclusion, what some academics describe as "giving voice." Restoration of voice necessitates equal support for community-driven research questions and clinical models as mechanisms for gaining knowledge and achieving health and well-being. Communities of color should be extended an open invitation to participate in the design and delivery of research protocols aimed at furthering medical technologies and education. Tangible strategies to build trust by inclusion and engagement of people of color in research development and the dissemination of findings should be a requirement for successful application for intra- and extramural funding. The addition of a checklist informed by community members and providing a filter for explicit and implicit biases in research protocol would support integrity in process. Adding a community lens to research and education endeavors would facilitate relationship building and critical dialogue necessary for the maximization of learning, fidelity in data collection, adaptability of program design, and valuable investment in new research, treatment, and program development.

Finally, for altruism to regain a real footing, it is necessary to revisit informed consent, taking note of key elements of consent: characteristics of knowledge (information dissemination), participant acumen (understanding and decisional competence), and voluntariness. Voluntariness must include two elements, the absence of external influence and the ability to choose from at least two options. At least one of the options must recognize the opportunity of the individual to decline to participate without undue consequences. Consent should provide a leveling of the playing field, which includes the removal of asymmetry in information and power and, where applicable, a discussion of the potential financial interests of researchers and institutions associated with developing scientific and medical technologies related to participant contribution. Reconsideration should be given to the wisdom of using consent waivers for some areas of clinical research, taking into account historic exploitation when consent is not firm.

PART III

Managing Markets in Contestable Commodities

Public and Private Regulation

7 The Perverse History of Dead Bodies under American Law

Ray D. Madoff

A corpse in some respects is the strangest thing on earth. A man who but yesterday breathed and thought and walked among us has passed away. Something has gone. The body is left still and cold, and is all that is visible to mortal eye of the man we knew. Around it cling love and memory. Beyond it may reach hope. It must be laid away. And the law – that rule of action which touches all human things – must touch also this thing of death.[1]

Throughout American history, people have been able to control what happens to their property after death. This right, called freedom of testation, is the fundamental principle on which American wills law is based. Most people believe that the same rule holds true for control of their bodies. (After all, if we own anything, surely it is the body in which we live.) This belief seems to be borne out in practice, where it is common for people to leave instructions in their wills about how to dispose of their physical remains. And yet, despite intuitions and practices, the rules governing the control of our bodies are founded on a vastly different principal, giving rise to a vastly different landscape. While the starting point for the control of a person's property is freedom of testation, the starting point for control of a person's body is *corpus nullius in bonis,* the body belongs to no one. With this principle as a starting point, the rules governing and the history of the treatment of bodies under American law have been able to shift over time to meet the changing needs of society. This chapter traces these changes from the country's earliest days to today.

[1] Louisville & N.R. Co. v. Wilson, 51 S.E. 24, 25 (Ga. 1905).

Dead Bodies in Early America

The most important rule regarding controlling bodies after death was one that the United States inherited from the common law of England, that is, the rule that a person does not have a property interest in his own body after death. The principle of common law is *corpus nullius in bonis* – the body belongs to no one. Although many posit that the root of this rule is in the view that the body is sacred, Professor Lori Andrews suggests another possible interpretation – that under the common law in England, there was a notion that people's bodies belonged to the Crown. This would be consistent with the feudal law that it was a crime to maim oneself because doing so rendered one less able to fight for the king.[2]

The decision most often cited for this proposition is the English case *Williams v. Williams*.[3] In that case, a man by the name of Henry Crookenden – an early advocate of cremation – provided in his will that upon his death, his body was to be given to his friend Eliza Williams, "to be dealt with in the manner provided for in a letter to her." In this letter, he laid out his wishes with specificity: he wanted his body burned under a pile of wood and the remains stored in a particular Wedgwood vase (that Crookenden had conveniently provided to Williams through his will).

When Crookenden died, rather than following the wishes laid out in his will, his family buried him with the rites of the Roman Catholic Church. Eliza Williams tried to enforce the provisions of the will. In refusing her request, however, the court ruled that "there can be no property in a dead body"[4]:

> [A] man cannot by will dispose of his dead body. If there be no property in a dead body it is impossible that by will or any other instrument the body can be disposed of.[5]

Although undoubtedly affected by the decedent's avant-garde choice of burial, the court went out of its way to state that its decision had much broader applicability: "if the purpose had merely been for burial in a

[2] Lori Andrews, *Who Owns Your Body? – A Patient's Perspectives on* Washington University v. Catalona, 34 J.L. MED. & ETHICS 398, 400 (2006).

[3] Williams v. Williams, 20 Ch. Div. 659 (1882).

[4] *Id.* at 662–63.

[5] *Id.* at 665.

particular cemetery, which would be entirely according to the law of this country, that would not make the direction to deliver the body to someone who was not an executor any more legal or enforceable."[6]

This common law rule, that there is no property interest in the body, was adopted in the United States and has been of critical importance in the subsequent development of the law of the body. The failure to recognize a property interest in a dead body has proven to be a significant impediment to the ability of an individual to control what happens to his body after death. The recognition of something as a property interest carries with it a wide range of protections. Most notably, the United States Constitution provides protections against the government's interference with property interests.[7] Therefore, the failure to treat a person's body as a property interest effectively precludes the use of a range of constitutional protections.[8] The other main value in having something designated a property interest is that when something is "property," then the law generally designates a particular person or entity as the property owner. This designation makes it much easier for claims to be asserted. As the law stands now, without a recognized property interest, much litigation occurs just to determine which person is the appropriate decision maker.[9]

It is perhaps due in part to this common law "no property in your body" rule that so many states have enacted statutes that purportedly provide people with the ability to control what happens to their bodies after death. These statutes typically allow people either to leave directions regarding the disposition of their bodies and/or to designate someone to make such decisions regarding disposition.[10]

[6] *Id.* at 665.

[7] U.S. CONST. amend. V.

[8] This has particular significance in the development of laws regarding organ donation.

[9] When Anna Nicole Smith died, there was a lengthy trial over who was authorized to make the decision regarding the disposition of her body: the executor of her will, her mother, or one of the two potential fathers of her newborn daughter. The probate court judge ultimately ruled that the infant daughter was the appropriate decision maker. This case was a more public version of a controversy that has played out since this country's inception – fights among family members and others about controlling the disposition of a person's body after death. Frances H. Foster, *Individualized Justice in Disputes over Dead Bodies*, 61 VAND. L. REV. 1351 (2008).

[10] ARK.CODE ANN. § 20-17-102 (Arkansas); COLO. REV. STAT. § 12-34-204 (Colorado); CONN. GEN. STAT. § 45 a-318 (Connecticut); DEL. CODE ANN. tit.12, § 262 (2004)

Thus, despite the fact that the statutes appear to be highly protective of people's rights to control what happens to their bodies after death, the reality falls short of appearances. The key reason for this is that these statutes are primarily the product of lobbying by the funeral industry, which was concerned with avoiding liability from dissenting family members. Thus, the focus of the statutes is to allow funeral directors to rely on instructions left by a decedent, provided they are expressed in a particular form. While these statutes might provide some protection for people who have survivors interested in carrying out their wishes, they provide no protection where these people are missing because the statutes have no mechanism for imposing liability for failure to fulfill the person's stated wishes. Moreover, many statutes that purport to grant rights of control actually limit this control in substantive ways. For example, some hold that the wishes only need to be carried out if they are "reasonable and do not impose an economic or emotional hardship"[11] or are "reasonable under the circumstances" (taking into account a variety of factors, including the size of the estate, cultural or family customs, and the person's religious or spiritual beliefs).[12] The effect of such qualifications is that these statutes provide more of a hope than a promise that a person's wishes regarding his or her body will be carried out.

Early American law affected the treatment of dead bodies in another context as well: that is, the practice of desecrating the body as punishment for certain, particularly egregious, crimes. As early as 1784, Massachusetts law required that a person slain in a duel would be either buried in a public place without a coffin with a stake through his body or given to a surgeon for dissection (in case death was not an adequate deterrent on its own).[13] These provisions served the dual purpose of (1) punishing perpetrators and (2) providing bodies for anatomical studies.

(Delaware); D.C. CODE § 3 - 413 (District of Columbia); 755 ILL. COMP. STAT. 65/40 (Illinois); Md. Code Ann., [Health-General] § 5-509 (Maryland); MINN. STAT. § 149A.80 (Minnesota); Nev. Rev. Stat. § 451.655 (Nevada); N.M. STAT. § 24-12A-1 (New Mexico); N.C. GEN. STAT. § 130A-420 (North Carolina); OR. REV. STAT. § 97.130 (Oregon); R.I. GEN. LAWS § 5-33.2-24 (Rhode Island); S.D. CODIFIED LAWS § 34-26-1 (South Dakota); UTAH CODE ANN. § 58-9-601 (Utah); WASH. REV. CODE § 68.50.160 (Washington).

11 Arizona, ARIZ. REV. STAT. ANN. § 36-831.01.

12 Delaware, 12 DEL. CODE ANN. tit. 12 § 265.

13 Aaron D. Tward & Hugh A. Patterson, *From Grave Robbing to Gifting: Cadaver Supply in the United States*, 287 J. AM. MED. ASS'N 1183 (2002).

The First Wave of Change: Bodies for Anatomical Study

The basic principles regarding the law of the body were stable for many years. As society developed new uses for dead bodies, however, there was pressure to change the laws governing the control and treatment of bodies. Increased interest in anatomical study triggered the first wave. In the United States, anatomical studies – and the growing need for corpses – were closely linked to the formalization of medical education. Michael Sappol explores this link in *A Traffic in Dead Bodies.*[14]

Beginning in the eighteenth century, with the development of medicine as a profession, hands-on anatomical study became a defining feature of medical education.[15] With these changes, the availability of corpses for dissection became an essential feature in a school's success or failure. Indeed, the reason Harvard Medical School moved from Cambridge to Boston in 1810 was motivated by the desire to increase access to cadavers, which were "utterly unattainable at Cambridge."[16]

Medical education expanded rapidly in the nineteenth century; while in 1800 there were 4 medical schools in the United States, by 1900 there were 160.[17] The perceived importance of anatomical study for medical students, combined with the expansion of medical schools, created a significant problem: how were schools going to find a sufficient number of corpses for dissection by their students? This problem was exacerbated by the fact that in the nineteenth-century United States, a significant number of Americans believed in the literal resurrection of the human body and therefore were deeply concerned that their bodies remain intact. Because the body's integrity was thought to be necessary for salvation in the afterlife, many people did not want their bodies to be subject to autopsy and research.[18] Moreover, in the nineteenth century, Americans of all classes and backgrounds were deeply concerned with having a proper burial. Given the value of a proper

[14] MICHAEL SAPPOL, A TRAFFIC OF DEAD BODIES: ANATOMY AND EMBODIED SOCIAL IDENTITY IN NINETEENTH-CENTURY AMERICAN (2002).

[15] In 1745 the University of Pennsylvania established the first formal course in the study of anatomy in the United States. *Id.* at 60.

[16] *Id.* at 60.

[17] *Id.* at 2.

[18] Dorothy Nelkin & Lori Andrews, *Do the Dead Have Interests? – Policy Issues for Research After Life,* 24 AM. J.L. & MED. 261, 263 (1998).

burial and the widespread religious belief in a physical afterlife, it is not surprising that finding cadavers for anatomical research became an increasingly pressing problem.

The first source of bodies was criminals. Many states provided that – as a form of super capital punishment for the most heinous crimes – the bodies of executed criminals would be given to medical schools for dissection. This rule still exists in many state statutes today, including in Massachusetts, which provides that:

> Upon conviction of murder in the first degree, the court may order the body of the convict after his execution to be dissected. The warden of the state prison shall in such case deliver it to a professor of anatomy or surgery in a medical school established by law in the commonwealth, if so requested; otherwise, he shall, unless the convict's friends desire it for interment, deliver it to any surgeon attending to receive it who will undertake to dissect it.[19]

However, as interest in anatomy grew, the supply of executed criminals did not keep pace with the demand (and the association of dissection with punishment hardly made it an attractive option for the public at large). Initially this gap in the market was met – as it often is – by the criminal element. Grave robbery (also called "body snatching" or "resurrectionism") became a profitable enterprise as anatomy departments paid handsomely for fresh dead bodies. At one time the going rate for a body was between ten and thirty-five dollars – this was at a time when the wages of a skilled worker were between twenty dollars and thirty dollars per *week* and a day laborer was paid a dollar a day or less.[20] Of course, sometimes if the bodies were not available, the providers needed to be creative. There were several cases in which providers of bodies did not wait for death – they simply killed people and then submitted their bodies for payment. In 1884 a family of three was killed in Cincinnati and sold to the Medical College of Ohio for $100. In 1886 an elderly woman in Baltimore was murdered and sold to the University of Maryland Medical School for $15.[21]

19 MASS.GEN. LAWS ch. 113, § 6. Dissection of bodies of executed murderers. The application of this statute is currently limited by the fact that Massachusetts does not impose a death penalty, although presumably it would apply to federal capital cases that are tried in Massachusetts.

20 SAPPOL, *supra* note 14, at 320.

21 SAPPOL, *supra* note 14, at 318.

In order to meet the pressing demand for cadavers, American medical schools became both directly and indirectly involved with the body snatching business. A letter from John Godman, one of the most distinguished anatomists of the early nineteenth century, to John Warren, a leading anatomist at Harvard University, provided insight to the supply of corpses for education:

> In both New York and Philadelphia, anatomists bribed public officials and burial-ground employees to gain unhindered access to the paupers buried in Potter's field. In New York, the superintending official divided the bodies into two categories. Those "most entitled to respect, or most likely to be called for by friends" were buried in Pit No. 1 and exempted from dissection; the rest were buried in Pit No. 2, which was plundered to supply the medical colleges. In Philadelphia, however, the anatomists were entitled to "all the subjects buried in the two public grounds." If schools or physicians differed over who should get an allotment of bodies, the dispute was to be settled by the mayor – a high reaching conspiracy that resulted in a harvest of about 450 bodies per school year.[22]

As a result, while grave robbery was sometimes left to the "professionals," it was also a rite of passage that many medical students undertook themselves. William James McKnight – a doctor who later became a state senator in Pennsylvania – published a number of articles describing his grave robbing experiences while in medical school.[23] Grave robbery by medical schools was deeply disturbing to the public and gave rise to mass opposition. During the period 1785–1885 there were at least seventeen anatomy riots in America as people expressed their anger at the anatomists. These riots affected nearly every institution of medical learning.[24] At Columbia University, the riot went on for two days and seven people were killed.

Moreover, this epidemic of grave robbing resulted in a crisis for a legal system that had adopted the principal that a corpse is *nullius in bonis*, meaning the dead person belongs to nobody. Because of this lack of proprietary interest, no one had the legal authority to complain when a body was stolen. Earlier cases focused on the theft of the clothes that the body wore, but this was only a misdemeanor and could not provide punishment commensurate with pain at the theft of the bodies of loved ones. One

[22] SAPPOL, *supra* note 14, at 4.

[23] Horace Montgomery, *A Body Snatcher Sponsors Pennsylvania's Anatomy Act*, 21 J. HIST. & MED. & ALLIED SCI. 374, 376 (1966).

[24] SAPPOL, *supra* note 14, at 4.

response to this was the widespread enactment of legislation prohibiting the desecration of graves and the stealing of corpses.[25] However, because the underlying need for corpses persisted, this criminalization did little to stop the activity.

The practice of grave robbery continued until the passage of new legislation, known as "anatomy acts". These laws essentially provided a legal venue for medical schools to do that which they were already doing illegally – taking the bodies of the poor and dispossessed, whose burial costs would otherwise have been borne by the state.[26] Thus, anatomy laws were sold to legislators as providing a double benefit: they saved local jurisdictions the cost of burying the dead while providing a stream of bodies to medical schools. Proponents of anatomy acts also argued that they would serve to discourage people from becoming wards of the state. Most importantly for the middle and upper classes, by providing a legal source of bodies for the medical schools, this would significantly decrease the risk that more affluent bodies would be stolen by the grave robbers.

The first anatomy act in the United States was passed in Massachusetts in 1831. This statute, "An Act ... to protect the Sepulchers of the Dead," was carefully crafted to limit controversy. First its purported goal – trumpeted in its name – was to prevent grave robbery. Second, to avoid charges that it was targeted at poor people, the law used the term "unclaimed," rather than "indigent" bodies. Thus, theoretically, a wealthy person could die and his body could remain "unclaimed." However, to protect against this actually happening, the law provided exemptions for "travelers" as well as a waiting period for other bodies to be claimed. It also limited its application to those living in the city and provided an exception for poor people who had been longtime residents of the area (called "town paupers"). After applying all of these rules, the anatomy act (as well as others that were to follow) most commonly applied to the growing population of German, Irish, Italian, and Jewish immigrants who had settled in the cities.[27]

[25] Sappol, *supra* note 14, at 101–02.

[26] Sappol, *supra* note 14, at 4. Massachusetts passed the first anatomy act in the United States in 1831.

[27] Kunal M. Parker, State, *Citizenship and Territory: The Legal Construction of Immigrants in Antebellum Massachusetts*, 19 Law & Hist. Rev. 583 (2001). Sappol notes that the 1830 Massachusetts act applied only to Boston, the 1854 "Bone Bill" was limited to cities with populations greater than 30,000 and the 1867 Pennsylvania "Armstrong Act" was limited to Philadelphia and Pittsburgh. Sappol, *supra* note 14, at 123.

Anatomy acts were enacted in several other states, but they remained a source of controversy. While many states passed anatomy laws in the antebellum period, including New Hampshire (1834), Connecticut (1833), Michigan (1844), New York (1854), and Pennsylvania (1867, and amended in 1881), the majority of these statutes were repealed shortly after enactment. By the end of the Civil War, only the Massachusetts and New York anatomy statutes remained in effect.[28]

After the Civil War, medical science began to produce significant advances that resulted in dividends for the American people and softened popular sentiment toward the medical profession. Along with this shift in sentiment was an acceptance of the necessity of anatomy acts. By the turn of the century, many states had anatomy acts, and Congress passed an anatomy act for the District of Columbia.

Today, many medical schools meet their need for cadavers through people's voluntary donation of their bodies. This is particularly true for the most prestigious institutions, some of which have such a surplus of cadavers that they purposely make it difficult to donate bodies.[29] However, less well-known institutions continue to have difficulty meeting their demand for bodies and in those cases, anatomy acts continue to play a role in meeting this demand.[30] Today's anatomy acts continue to apply to "unclaimed bodies." However, rather than being directed to residents of poorhouses, today's acts are more likely to apply to people in prisons and hospitals who would otherwise have to be buried or cremated at government expense. The statutes continue to provide protections to prevent more affluent people from being unwittingly caught by retaining an exception for travelers and sufficient waiting periods. In addition, modern anatomy statutes have added exceptions for those who have served in the military. However, those who do not meet these exceptions generally give up their rights to control

[28] SAPPOL, *supra* note 14, at 123–24.

[29] One side effect of these excess cadavers has been several scandals involving cadaver trafficking by officials at some of these institutions. For example, an article in the Los Angeles Times in March 2007 reported that criminal charges were filed against the director of the "willed body" program and another man who allegedly sold parts of donated bodies for a profit. According to authorities, they made in excess of $1 million through their illegal activities. Charles Ornstein & Andrew Blankstein, *2 Men Charged in Sale of Donated Bodies*, L.A. TIMES, Mar. 8, 2007, at 1.

[30] Tward & Patterson, *supra* note 13; Lindsey Gruson, *Signs of Traffic in Cadavers Seen, Raising Ethical Issues*, N.Y. TIMES, Sept. 25, 1986, at A14.

what happens to their bodies after death, as only a small number of states allow people to choose to opt out of these provisions.

The Second Wave of Change: Bodies for Transplant

Just as societal changes brought about more uses for dead bodies, scientific and technological developments also changed the landscape. Nothing has done more to change the legal regime governing dead bodies than the development of the ability to transplant organs.

Early in December 1967, a young South African surgeon took the healthy heart of a young woman fatally injured in an automobile accident and transplanted it to the body of a man dying of heart disease. The surgeon, Dr. Christiaan Barnard, later said that he knew it was a surgical success when he first applied electrodes and the heart resumed beating. Although the transplant recipient died eighteen days later from pneumonia, this was a milestone in a new field of life-extending surgery that dramatically increased awareness of the potential value of human cadavers and transformed legal issues involving the dead in fundamental ways.[31] As one scholar described it:

> Organ transplantation radically changed the nature of the problem by bringing into the picture for the first time the highest principle of law, medicine, ethics and religion: saving human life. This principle was not previously relevant in the disposition of corpses.[32]

Over the next twenty years, with the development of new antirejection treatments, organ transplants offered promises of treatment to more and more people. Yet, for these promises to be fulfilled, the legal regimen needed to be transformed yet again. The greatest difficulty was in providing an adequate source of organs for the rapidly increasing number of people who could potentially benefit from transplants.[33] To address this problem, a

[31] *A Science Odyssey, People and Discoveries: Christiaan Barnard 1922–___*, PUB. BROAD. CO., (1998), http://www.pbs.org/wgbh/aso/databank/entries/bmbarn.html.

[32] Jesse Dukeminier Jr., *Supplying Organs for Transplantation*, 68 MICH. L. REV. 811, 818 (1970).

[33] Indeed, from the very early days of transplants, through to today, there has been a persistent and significant shortfall in the number of organs available to transplant. In 2006 there were more than 95,000 people on the waiting list awaiting an organ. On

proliferation of new laws was enacted to allow and encourage the donation of organs. These laws had to provide new rules for controlling the disposition of dead bodies, but they also needed to alter the rules regarding the very definition of death itself.

The first problem was that it was not clear who had the power to donate a human body to provide the organs for transplant. American law had developed on the basis of the common law legal principle that a corpse is *nullius in bonis,* that is, belongs to no one. This rule may have been adequate at a time when a body was primarily an obligation, something to be handled and disposed of, but it became deeply problematic as the potential value of – and thereby the number of people interested in – dead bodies increased.

To address this problem, shortly after the famous heart transplant, a group of influential lawyers, judges, and professors were commissioned in 1968 to draft model legislation aimed specifically at addressing the issue of cadaver organ donation. This model statute, called the Uniform Anatomical Gift Act (UAGA), provided a mechanism for the donation of bodies at death for transplant and was highly successful in that it was adopted by all fifty states and the District of Columbia within five years of first being proposed.

The 1968 UAGA accomplished several goals. Most importantly, it provided a clear mechanism through which people could donate organs at death. Prior law had been a mishmash of rules that considered a variety of factors in determining who could make decisions regarding a person's body after death. Under the UAGA, an individual could state his wishes to donate his body either through a provision in a will or by a witnessed document (usually in the form of an organ donor card issued by a state's department of motor vehicles). The UAGA also provided a mechanism through which family members (in ranked order) could donate part or all of the decedent's body. By creating a statute that was adopted throughout the United States, the UAGA also provided national uniformity for the laws governing organ donation. This was particularly important because a nationwide program increased the ability to find compatible matches between organ donors

average 18 people die each day because no organ is available for transplant. UNITED NETWORK FOR ORGAN SHARING, http://www.unos.org/index.php (last accessed Dec. 28, 2012).

and organ recipients. Finally, the UAGA established standards for which organs could be donated and which organizations could be recipients of organ donations.[34]

The 1968 UAGA was extremely successful in providing mechanisms for donation and national uniformity. However, it was less successful in terms of procuring sufficient donors to meet the burgeoning demand of potential transplant recipients. Almost twenty years after the enactment of the 1968 UAGA, the problem was described as follows:

> An overriding problem common to all organ transplantation programs as well as to the well-established programs in tissue banking (for corneal, skin and bone transplantation) is the serious gap between the need for the organs and tissues and the supply of donors. Despite substantial support for transplantation and a general willingness to donate organs and tissues after death, the demand far exceeds the supply. At any one time, there are an estimated 8,000 to 10,000 people waiting for a donor organ to become available.[35]

In response to the problem of insufficient organ donations, states incorporated two types of provisions into their statutes (required request and presumed consent). These provisions sought both to increase the number of available organs and take into account the desire of individuals to control what happens to their bodies or the bodies of their loved ones. However, the balance was struck very differently in the two different provisions.

[34] The UAGA was expansive in this area and provided for the donations of any human body or body part to

(1) any hospital, surgeon, or physician, for medical or dental education, research, advancement of medical or dental science, therapy, or transplantation; or
(2) any accredited medical or dental school, college or university for education, research, advancement of medical or dental science, or therapy; or
(3) any bank or storage facility, for medical or dental education, research, advancement of medical or dental science, therapy, or transplantation; or
(4) any specified individual for therapy or transplantation needed by him.

Unif. Anatomical Gift Act § 3 (1968).

[35] 1987 UAGA Prefatory note, quoting *Organ Transplantation: Issues and Recommendations* (1986), Task Force on Organ Transplantation. The problem has only become worse over the last 20 years. As described in the Prefatory Note to the 2006 UAGA: As of January 2006 there were more than 92,000 individuals on the waiting list for organ transplantation, and the list keeps growing. It is estimated that approximately 5,000 individuals join the waiting list each year.... Every hour another person in the United States dies because of the lack of an organ to provide a lifesaving organ transplant. *Revised UAGA (2006) Prefatory Note*, http://www.law.upenn.edu/bll/ulc/uaga/2006final.htm.

Required request provisions sought to encourage more people to think about organ donation by requiring hospitals to ask people about organ donation upon admission to the hospital and to ask family members for permission to retrieve organs from patients who died.[36] States generally accepted these provisions, and they remain in force today.[37] In addition, the federal government put its own imprimatur on the required request approach by making it a condition if hospitals are to receive Medicare and Medicaid reimbursement.[38]

Presumed consent provisions also had as their goal the procurement of more organs for donation. Under presumed consent statutes, however, the focus is more directly on society's needs for organs and less on preserving control by individuals or their families. Presumed consent statutes seek to increase the number of organs available for transplant by presumptively eliminating the need for consent in certain situations. These statutes provide that in any case in which a body is subject to autopsy, the coroner is entitled to donate parts of the decedent's body for transplant purposes, unless the coroner has direct knowledge of a refusal or contrary indication by the decedent or the decedent's family.[39] This last provision might seem to provide some protection for the decedent or his or her family in that their objections must be taken into account. However, because the coroner is under no obligation to make any inquiry about the preference of the deceased or her family members, and he is relieved of liability so long as he does not know of any contrary instructions, this arrangement encourages coroners to embrace ignorance rather than to search for true intent.

Presumed consent statutes apply only to cases in which the body is under investigation by a state medical examiner. (These autopsies should not be confused with private autopsies requested by family members.) Bodies are typically subject to investigation by state coroners in the case of homicide or suspicious death. Who is most likely to be subject to these

[36] Unif. Anatomical Gift Act § 5 (1987).

[37] Erik S. Jaffe, *'She's Got Bette Davis['s] Eyes': Assessing the Nonconsensual Removal of Cadaver Organs under the Takings and Due Process Clauses*, 90 Colum. L. Rev. 528, 535 (1990).

[38] 42 U.S.C. § 132b-8 (2002).

[39] Unif. Anatomical Gift Act § 4 (1987).Some state versions of presumed consent limit its application to certain body parts, such as corneas, pituitary glands, and other tissues. Other versions, including the UAGA apply to all organs.

mandatory autopsies? Most commonly it is young black and Latino men who have been victims of gang violence or drug overdose. As Professor Michele Goodwin points out in her book *Black Markets*, "during this period of violence in the 1980's and into the 1990's came rising death tolls of young Blacks and Latinos and the promulgation of presumed consent laws. These two overlapping occurrences were a tragic coincidence."[40]

Presumed consent statutes have been subject to court scrutiny because several families have complained about the removal of corneal tissue for donation to eye banks without the family's consent.[41] These statutes have generally been upheld on the theory that (1) neither the decedent nor his family member has a property interest in his body, and (2) whatever constitutional right of privacy may exist with respect to the integrity of the body, such right is personal and ends with death.[42] The one case that ruled in favor of the family, *Brotherton v. Cleveland*, failed to find a property right in the decedent's body but nonetheless held that the decedent's wife had a legitimate claim of entitlement protected under federal law.[43]

Many other countries have presumed consent statutes.[44] However, these statutes differ from U.S. law in two important ways: (1) these statutes provide mechanisms through which people can opt out of presumed consent and they know that such wishes will be upheld; and (2) these statutes apply to all individuals – not just those whose deaths are subject to state investigation.

While some people's bodies are being used for organ transplants without their consent or the consent of their families, there is another group of people who have expressed interest in becoming organ donors but have been unable to do so: death row inmates. Jonathan Nobles was sentenced to

[40] MICHELE GOODWIN, BLACK MARKETS: THE SUPPLY AND DEMAND OF BODY PARTS 121 (2006).

[41] Brotherton v. Cleveland, 173 F.3d 552 (6th Cir. 1999); State v. Powell, 497 So.2d 1188 (Fla. 1986), *cert. denied*; Georgia Lions Eye Bank v. Lavant, 335 S.E.2d 127 (Ga. 1985); Tillman v. Detroit Receiving Hosp., 360 N.W.2d 275 (Mich. Ct. App. 1984).

[42] *Tillman*, 360 N.W.2d at 277.

[43] *Brotherton*, 173 F.3d.

[44] Presumed consent laws have been implemented in 22 countries, including Austria, Spain, Portugal, Italy, Belgium, France, Luxembourg, Norway, Denmark, Finland, Sweden, Switzerland, Latvia, Czech Republic, Slovak Republic, Hungary, Slovenia, Poland, Greece, Israel, and Singapore. *See* Marie-Andrée Jacob, *On Silencing and Slicing: Presumed Consent to Post-Mortem Organ "Donation" in Diversified Societies*, 11 TULSA J. COMP. & INT'L L. 239 (2003).

death in Texas for the murder of two young women. While in prison, Nobles went through a religious conversion and sought to donate his organs so that he could do something positive after "bringing so much darkness into this world."[45] Nonetheless, his request was denied by the Texas Department of Criminal Justice.

Death row inmates cannot donate their organs primarily because of the methods of execution used in the United States. There are currently five methods of execution in the United States: electrocution, lethal injection, gas chamber, hanging, and firing squad. Although these methods differ, they share one important feature: each of these methods prevent effective organ procurement from executed prisoners because the organs are either destroyed or rendered useless during the time that elapses between the administration of the execution and the pronouncement of death.[46] What this means is that people executed for crimes are not able to donate their organs for transplant.

Some states have attempted to adopt legislation that would make it easier for inmates to donate their organs. In 2000 a representative in the Florida legislature proposed a bill to allow death row inmates to donate their organs upon execution, if the organs were still usable. There was strong opposition to this bill from organ procurement organizations and many were concerned about the ethical, scientific, and legal issues. This opposition prevented the bill from becoming law. In Missouri a "Life for a Life" bill was proposed to allow an inmate to donate a kidney in exchange for a commuted sentence. This bill failed as well, as a result of the ethical concerns over offering such an incentive.[47]

As is made clear in Professor Jamila Jefferson's companion chapter in this book, there is a lot of complexity underlying the decision whether to allow executed criminals to donate their organs (including whether the prisoners have truly consented to have their organs donated as well as the perceived opportunities for abuse). This issue has been made even more complex by the situation in China, where prisoners are routinely executed

[45] AP, *An Organ Donation Offer on Death Row is Refused*, N.Y. Times, Sept. 9, 1998, at A23.

[46] Laura-Hill M. Patton, *A Call for Common Sense: Organ Donation and the Executed Prisoner*, 3 Va. J. Soc. Pol'y & L. 387 (1995).

[47] Donnye Perales, *Rethinking the Prohibition of Death Row Prisoners as Organ Donors: A Possible Life Line to Those on Organ Donor Waiting Lists*, 34 St. Mary's L.J. 687 (2003).

and their organs reputedly sold by the Chinese government at large profits.[48] However, undoubtedly there is another concern at play here. That is, the opportunity to donate organs is an opportunity to leave a positive mark on the world, and people who have committed the most heinous crimes should not be allowed this opportunity to have this legacy. The mother of one of the victims of Nobles said that the convict lost his rights, including the right to donate organs, when he murdered her daughter.[49]

Redefining Death

The most significant, and in some ways stunning, change of law that was required by the ability to transplant organs was the very definition of death itself. There are significant differences between legal and moral duties owed to living persons as opposed to dead persons. Therefore, the distinction between the living and the dead is a critical one. Yet, the question of when death occurs is surprisingly more complicated than one might initially imagine. This problem has both practical and theoretical dimensions.

The challenge of determining when death occurred was historically a practical one. People knew (or at least thought they knew) what death was; they just did not have the tools to determine whether death had in fact occurred. Thus, the problem of premature burial was a very real one. One contemporaneous compilation from the seventeenth century revealed that there were 219 instances of narrow escape from premature burial, 149 cases of actual premature burial, 10 cases in which bodies were accidentally dissected before death, and 2 cases in which embalming was started on the not-yet-dead.[50]

This fear of premature burial prompted people to invent ingenious solutions. In 1868 a New Jersey man was granted a patent for his design of a coffin outfitted with a tube that contained a bell and a ladder, enabling the entombed individual to climb to safety or to summon help.[51] Another

[48] *Organ Sales "Thriving" in China*, BBC NEWS, Sept. 27, 2006, http://news.bbc.co.uk/2/hi/asia-pacific/5386720.stm.

[49] Patton, *supra* note 46.

[50] Brian Olshansky, *For Whom Does the Bell Toll?*, 12 J. CARDIOVASCULAR ELECTROPHYSIOLOGY 1002, 1002–03 (2003).

[51] JOANNA BOURKE, FEAR: A CULTURAL HISTORY 41–42 (2006).

response was the development of the waiting mortuary. This was a holding place where the presumed dead could be kept before burial, giving them a last opportunity to show that they had life in them before being buried. Some mortuaries had procedures whereby they placed a bell on a person's foot. If the person moved, the bell would ring, notifying the attendant that the person was still alive.

There was also more organized response to this fear as well. In 1899 the Association for Prevention of Premature Burial was formed in London, England, and a year later its American counterpart, the Society for the Prevention of Premature Burial, was established. These organizations sought the enactment of laws to include professional medical personnel in the determination of whether death had occurred. We see the results of their work today in statutes that require death certificates to be issued with the signature of a licensed physician who can attest to the fact of the person's death.

The practical problem of discerning whether the signs of death had occurred largely abated in the twentieth century with the development of medical technology that provided the physician with more accurate ways of measuring heart and brain activity. Though one practical problem was solved, a more significant problem remained. This was the theoretical problem of defining what constitutes death. This issue is not as clear-cut as many people think. The primary reason is that although people think of death as occurring in a single moment (and the legal world requires this as well), in biological terms, death is not a discrete event, but instead is a gradual process.[52] Thus, even after a person's heart stops beating, other muscle, skin, and bone cells may live on for several days. Picking a moment in this process and calling that the moment of death is in some ways arbitrary and has had a complicated history.

The debate about what constitutes death began in earnest in 1740 with the writings of the French physician and anatomist Jacques Winslow. Winslow was terrified by the thought of premature burial and sought – unsuccessfully – to discover a definitive surgical test to determine whether death had occurred (considering, but ultimately rejecting such tests as pinpricks and incisions). Winslow came by his fear honestly. As a child he had

[52] Kenneth V. Iserson, Death to Dust: What Happens to Dead Bodies 13 (1994).

twice been abandoned for dead, only to revive and discover that he had been placed in a coffin.[53]

Building on the work of Winslow, some argued that all signs of death, except for putrefaction (decomposition of the body), were inconclusive and therefore that a corpse should only be dissected, embalmed, or buried after it had begun to decompose because "the laws of Religion and of humanity forbid advancing death even one moment."[54] However, while putrefaction of the body as a standard for death protected people against premature burial, the standard created significant problems of its own. First of all, at a time when most people died at home, waiting for a body to decay was not simply an inconvenience, but also a health risk to the family and neighbors of the deceased. Second, the putrefaction standard also posed a problem for anatomists (a growing group in the eighteenth and nineteenth centuries), who needed to study cadavers before they had been changed by decay.[55]

Fortunately for neighbors and anatomists, medical tools were developed that enabled medical professionals to adopt a new standard for death: the cessation of the beating heart and the breathing of the lungs. These "cardiopulmonary criteria" became widely adopted by the medical profession and in turn allowed the definition of death to be viewed as a technical problem that could be solved by the application of medical expertise.[56] This resulted in the development of the almost universal law that "a person is dead when a physician says so."[57]

Although for a brief period, there seemed to be some certainty on the status of death– an agreed upon standard (cessation of heartbeat) and a mode of determining whether the standard had occurred – such certainty was not to last. The reason was the continuing development of medical technology that raised new issues as to the appropriateness of the cardiopulmonary standard of death.

The first of these was the development of the mechanical ventilator, which made it possible to support a person's heart and lung function even

[53] Marc Alexander, *"The Rigid Embrace of the Narrow House": Premature Burial at the Signs of Death*, HASTINGS CTR. REP. 25, 26 (1980).

[54] *Id.*

[55] *Id.*

[56] *Id.* at 31.

[57] ISERSON, *supra* note 53, at 19 quoting in 26. *See also* 22nd WORLD MED. ASSEMBLY, Sydney, Australia (1968).

after brain function had ceased. A person's heartbeat could now continue even when he or she had no discernible brain activity and respiration was mechanically sustained. This put hospitals in the difficult position of maintaining care for individuals who seemed to be more dead than alive.[58] It also raised an additional problem that under a cardiopulmonary definition of death, the removal of a mechanical ventilator from a person with no brain activity technically constituted murder. This resulted in some peculiar legal cases, including one case in which a defendant charged with murder argued that the doctors who removed the life support, rather than he, caused the death of the victim.[59]

The possibility for organ transplants raised another problem for using the cardiopulmonary definition of death. That is, after the heart stops pumping, organs quickly begin to decay and soon are no longer suitable for transplant. Therefore, the cardiopulmonary definition of death impeded the availability of organs for transplant. A highly influential report by an ad hoc committee at Harvard Medical School came to the rescue by proposing a new definition of death: cessation of brain function. This definition made a certain degree of sense in a society that associates personal identity with the brain. Happily, it also served the goals of organ transplants by providing that organs could be harvested from a body after the brain had ceased functioning, even if the person was still breathing and still had a heart rate (due to mechanical ventilation). Shortly after this report appeared, all fifty states had adopted some version of the brain death standard either by statute or via case law.

The most widely adopted statute, the Uniform Definition of Death Act, provides that a person can be declared dead when he has sustained either (1) irreversible cessation of circulatory and respiratory functions or (2) irreversible cessation of all functions of the entire brain.[60] This statute has been adopted in forty-three states; states that have not adopted the Uniform Definition of Death Act have either adopted their own statutes or

[58] John P. Lizza, Persons, Humanity, and the Definition of Death 7 (2006).

[59] State v. Schaffer, 574 P.2d 205 (1977); *see also* People v. Eulo, 472 N.E.2d 286 (N.Y. 1984).

[60] This is the standard set out in the Uniform Determination of Death Act. As of 2009, this statute had been adopted in some form in 40 states. This standard is different from a permanent vegetative state (PVS) in that the brain of a person in a PVS still functions, albeit at a very rudimentary state.

developed case law allowing the use of brain death as a standard for death. Brain death has been adopted as a standard throughout much of the rest of the world as well.

Despite this near-universal adoption of the brain death standard, this is not likely to be the end of the issue. There are several reasons. First, a person who is brain dead does not necessarily appear dead to outsiders. To many people, it is disconcerting to call a person who is warm and has a heartbeat "dead." Moreover, many religions have their own official views of when death occurs, and these standards are sometimes at odds with the brain death standard. Finally, as technology develops, it is able to detect more and more subtle levels of brain activity, calling into doubt the ability to measure brain death with any accuracy.

As a result of these issues, disagreements can arise regarding whether a person is in fact dead. This conflict played out in a 2007 case involving Cho Fook Cheng, a seventy-two-year-old grandfather, who suffered a heart attack the day after Thanksgiving. He was taken to the hospital and placed on a ventilator. Soon thereafter, the doctors declared Cheng dead on the basis of the brain death standard and sought to have him removed from life support. The family, however, practiced a Taiwanese form of Buddhism, in which a person is not considered dead until his heart stops beating. The case headed for a court showdown but was rendered moot when Cheng's heart stopped on its own.[61] Yet, in terms of the plain meaning of the governing statutes, as well as case law from other jurisdictions, it seems likely that the hospital would have been within its legal rights to remove life support. Once a person is declared dead under the governing authority, the family is not entitled to demand life support measures.[62]

In response to such difficulties, some scholars have suggested that the moment of death be at least partially a function of individual choice. New Jersey has enacted a statute that does this by allowing a patient's religious belief to be taken into account in determining whether death has occurred. New Jersey's law is similar to the law of other jurisdictions in providing for doctors to apply either the cardiopulmonary or brain death standard, but

[61] Megan Tench, *End-of-Life Lawsuit Outliving Its Subject: Kin to Appeal Dismissal Ruling*, Bos. Globe, Dec. 6, 2006, at 3B; Megan Tench, *After Buddhist Dies, Legal Battles Continues: Kin, Hospital Split on When Death Occurs*, Bos. Globe, Dec. 3, 2006, at 1A.

[62] *See In re* Welfare of Bowman, 617 P.2d 731, 738 (Wash. 1980); *In re* Long Island Jewish Med Ctr., 651 N.Y.S.2d 989 (Sup. Ct. 1996).

it goes on to provide that the brain death standard is not to be used if the physician authorized to declare death has reason to believe that the brain death standard would violate the person's religious beliefs. In such a case, only the cardiopulmonary standard is to be used.[63]

These issues have caused some American scholars to argue that each individual should be allowed to choose which standard of death he or she wants to use. Indeed, one scholar has argued that the ability to choose one's definition of death is mandated by the Constitution's protection of the free exercise of religion.[64]

Commodifying Dead Bodies Today: Posthumous Conception, Cryonics, and Beyond

Scientific advances keep expanding uses for human bodies after death and challenging the boundaries of commodification. Matters once firmly in the realm of science fiction – like reproducing after death – have become commonplace. However, such practices are demanded for in the contemporary biotechnological marketplace. Moreover, there is no end in sight for scientific developments and one can easily imagine a time in the not too distant future when human cloning and cryonics become viable as well. Today, these technologies are contested. Yet, just as the growth of anatomical studies and the development of organ transplant technology put pressure on prior legal structures, these most recent developments pose many unresolved challenges to our current legal system. To be sure, if history provides any lessons for the future, one thing for certain is that the law will continue to develop to address these latest waves of change.

[63] N.J. Stat. Ann. § 26:6A-5.

[64] Tom Stacy, Death, Privacy, and the Free Exercise of Religion, 77 Cornell L. Rev. 490 (1992).

8 Taxing the Body

Dorothy A. Brown

The fall will probably kill you.

Butch Cassidy to the Sundance Kid
(Twentieth Century Fox)

Introduction

As I like to tell my students – tax is everywhere. It is the reason why Al Capone wound up in prison. The federal government could not prove illegal activities, but they could prove tax evasion. It is the reason why former New York Governor – and possible presidential hopeful – Eliot Spitzer, was initially investigated, which led to his very public political downfall. In both cases – an icon of the mafia and the champion of Wall Street reform – fell from what they believed were fairly secure perches, because the federal government suspected unreported income. It is the reason why Tom Daschle withdrew his nomination to be secretary of Health and Human Services. He had unreported income. It is also the reason why the Hollywood actor, Wesley Snipes, was eventually sent to prison; he had misdemeanour convictions for failing to file three years of tax returns. Tax is indeed everywhere.

Professor of Law, Emory Law School, B.S. Fordham University; J.D., Georgetown University Law Center; L.L.M. (Taxation), New York University. I would like to thank Professor Michele Goodwin for inviting me to take on this project. I also thank the faculty participants at the University of Chicago's symposium Contested Commodities: Reframing the Debate on Financial Incentives in the Supply of Genetic Material for commenting on an earlier draft that I presented in April 2008. I also thank June Carbone for reading an earlier draft. I thank Ms. Erika Beck for outstanding library assistance. I thank Melissa D. Johnson and Daniel Reach for excellent research assistance. I would also like to thank Daniel Reach for outstanding editorial assistance as well.

This chapter picks up where the robust debates of the prior chapters taper. Goodwin, Jefferson, Spar, and Epstein speak of markets; Goodwin and Jefferson critique the linguistics of altruism - and Jefferson goes so far as to suggest that altruistic exchanges in the human biological realm are sometimes quid pro quo transactions. Spar and Epstein are quite explicit about markets in and of the human body. Yet, all the authors, including Dickenson and Duke offer sophisticated analyses about externalities, leaving out an important sphere of the monetary - the taxable - consequences. This chapter picks up where they left off.

This chapter argues that any discussion about creating a market for organ sales must include an analysis of the tax consequences of those sales. Under current tax law, if the sale of organs were legal, the seller would have taxable income. The only question is whether the tax rate that applies would be the lower capital gains rate or the progressive tax rate with a current maximum of 35 percent. Tax consequences must not be ignored.

This chapter will draw upon the few reported cases and Internal Revenue Service pronouncements that deal with the donation or sale of blood, blood plasma, and mother's milk - not the sale of kidneys. You might think that because it is, after all, illegal to sell kidneys, there really cannot be any tax consequences. Tax laws, however, are not limited by anything as mundane as what is legal - ask Al Capone.

Tax Treatment of the Body

There are two fact patterns that raise tax issues relating to body parts and/or fluids. In the first a taxpayer has donated either blood or breast milk to a charitable organization and has attempted to take a tax deduction for the value of the blood or breast milk donated. In the second a taxpayer has sold blood or blood plasma and the question is whether the amounts are taxable income. (Curiously, there have been no reported cases dealing with sperm donations or sales.) In the former, the deduction has been denied and in the latter the amounts received have been found to be taxable income. Either way, taxpayers lose.

Donating Blood Is not Deductible.

The first time that the Internal Revenue Service (IRS) addressed the issue of whether a taxpayer who donated blood could take a deduction, the taxpayer won.[1] The victory was short-lived, however, because in 1942 in a General Counsel Memorandum, the same question resulted in the opposite conclusion – a taxpayer was denied a tax deduction for donating blood.[2] In 1953, the IRS again addressed the issue and held that providing blood for a transfusion or to a blood bank is rendering a personal service rather than making a contribution of property and is not deductible.[3] The tax law denies a charitable contribution deduction for donated services. As a result, the IRS held that an individual who donates blood to a charitable organization is denied the deduction.

In 1975, the IRS had the occasion to reexamine the law, but in a slightly different context.[4] The facts involved the donation of a mother's milk to a charitable organization, and the IRS considered whether the mother would be eligible for a charitable contribution deduction. The IRS found that no charitable deduction was allowed. Instead of finding that the donation is of services, the IRS conceded that the milk was property, just not the right kind of property. In order for the deduction to be valid, the property donated had to be the type of property that, if sold, would result in long-term capital gain treatment.

In order to be the right kind of property, it had to have two elements that are relevant for our purposes: first, it had to be a capital asset;[5] second, it had to have been held for a certain period of time (holding period).[6] A very basic definition of a capital asset is an asset that is not associated with a taxpayer's trade or business or an asset that is not held primarily for sale to customers. To give you an example, a real estate dealer who regularly sells real estate to the public cannot get capital gains from the sale of that real estate. But if you or I had one piece of land that we sold, we should receive

[1] *See* I.R.S. Gen. Couns. Mem. 36,418, n. 1 (Sept. 15, 1975) (describing the original position of the IRS in which a taxpayer was allowed a deduction for blood donation and noting that this position was later reversed by I.R.S. Gen. Couns. Mem. 23,310 (July 6, 1942)). Because of the age of this original position, the underlying document is not readily available for citation. My research assistant submitted a Freedom of Information Act (FOIA) request to the IRS, seeking evidence of these underlying documents. Unfortunately, the IRS could not locate the relevant material. The IRS letters in response to this request are on file with the author.

[2] I.R.S. Gen. Couns. Mem. 23,310 (July 6, 1942).

[3] Rev. Rul. 162, 1953-2 C.B. 127.

[4] I.R.S. Gen. Couns. Mem. 36,418 (Sept. 15, 1975).

[5] I.R.C. § 1221 (2006).

[6] I.R.C. §§ 1222, 1223 (2006).

capital gains treatment (assuming we held it long enough) because we are not in the business of selling real estate. We simply sold real estate one time. (If the wheels are turning, then you can imagine the argument that a tax attorney would make on behalf of her kidney-selling client, right?)

According to the IRS analysis, mother's milk, if sold, would not result in long-term capital gain treatment because it would not have been in the taxpayer's body long enough. (In 1975, the holding period for long-term capital gains treatment was six months.)[7] The taxpayer could not prove that her milk was in her body for more than one year before she donated it. As a result, she was ineligible for the charitable contribution deduction. In determining that milk was property, the IRS stated, "Milk is a commodity, whether from a human being or a cow."[8] Nice, huh? You can see your tax dollars at work.

The IRS next announced that it would treat blood plasma (as it had previously treated mother's milk) as property, and not a service, when it acquiesced to a 1980 Tax Court decision that held that blood was property.[9] The IRS made clear that its earlier position that the donation of blood was a service was incorrect. The IRS position, which remains their position today, is that donating blood plasma will not result in a charitable contribution. Taxpayers lose because their blood cannot satisfy the holding period requirements. Blood does not stay in the body long enough.

In 1976, the Eleventh Circuit in *Lary v. United States*[10] also denied a deduction to the taxpayer (a doctor) for the value of a pint of blood he donated to the Red Cross. The court did not decide whether the donation of blood constituted performing services or contributing a product because either way, the taxpayers were prevented from taking a tax deduction. If the donation was the performance of a service, the charitable contribution regulations prohibit deductions for performing services. If, on the other hand, the donation was of a product, because the sale of blood would result in ordinary income and not long-term capital gain (holding period was not satisfied), no deduction was allowed. This view is the result of treating red blood cells in the body as generally not being older than

[7] I.R.C. § 1222 (1970). In 1976, the holding period for long-term capital gains treatment was increased to nine months. I.R.C. § 1222 (1976).

[8] I.R.S. Gen. Couns.Mem. 36,418 (Sept. 15, 1975).

[9] *See* Green v. Comm'r, 74 T.C. 1229 (T.C. 1980)

[10] 787 F.2d 1538 (11th Cir. 1986).

four months, which is shorter than the period required to attain long-term capital gain status.

Proceeds from the Sale of Blood Are Taxable Income

Instead of donating their blood, some taxpayers sell their blood. In 1979, the Fifth Circuit in *United States v. Garber*[11] considered whether the taxpayer should have been convicted of "knowingly misstating her income" for the years 1970, 1971, and 1972. She was sentenced to eighteen months in prison with all but sixty days suspended and placed on probation for twenty-one months. On appeal, her conviction was reversed. The issue was whether her failure to report amounts received from the sale of her blood plasma was willful. The conviction was reversed because it was an open question whether the amounts received from the sale of her blood plasma were taxable.

Dorothy Garber filed joint returns with her husband during the years in question, but by the time the case came to trial, she was divorced. In the late 1960s, after she gave birth to her third child, Dorothy Garber was told that her blood had a rare antibody. A company, Dade Reagents, Inc., entered into a contract with her in 1967 for the purchase of her blood plasma. Dade Reagents agreed to pay her for each "bleed" an amount to be determined by the strength of the plasma obtained – the greater the strength of the plasma, the higher the payment. The court noted that this process was both painful and risky.

Dorothy Garber's blood was so rare that at the time she was one of only two or three known persons in the world with the antibody. She was also approached by other laboratories with offers of higher prices for her blood plasma. A bit of a bidding war ensued and she ended up signing contracts with two different laboratories: Associated Biologicals, Inc. and Biomedical Industries, Inc. Payments to Dorothy Garber were a function of the strength of the antibody in the blood plasma she gave. In addition, Biomedical gave her a weekly salary of $200, provided a leased automobile, and in 1972 added a $25,000 bonus. That bonus paid off for Biomedical, because in 1972, Dorothy Garber sold her plasma to them exclusively as often as six times a month. The amount of income at issue was substantial.

[11] 607 F.2d 92 (5th Cir. 1979).

In 1970, the sale of her plasma was alleged to be $80,200, in 1971 it was $71,400, and in 1972 it was $87,200. Dorothy Garber only included the $200 weekly payments from Biomedical as taxable income on her tax returns. An added complication was that Dorothy Garber seemed more concerned with hiding the additional amounts from her husband than from the Internal Revenue Service.

Although this was a case of first impression, the government's view was that Dorothy Garber was either (i) selling a product and the entire sales price would be taxable gain under §61(a)(3), or (ii) rendering a service and the entire sales price would be taxable under §61(a)(1). In either case the income would not be eligible for the lower capital gains rate. Dorothy Garber argued that the amounts she received were not within the definition of income, and therefore she participated in a series of tax-free exchanges. Her expert relied on 1918 case law as well as an Attorney General opinion that considered the human body a kind of capital asset and the amounts received a tax-free return of capital. That position found further support in a 1967 IRS Revenue Ruling, which found a basis equal to value, and therefore no taxable gain when what was being sold was so personal that its value was not capable of measurement. The argument by analogy was that blood plasma, being intensely personal, must also be worth its market value, and that its exchange was not a taxable event.

The trial court found as a matter of law that the amounts Dorothy Garber received were taxable income – whether the blood plasma was determined to be the sale of a product or service. On appeal, the Fifth Circuit, however, found that because no court had yet determined that the payments in question were taxable income, Dorothy Garber should not have been convicted of willful tax evasion without having a chance to present evidence that there was a question as to what the proper tax treatment should be. The court stated that "we need not and do not undertake the complex task of resolving what the law should be."[12] There is no subsequent history on the case after remand.

The following year, the Tax Court decided the case of Margaret Cramer Green, who represented herself.[13] The issue in that case was not whether

[12] *Id.* at 97. The dissent argues that the majority in effect was deciding that the amounts constituted taxable income or there would not have been a need for a remand. *Id.* at 101–02.

[13] *Green*, 74 T.C. at 1230.

amounts received were taxable income, but whether she was entitled to take certain deductions in producing that income. Margaret Cramer Green was a single mother of three teenaged children during 1976, the tax year at issue. She also had income from three sources: $4,080.59 from Wiggins, Inc.; $368.50 from the Shirt Shop; and $7,170 from Serologicals, Inc. Margaret Green had been a blood plasma donor for about seven years. The amounts from Serologicals, Inc. were the result of her donations of blood. After removal, the plasma is separated and the remaining red blood cells were returned to her body. This process was generally repeated because two bleeds produce one pint of plasma. Margaret Green's blood type was AB negative.

Margaret Green included in income the amounts she received from Serologicals, Inc., but the issue in the case was over whether she had taken appropriate deductions. Because the case presented "novel legal questions,"[14] the court carefully analyzed whether this was in fact income, and whether the income was capital (which would be taxed at the reduced capital gains rate) or ordinary (and taxed at the higher ordinary income rate).

The court began by observing that the amounts received from Serologicals, Inc. were indeed income and turned next to whether there were any tax provisions that would exclude the amounts. The court found that no exclusions applied. The court then considered the character of the income, namely, whether Margaret Green sold a product that could perhaps be a capital asset subject to a lower capital gains rate, or whether she provided a service that would result in ordinary income treatment and be taxed at the higher ordinary income rate. The court concluded that Margaret Green did not provide a service, but had in fact sold a "tangible product."[15] Nevertheless, the court declared that Green was ineligible for capital gains treatment. The court reasoned that Green was ineligible for capital gains treatment because capital gains treatment can not be received for property held for sale to customers in the ordinary course of business – which is what Margaret Green was doing. The court stated:

Petitioner performed no substantial service. She was paid for the item extracted by the lab. Except for the unusual nature of the product involved, the contact

[14] *Id.* at 1232.
[15] *Id.* at 1233–34.

between petitioner and the lab was the usual sale of a product by a manufacturer to a distributor or of raw materials by a producer to a processor. *A tangible product changed hands at a price, paid by the pint.*[16]

The court also found that Margaret Green's activity constituted a trade or business within the meaning of the Internal Revenue Code. The facts the court relied upon included (i) that Green sold her blood plasma on a regular basis for more than seven years; (ii) that she paid daily attention to her diet; and (iii) that she went to the extracting lab weekly or biweekly. The court found therefore that Margaret Green was in the trade or business of selling blood plasma. The court then considered whether certain expenses would be deductible by Margaret Green as ordinary and necessary trade or business expenses.

Health insurance premiums were disallowed because they were primarily personal and nondeductible. A portion of expenses for special high-protein foods, "special drugs," and diet supplements were found to be deductible.[17] Although commuting expenses from home to work are generally not deductible, the court allowed a deduction representing transportation expenses for her ninety-five trips to the lab in 1976. The court concluded that Margaret Green's trips to and from the lab were solely for business purposes and not for personal reasons. The court reasoned as follows:

The nature of her product was such that she could not transport it to market without her accompanying it. Of necessity, she had to accompany the blood plasma to the lab. *Unique to this situation, petitioner was the container in which her product was transported to market.* Had she been able to extract the plasma at home and transport it to the lab without her being present, such shipping expenses would have been deductible as selling expenses.[18]

The Tax Court struggles mightily with this duality – if we tax the sale of body parts the way we do other forms of property, should we treat them the exact same way we treat other property sales? For example, donating blood plasma results in a loss of blood mineral content and the blood's ability to regenerate. Can Margaret Green get a depletion deduction – the way we allow oil companies to receive a depletion allowance? Margaret Green in fact made that argument, but the court rejected it and stated that "bodies

[16] *Id.* at 1234 (emphasis added).

[17] *Id.* at 1236–37.

[18] *Id.* at 1238 (emphasis added).

and skills of taxpayers are not among the 'natural deposits' contemplated by Congress in those depletion provisions."[19] Perhaps the court was too quick to dismiss the argument or perhaps the court was correct, because blood cells regenerate themselves, but oil does not.

The court's sensitivity to treating parts of the body like property was apparent when it noted:

> Although we recognize the traditional sanctity of the human body, we can find no reason to legally distinguish the sale of these raw products of nature from the sale of petitioner's blood plasma. Even human hair, if of sufficient length and quality, may be sold for the production of hairpieces.[20]

The Tax Court recognizes the uniqueness of the human body, but was compelled to decide the case before it under existing tax laws. The taxpayer, when she sold her blood plasma, had income. However, the Tax Court did gloss over the basis question. What is Margaret Green's basis in her blood plasma? I would argue zero because Margaret has not "paid" anything for her blood. The IRS has rejected the *Garber* view that Margaret should receive a basis equal to the plasma's fair market value, because of the inherent personal nature of blood.

Subsequent to that decision, the IRS in a private letter ruling held that amounts received by the taxpayer for the "donation" of blood are taxable income.[21] In that case, a taxpayer was a professional blood donor for a particular corporation. The taxpayer had a rare factor in his or her blood plasma. Although the request for a ruling was made in 1987, the taxpayer had been receiving payments in exchange for the blood "donations" since 1973. The IRS cited the *Green* and *Lary* decisions as support for their conclusion that the amounts received by the taxpayer were taxable income. Again, since the blood was sold over a period of years, the taxpayer was engaged in a trade or business. As a result, the taxable income would not be eligible for the preferential capital gains rate.

Tax Treatment of Organ Donations and/or Sales

The current state of the law suggests that income from a one-time kidney (or any other organ) sale would result in taxable income. I would also

[19] *Id.*

[20] *Id.* at 1234.

[21] I.R.S. Priv. Ltr. Rul. 88-14-010 (Dec. 30, 1987).

expect that reasonable expenses incurred to produce such income would be deductible either as an ordinary and necessary expense or as a medical expense. I would argue further that a one-time kidney (or other organ) sale would be the sale of a capital asset and not the sale of an asset connected with a trade or business. I would further argue that since a kidney would be held long enough to satisfy long-term capital gains treatment of one year, that income would be taxed at the lower capital gains rate. Unlike in the case of Margaret Green, who was in the business of selling her blood, a one-time sale of a kidney that goes to the highest bidder would generally not be considered as property held primarily for sale to customers in the ordinary course of a trade or business. For the lower capital gains rate to apply, the taxpayer would have to prove that she had the organ for more than one year, a requirement that should not prove difficult.

If, however, the taxpayer were to sell an organ that could regenerate itself, such as lobes of a liver and/or somehow result in multiple sales, then the taxpayer would be susceptible to the argument that he or she was in a trade or business. In those circumstances the income would be subject to the higher 35 percent rate and not treated as the result of a sale of a capital asset. I would argue that a taxpayer who sells more than one body part runs the risk that all of the sales will be viewed in totality and the taxpayer may be viewed as being in the business of selling body parts. While we can anticipate the answers to many of these questions with some certainty, there are still open questions.

What if someone who regularly sells blood also sells her kidney? Could the argument be made that her blood-selling business would taint her kidney sale, which would subject all the payments to ordinary income treatment? Would you advise such a blood-selling client to stop selling blood for a period before selling her kidney? Would you advise such a client never to sell blood again if she sold her kidney and wanted to ensure capital gains treatment on the kidney sale?

Assuming that the sale of organs would result in taxable income, an economic analysis would suggest that the price of organs would increase. For example, if a compensated organ donor who has to pay taxes on any amount that she receives, may want to receive more money in order to pay off the tax bill. Is it good for society if taxes increase the cost of organs? If you think not, then you might argue that Congress should pass a law that excludes from income amounts received from organ sales. Currently, there is no exclusion that would prevent taxation of those amounts.

If Congress were to determine that it was in society's best interest to encourage organ sales, it could pass a law that excluded from income any amounts received from such sales. No deductions would be allowed, however. If the income is not taxable, then expenses to incur nontaxable income are not deductible. The exclusion is similar in some respects to two existing tax provisions: the exclusion for amounts received from personal physical injuries[22] and the exclusion for gifts.[23]

Currently, we have a provision that excludes from income amounts received on account of personal physical injuries. The policy reason is that the taxpayer has suffered enough and is merely being compensated for a loss that he or she did not cause. The difference with a kidney sale is that the taxpayer signs up for the pain and suffering and in exchange receives a payment. The payment does, however, represent compensation for the loss of an organ. Congress could decide to encourage this type of behavior with tax-free treatment because society is better off when organs are sold to save lives.

Currently, we have a tax provision that excludes gifts. Since cash is passing hands, this is not a gift, but it is also not an entirely commercial transaction. How can you put a price on saving a life or improving the quality of the recipient's life? You could argue that payments for organs should be excluded in order to encourage the altruistic benefits of lifesaving organ exchanges, just as the benefits of gift giving are encouraged by providing an exclusion for amounts received.

After having said this, I am not at all convinced that the right answer is to amend the tax laws and further complicate tax administration. But the tax treatment of organ sales could impede an efficient functioning of the market and therefore must be addressed, whatever your point of view.

The IRS could administratively decide that my basis in my kidney is equal to its fair market value, resulting in no taxable income to me. It could resurrect its 1967 Revenue Ruling.[24] This would not require an act of Congress, although if Congress did not like the result, it could then override the IRS decision by passing a law more to its liking.

22 I.R.C. § 104 (2006).

23 I.R.C. § 102 (2006).

24 Rev. Rul. 67-221, 1967-2 C.B. 63 (husband transferred property to his former wife in exchange for her dower rights and it was held that the marital rights of the former wife are equal in value to the property she received, resulting in no gain or loss to the former wife upon receipt of the property).

Tax law is ahead of the curve when discussing the creation of a market for organ sales. That may make us uncomfortable, especially when mother's milk is compared to cow's milk, or when we discuss whether taxpayers should get a depletion allowance for blood. Nevertheless, such discomfort should not cause us to ignore tax law. I can hear Butch Cassidy's tax counterpart saying: It's the tax law that's going to kill you.

Conclusion

Can tax policy be used to encourage or discourage organ donation? Even if you do not believe that tax policy can encourage donations, most would agree that, at the very least, tax policy should not discourage organ donation. If I want to sell an organ and I know that I am going to get hit with a large tax bill, I may be less inclined to sell if I cannot be adequately compensated. Given that obvious reality, tax policy must not be overlooked in the current debate concerning creating a market for contested human commodities.

9 Criminal Policing of Human Experimentation

L. Song Richardson

Introduction

An unacknowledged problem exists in the realm of human subject experimentation: criminal acts are committed without consequence. Those escaping punishment are no ordinary individuals; rather, they are medical researchers whose exalted social status combined with the social benefits of their research appear to immunize them from punishment. Consider the following examples:

- Pregnant women become unwitting guinea pigs in an experiment testing a medication to prevent miscarriages. As a result, their daughters and sons are at higher risk for cancer. The researchers are never prosecuted.[1]
- A patient becomes an unsuspecting participant in an experiment to test the safety and effectiveness of an ocular implant. Before implanting the device, the researcher tells the patient that it is "quite safe" and a "tried and true method" of vision correction, rather than the truth – that the FDA has not approved the device. The victim suffers permanent damage to his eye.[2] The researcher is never prosecuted.

A healthy twenty-four-year-old woman participates in an asthma study. Doctors ask her to inhale a drug without telling her that this is an

[1] Mink v. Univ. Chi., 460 F.Supp. 713 (N.D. Ill. 1978).

[2] Kus v. Sherman Hosp., 644 N.E.2d 1214, 1216 (Ill. App. Ct. 1995).

Reprinted by permission from L. Song Richardson, *When Human Experimentation is Criminal*, 89 *Journal of Criminal Law and Criminology* 133 (2009). Extensive citations supporting the assertions made here are available in the original version.

experimental use of the drug, previous inhalations resulted in death, and the FDA has not approved the procedure. She dies.[3] The researchers are never prosecuted.

This chapter addresses the significant, yet largely unexplored, question of why medical researchers escape criminal punishment. Whereas other actors who violate bodily integrity and autonomy are routinely punished with convictions for assault, fraud, and homicide, researchers walk away from similar crimes unsanctioned. This chapter is meant to begin a conversation that considers why criminal sanctions are not utilized in the context of human subject research and scrutinizes whether criminal punishment is an important, but overlooked, mechanism for protecting the dignitary interests of human subjects. Given the rise in human subject experimentation as a result of biotechnology research, this is a critical and timely question.

This chapter examines two forms of intentional misconduct. Each, like the illustrations above, involves a researcher's purposeful and deliberate failure to obtain consent, thereby violating an individual's interest in self-determination and autonomy. The first type of misconduct is that of researchers who conduct experiments on individuals without their knowledge. The second is that of researchers who deliberately fail to disclose to individuals the known and obvious risks of participation in an experiment. This occurs, for example, when a researcher intentionally fails to utilize, or significantly alters, an approved informed consent document. The misconduct involves acts that the criminal law typically punishes: intentional, deceptive, and nonconsensual contact with the person of another. These acts are customarily prosecuted because they violate one of our most cherished entitlements - freedom from intentional and nonconsensual contacts with our person.

There is no question that informed consent is lacking in these cases. I focus upon these "easy" cases of nondisclosure in order to center full attention on the question I seek to consider: why culpable acts in human experimentation, which eliminate an individual's right to make informed choices

[3] *See* Letter from the Office of Human Research Prot. (OHRP) to Dr. Edward D. Miller, Johns Hopkins Univ. Sch. of Med. (July 19, 2001), *available at* http://www.sskrplaw.com/bioethics/letter.html; Warning Letter from the Joanne L. Rhoads, Ctr. For Drug Evaluation & Research, FDA, to Dr. AlkisTogias, Johns Hopkins Asthma & Allergy Ctr. (Mar. 31, 2003), *available at* http://www.sskrplaw.com/bioethics/warningletter.pdf.

about what will be done to her body, are not punished. While other forms of misconduct in human subject research exist, the fact that these straightforward cases of misconduct do not result in criminal punishment demonstrates the need to explore the initial question of why the criminal sanction is overlooked.

This chapter provides the first framework for understanding why research misconduct in the form of deceit and violations of bodily integrity currently escapes criminal punishment. The framework has two components, which I label "idealization bias" and "social benefit bias." Idealization bias refers to the difficulty individuals may have in viewing researchers, who are often doctors, as criminals deserving of punishment. Social benefit bias refers to the hypothesis that research misconduct is often ignored or forgiven because of the perceived societal value of the research.

This chapter posits that idealization and social benefit biases may affect decision-making in ways that can result in researchers' being immunized from criminal punishment. This implicit immunity is harmful because the state's failure to punish researchers creates expressive harms by displaying attitudes toward victims and perpetrators that negatively affect the values of autonomy and dignity in medical research. While sanctions outside the criminal context do exist, these alternatives not only lack the same expressive impact, but also may inadequately police criminal harm.

The Two Biases

Lessons from social cognition research, which studies how individuals process information and draw conclusions, can explain why culpable medical researchers escape criminal punishment. The research demonstrates that people regularly employ "schemas" to categorize and assimilate information quickly.[4] A schema can be "conceptualized as a mental structure which contains general expectations and knowledge of the world."[5] It "represents knowledge about a concept…, including its attributes."[6] Stereotypes are the

[4] *See generally* Ronald Chen & Jon Hanson, *Categorically Biased: The Influence of Knowledge Structures on Law and Legal Theory*, 77 S. CAL. L. REV. 1103 (2004) (summarizing research).

[5] *Id.* at 1133 (citation omitted).

[6] Jerry Kang, *Trojan Horses of Race*, 118 HARV. L. REV. 1489, 1498 (2005) (citation omitted).

best-known example of a schema. Essentially, schemas provide a mechanism for people to make quick predictions, decisions, or judgments about the overwhelming amount of information they encounter.

Despite the necessity of employing schemas, they create the risk of biased decision-making because they "guide what we attend to, what we perceive, what we remember and what we infer."[7] Two possible biases may result from the schema we apply to researchers and to the work that they perform. These biases create the risk of faulty decision-making in the human subject research context and, thus, may explain the failure to utilize the criminal sanction to punish culpable medical researchers. The purpose of identifying these potential biases is to call attention to the possibility of their existence and encourage further empirical inquiry.

Idealization Bias

Role schemas, as the name suggests, help people decide what conduct to expect from those in certain roles.[8] Generally, people do not expect criminal behavior from a doctor, despite substantial documentation of the commercialization of science and medicine and the incentives this creates for misconduct. Instead, doctors are often placed on a pedestal. They are perceived as healers and altruistic, honest actors who toil tirelessly for the betterment of mankind. Evidence of this schema can be seen in television portrayals and public opinion polls. In 2006, for example, a nationwide public opinion poll found that doctors and scientists are among the most trusted of occupations and professions.[9] In fact, doctors are the most trusted occupation and scientists among the top three, above police officers and professors.[10]

The role schema applied to doctors and researchers creates the risk of an idealization bias. This bias may affect how the acts of researchers are judged. Individuals may interpret the culpable acts of researchers as

[7] Chen & Hanson, supra note 4, at 1133 (citation omitted).

[8] *Id.* at 1137 (citation omitted).

[9] The Harris Poll, *Doctors and Teachers Most Trusted Among 22 Occupations and Professions: Fewer Adults Trust the President to Tell the Truth*, Harris Interactive, Aug. 8, 2006, available at http://www.b2i.us/profiles/investor/NewsPDF.asp?b=1963&ID=34138&m=rl.

[10] *Id.* Scientists were trusted to be truthful by 77% of those surveyed, compared with police officers at 76% and professors at 75%.

innocent mistakes or, at most, negligence, rather than as criminal. Hence, the idealization of doctors may explain the reluctance to prosecute them when they are involved in research misconduct.

The evolution of tort doctrine in informed consent cases provides some evidence of this bias. Prior to the 1960s, courts strongly protected an individual's autonomy interests by recognizing the torts of assault or battery against doctors who either failed to adequately inform their patients about the risks of treatment or failed to abide by the consent obtained. The attitude of courts during this period is best expressed by Justice Cardozo's oft-quoted language: "Every human being of adult years and sound mind has a right to determine what shall be done with his own body; and a surgeon who performs an operation without his patient's consent commits an assault, for which he is liable in damages."[11]

By recognizing the torts of assault or battery in informed consent cases, courts placed the individual's right to self-determination at the fore. Doctors were held liable for violations of consent, whether or not the patient suffered any physical harm, because "the essence of the plaintiff's grievance consists in the offense to the *dignity* involved in the unpermitted and intentional invasion of the inviolability of his person."[12] The doctor's good or bad faith was irrelevant because the injury justifying compensation was to the patient's right to be free from nonconsensual contact with her person.

However, in the 1960s and 1970s, courts began to shield doctors from battery liability because they presumed that doctors were acting in good faith and for the benefit of the patient. As one court put it:

> We believe that medical treatment beyond the scope of a patient's consent should not be considered as an intentional tort or species of assault and battery as it has been viewed in the past. The doctor in a malpractice case is ordinarily not an actor who intends to inflict an injury on his patient and any legal theory which presumes that intent appears to be based upon an erroneous supposition. Instead, *the doctor is not one who acts antisocially as one who commits assault and battery, but is an actor who in good faith intends to confer a benefit on the patient.*[13]

[11] Schloendorf v. Soc'y of N.Y. Hosp., 105 N.E. 92, 93 (N.Y. 1914) (citing Pratt v. Davis, 79 N.E. 562 (Ill. 1906)).

[12] RESTATEMENT (SECOND) OF TORTS § 18 18 cmt.c (1965) (emphasis added).

[13] Dries v. Gregor, 424 N.Y.S.2d 561, 564 (App. Div. 1980) (citations and emphasis added).

Idealizing doctors in this fashion caused courts to view the consequences of battery liability as overly punitive. For example, if found liable in battery, a doctor might be required to pay damages out of pocket because malpractice insurance would not be available for an arguably criminal act. Additionally, the possibility of an award of punitive damages raised concerns. Since courts presumed that doctors were acting in good faith and for the benefit of the patient, these outcomes seemed unduly harsh. Thus, courts began to treat nonconsensual encroachments upon the sanctity of the body as a form of medical malpractice sounding in negligence. The concern for doctors appeared to overshadow considerations of individual dignity, autonomy, and self-determination.

The courts' idealization of the medical profession persists even in cases involving researchers who act in bad faith. For instance, *Heinrich v. Sweet*[14] was a class action lawsuit filed on behalf of terminally ill brain cancer patients who were subjects in radiation experiments without their knowledge. The patients thought they were receiving treatment and were unaware of the deception until a government report uncovering the experiments was published more than forty years later. The plaintiffs sued in battery, alleging that the defendants "intentionally injected the class' decedents with toxic substances and irradiated the class' decedents *without consent*." The researchers acted in bad faith. The victims had not agreed to become research fodder, or to be injected with the experimental radioactive substance. However, despite evidence of intentional deceit, the court dismissed the battery claim and held that the action should be treated as a form of medical malpractice or negligence.

Idealizing doctors, even those acting in bad faith, demonstrates the efficacy of idealization bias. Indeed, such reverence overshadows concern for the patient's right to make informed decisions about what is done to her person and relegates protection of the individual's interests in her bodily integrity to a secondary status. The idealization phenomenon is not new. For example, the long-standing therapeutic exception to informed consent allows doctors, in their sole discretion, to withhold information from a patient if they believe the information would cause psychological harm and thus hurt the patient's physical well-being. This exception implicitly assumes doctors' acting in good faith and failing to

[14] 44 F.Supp.2d 408 (1999).

disclose relevant information, not to serve their own ends, but for the benefit of the patient.

Importantly, idealization bias can be overcome in individual cases. After all, some doctors are prosecuted for criminal conduct. However, when these prosecutions occur, there is usually an explanation for why the role schema was conquered. In some cases, the person's role as a doctor was merely coincidental to the conduct, for example, when a doctor is prosecuted for rape or murder. In others, alternative schemas were more salient. For example, the so-called War on Drugs likely primes prosecutors and law enforcement to be ever vigilant for evidence of improper drug distribution. Hence, doctors are prosecuted for allegedly improperly prescribing narcotic painkillers to patients. In sum, when doctors are prosecuted, it appears that alternative schemas are more salient and thus defeat idealization bias.

Social Benefit Bias

Another explanation for the failure to prosecute culpable researchers is that they are engaged in socially beneficial research. Researchers perform a service that society believes is worthy, beneficial, and important. Generally, our society accepts the practice of human subject research, despite the fact that serious injury and death can result, because it may lead to cures or treatments for devastating diseases. The desire to foster research that holds the promise of substantial potential benefits may create a willingness to turn a blind eye to intentional misconduct or an unawareness that one's interpretation of conduct is influenced by the motivation to encourage research. This is what I refer to as social benefit bias.

Social cognition research establishes that an individual's motivations can play a significant role in determining "which concepts, beliefs, and rules we apply to a judgment; we may be especially likely to apply those that are congruent with our goals."[15] In fact, motivations may be the most important factor affecting the schema an individual adopts. The failure to punish culpable researchers may stem from fear that punishment would stymie medical research that we are motivated to promote. This desire to advance research may affect how decision makers interpret researchers' conduct and victims' harm.

[15] Chen & Hanson, *supra* note 4, at 1183 n.4 (citation omitted).

Perhaps the best example of social benefit bias, and its close relationship to idealization bias, is *Moore v. Regents of the University of California*, a case involving surreptitious research.[16] Mr. Moore had a rare and deadly cancer known as hairy-cell leukemia in his spleen. He sought treatment from Dr. David Golde, a prominent cancer specialist at the UCLA Medical Center. He gave Dr. Golde permission to conduct a splenectomy (the surgical removal of his spleen) to treat his leukemia. After the successful procedure, Moore moved to Seattle.

When Dr. Golde asked Moore to return for follow-up treatments, Moore was not suspicious. For the next seven years, Moore dutifully flew from Seattle to California every few months and underwent sometimes-painful medical procedures that included withdrawing samples of "blood ... skin, bone marrow aspirate, and sperm." He made the trek because Dr. Golde asserted that the procedures were medically necessary and that only he could perform them. Neither assertion was true.

What Moore did not know was that prior to his surgery, Dr. Golde had developed research and financial interests in Moore's cells. The procedures Dr. Golde performed after the successful surgery had nothing to do with treating Moore's leukemia, which was in remission. Instead, Dr. Golde was actively conducting research on Moore's cells solely for financial gain and commercial advantage. Dr. Golde exploited the doctor-patient relationship to ensure that he had exclusive access to Moore's cells. When Moore specifically asked Dr. Golde whether there was any possible research interest or financial benefit in his bodily substances, Dr. Golde repeatedly told him no and "actively discouraged such inquiries." In fact, Dr. Golde went so far as to say that "there was no commercial or financial value" in Moore's tissue.

Dr. Golde never asked Moore for express consent to the removal of his blood and tissue. However, at the close of seven years, Dr. Golde asked him to sign a consent form giving UCLA permission to use the withdrawn tissue for research purposes. Dr. Golde presented the consent form as a mere formality and Moore signed. However, Moore became suspicious when, after he later declined to sign a similar consent form, Dr. Golde offered to pay for his airfare and accommodations at a ritzy Beverly Hills hotel.

Moore hired a lawyer. During his investigation, the lawyer discovered that Dr. Golde had obtained a patent on the cell line developed from Moore's

[16] 793 P.2d 479 (Cal. 1990).

cells. He learned that Dr. Golde had a contract with a biotechnology company that gave Dr. Golde stocks and financing worth more than $3.5 million to "commercially develop" and "scientifically investigate" the cell line.[17] The market value of the cell line was predicted to reach $3 billion.[18] Upon learning of the deception, Moore said that he felt "violated for dollars," "invaded," and "raped."[19] Moore sued Dr. Golde for conversion. His lawsuit was dismissed by the trial court, was reinstated by the court of appeals, and finally made its way to the California Supreme Court.

Over strongly worded dissents, the majority refused to extend conversion liability to Moore's situation. It acknowledged that the tort of conversion would protect individual autonomy.[20] However, the court decided against extending the theory to the medical research context because recognition would "create[] disincentives to the conduct of socially beneficial research" that was "of importance to all of society." In so holding, the court touted protection of "innocent researchers" despite the fact that Dr. Golde was not an innocent researcher acting in good faith.

Invocation of the innocent researcher ideal demonstrates the sometimes-intimate relationship between the social benefit and idealization biases. The entire court agreed that Dr. Golde deliberately failed to obtain consent in order to mine Moore's body for cells in furtherance of Dr. Golde's financial interests. Despite this, the majority's primary concern was to avoid stymieing socially useful conduct.

The *Moore* decision marks an unwillingness to recognize insults to human dignity that result from intentional fraud. What appear to distinguish the *Moore* case from a typical assault or fraud case customarily subject to the criminal sanction are the potential social benefits of the researcher's conduct and a fear that recognition of Moore's interests would stymie future research.

Researchers engaged in intentional misconduct have taken advantage of social benefit bias, intentionally or unintentionally, to deflect attention from their bad acts, demonize the victim, and shape public opinion. They

[17] Rebecca Skloot, *Taking the Least of You*, N.Y. Times Mag., Apr. 16, 2006, *available at* http://www.nytimes.com/2006/04/16/magazine/16tissue.html.

[18] *Id.*

[19] Lori Andrews & Dorothy Nelkin, Body Bazaar: The Market for Human Tissue in the Biotechnology Age 28 (1998).

[20] *See Moore*, 793 P.2d at 494.

have become "availability entrepreneurs"[21] who can package events to benefit from social benefit bias. For example, in defending against accusations that his surreptitious mining of Moore's body was for his own financial benefit, Dr. Golde stated, "If there is economic gain, it will be to the people of California."[22] Dr. Golde's attorney described Moore to others as "an ingrate"; "Golde saved Moore's life.... 'Most people would embrace the doctor with all the gratitude they have.'"[23] One newspaper reported, "Moore's suit has raised the passions of the scientific community, which warns that if he is successful he will strike a blow against future medical research."[24] It is not surprising, then, that the general public, who stand to reap the benefits of research, are affected. As one letter to the editor stated:

> While I am not given to emotional outbursts over the numerous atrocities we humans seem hellbent on committing against one another, I was compelled to comment on the article "Medical Community Rocked by Tissue-Ownership Battle" [Jan. 8]. Instead of hoping the medical community might one day save a life with their research, it appears John Moore and his lawyers have regressed to the ultimate in greed and self-degradation. While not always a staunch supporter of many of today's medical advances and research tactics, I nonetheless believe these advances will ultimately benefit mankind in the long run. The only hope I was left with after reading this article was that the research conducted on Mr. Moore's spleen would one day prove vital and essential to extending the lives of Mr. Moore and his lawyers, and that they would be denied this life-extending help solely for financial reasons.[25]

Hints of social benefit bias can also be seen in the failure to acknowledge systematically and consistently the history of research misconduct that accompanies many important medical advances, procedures, and products. For example, Dr. James Marion Sims is recognized as the "father of American gynecology" and revered as a benefactor of women, having opened the first hospital in the nation for the care of women in New York City and dedicated his career to the treatment of women's

[21] Christine Jolls, et al., *A Behavioral Approach to Law and Economics, in* BEHAVIORAL LAW AND ECONOMICS 13, 38 (2000).

[22] *See Moore*, 793 P.2d at 494.

[23] Frank Swoboda, *It Was My Spleen, and Now it Could Be Anywhere*, WASH. POST, Jan. 26, 1988, at Z10 (statement of Anthony Murray).

[24] *Id.*

[25] Diane M. Burrows, Letter to the Editor, *John Moore's Spleen*, WASH. POST, Jan. 14, 1989, at A22.

disorders.[26] Hospitals carry his name, and marble monuments bearing his likeness and accolades stand in prominent locations. Very rarely, however, does anyone acknowledge the history of his abuse of female slaves, which formed the basis of his extensive knowledge. Importantly, this observation is not meant to condemn the use of the knowledge he gained (this chapter offers no opinion on that question), but rather to point out that the silence regarding his methods is perhaps the result of a desire to enjoy the fruits of his labor without the constant reminder of the methods used to obtain them.

In conclusion, both idealization bias and social benefit bias may explain why researchers engaged in misconduct escape punishment. They are not viewed as criminals deserving of punishment.

The Importance of Criminal Punishment

Punishing culpable researchers would send a clear message: violations of autonomy and dignity are wrong whether or not they take place in the context of socially beneficial research. But that begs the question – what is punishment? This chapter subscribes to the familiar view that what distinguishes punishment from other penalties is that punishments express moral condemnation. According to the philosopher Joel Feinberg's well-known formulation, punishment is a "*conventional* device for the expression of attitudes of resentment and indignation, and of judgments of disapproval and reprobation, on the part either of the punishing authority ... or of those 'in whose name' the punishment is inflicted."[27] Under this definition, a necessary condition of punishment is that it expresses censure, judgment, and disapproval in a socially conventional manner.

Viewed in this way, punishment is not necessarily limited to the criminal sanction. If other penalties are understood to carry similar messages of denunciation and disapproval, they too could constitute punishment. What I will consider next is the expressive meaning of criminal punishment and whether alternative sanctions carry the same expressive meaning.

[26] Harriet A. Washington, Medical Apartheid: The Dark History of Medical Experimentation on Black Americans from Colonial Times to the Present 1, 61 (2006).

[27] Joel Feinberg, *The Expressive Function of Punishment, in* Doing & Deserving: Essays in the Theory of Responsibility 98 (1970) (emphasis added).

What Criminal Sanctions Express

How a society conventionally expresses censure is important. For example, Dan Kahan argues that verbally castigating a wrongdoer could be considered punishment if social norms within the community make it appropriately condemnatory.[28] In our society, the criminal sanction is viewed, uncontroversially, as *the* most serious statement of moral blameworthiness. In his famous treatise, Henry Hart asserted that what differentiates criminal punishment from the civil remedy is "the judgment of community condemnation which accompanies and justifies its imposition."[29] The criminal sanction is the socially conventional method for expressing public censure and is well understood in this society as a way for the state to condemn an act and to disavow it. To paraphrase Hugo Bedau, use of the criminal sanction may not be the only way to punish, or the best way, but in our society, it is the usual way.

One feature of the sanction that makes it a unique method of expressing moral censure is the stigma that attaches to the individual. As one commentator describes it: "In modern criminal law, the stigma of a criminal sanction has become a special kind of remedy because of its burdensome and sometimes destructive consequences for the individual."[30] The stigma is not limited to a conviction. The state's decision to charge an individual also carries meaning, for it expresses that the accused probably deserves moral censure because his acts justify placing him at risk of a conviction and its attendant consequences. This explains the feelings of shame and humiliation that often accompany a criminal charge.

Furthermore, the criminal brand or mark continues to express condemnation long after it is imposed. Except in rare circumstances, a person convicted of a crime must, for the remainder of his life, inform others of his culpability and blameworthiness by disclosing his conviction on employment, education, housing, and licensing applications. A conviction also has political, economic, and social consequences. In many instances, it results in the loss of the rights to vote and to carry a weapon, and of the ability to

[28] Dan M. Kahan, *What Do Alternative Sanctions Mean?*, 63 U. CHI. L. REV. 591, 600 (1996).

[29] Henry M. Hart Jr., *The Aims of the Criminal Law*, 23 LAW & CONTEMP. PROBS. 401, 404 (1958).

[30] Kenneth Mann, *Punitive Civil Sanctions: The Middleground Between Criminal and Civil Law*, 101 YALE L.J. 1795, 1809 (1992).

obtain public benefits, live in certain neighborhoods, and engage in certain types of employment. These are just a few collateral consequences of a conviction.

When the state utilizes the criminal sanction, it "goes on record" and "testif[ies] to the recognition" that the conduct in question is wrong and the offender is deserving of condemnation and reprobation. The use of the sanction "tells the world that [the offender] had no right to do what he did, that he was on his own in doing it, that his government does not condone that sort of thing."[31] Through criminal punishment, the state vindicates the victim's value or worth. The victim has been wronged, and the state is stepping up to defend her honor, so to speak.

The state's failure to utilize this powerful method of condemnation is also expressive. "What a community chooses to punish and how severely tells us what (or whom) it values and how much."[32] When the state permits an identifiable group to commit criminal acts without punishment, it sends a message of official complicity and solidarity with the offender, approval of the conduct, and dissociation from the victim. As a result, wrongdoers may believe that they are entitled to act as they did. Punishment is meant to humble the offender, to make him feel some inner experience of humiliation and shame, in order to "annul or counter" the message sent by his conduct.[33] Letting the offender "get away with it" may lead to further bad acts as offenders and potential offenders come to believe that their treatment of the victim or class of victims is permissible.

The problems associated with failing to punish are apparent in the treatment of a well-known and respected researcher and professor, Dr. Albert Kligman. In 1951, Dr. Kligman, a professor of dermatology at the University of Pennsylvania School of Medicine, was called to Holmesburg Prison to treat an outbreak of athlete's foot. Describing how he felt when he first arrived at the prison, Dr. Kligman exclaimed, "All I saw before me were acres of skin. It was like a farmer seeing a fertile field for the first time."[34] For the next twenty-five years, Dr. Kligman conducted experiments on prisoners for the benefit of at least thirty-three major pharmaceutical and cosmetic

[31] Feinberg, *The Expressive Function of Punishment, supra* note 27, at 103.

[32] Dan M. Kahan, *Social Meaning and the Economic Analysis of Crime*, 27 J. Legal Stud. 609, 615 (1998).

[33] Jeffrie G. Murphey & Jean Hampton, Forgiveness and Mercy 124–28, 130 (1988).

[34] Washington, *supra* note 26, at 249.

companies, including Merck, DuPont, and Johnson & Johnson. He also created his own company to profit personally from his research and became a millionaire after he created the antiacne medication Retin-A as a result of his research.

The prisoners were not fully or accurately informed about the nature of the experiments conducted on them. As one explained, "We were never told what was going on. We never had [a copy of] anything we signed."[35] One of Dr. Kligman's students acknowledged that "uninformed patients were the rule,"[36] and Dr. Kligman admitted, "It was years before the authorities knew that I was conducting various studies on prisoner volunteers.... No one asked me what I was doing. It was a wonderful time."[37]

Dr. Kligman faced no lasting repercussions for his conduct, even after the U.S. Food and Drug Administration (FDA) discovered his questionable practices. The FDA initiated an investigation after Dr. Kligman published an article that described covering inmates' torsos with an industrial solvent that the FDA had banned from human tests. The FDA investigation revealed additional questionable practices. Consequently, the agency banned Dr. Kligman from receiving and testing investigational drugs on human subjects. This was only the second time in its history that the FDA used this sanction. However, prominent doctors and researchers spoke out in his defense and pressured the FDA to reverse its decision.[38] Less than a month later, the FDA gave in to the pressure. The agency's capitulation sent a clear message to Dr. Kligman and the research community that his actions were condoned.

Dr. Kligman received that message. He recently stated, "My view is that shutting the prison experiments down was a big mistake.... I still don't see there having been anything wrong with what we were doing."[39] He is still praised for his prison work and currently sits on the ethics committee at the University of Pennsylvania School of Medicine, where he is an emeritus professor of dermatology.

[35] *Id.* at 245 (quoting Jesse Williams's statement during a 2004 interview with Washington).

[36] Wolfgang Weyers, The Abuse of Man: An Illustrated History of Dubious Medical Expiermentation 435 (2003).

[37] Washington, *supra* note 26, at 251.

[38] Weyers, *supra* note 36, at 559–60.

[39] Ian Urbina, *Panel Suggests Using Inmates in Drug Trials*, N.Y. Times, Aug. 13, 2006, at 1, *available at* http://www.nytimes.com/2006/08/13/us/13inmates.html?r=1&pagewanted=1&oref=slogin

The failure to punish creates expressive harms. "A person suffers expressive harm when she is treated according to principles that express negative or inappropriate attitudes toward her."[40] When researchers are permitted to commit criminal acts against individuals without punishment, it sends the message that research subjects can be harmed to serve the ends of research. The state's failure to act makes this message all the more powerful because "the state is – or at least purports to be – an impartial agent of morality, with greater capacity to recognize the moral facts than any involved individual citizen."[41] To paraphrase John Braithwaite, what is needed is punishment for crime that maximizes the sense of shame and communicates the message that crime in human experimentation "is as abhorrent to the community as crime in the streets."

Scrutinizing the Alternatives

If punishments are "sanctions ... expressing public reprobation and moral censure of the harm-causing wrongdoer,"[42] then civil liability and institutional penalties may not constitute punishment.

Civil Liability

Generally, civil liability is viewed as a means to compensate an injured victim and return her to the status quo ante, as opposed to a punitive device. Unlike criminal punishment, tort liability is not reserved for culpable actors; even accidental conduct can result in a compensatory damages award. Setting aside the issue of punitive damages for a moment, compensatory damages do not express moral censure in the same way as criminal punishment, and thus do not carry the same stigma. Whether a harm is the

[40] Elizabeth S. Anderson & Richard H. Pildes, *Expressive Theories of Law: A General Restatement*, 148 U. PA. L. REV. 1503, 1527–8 (2000). Expressive harms can occur whether or not communication is intended. *Id.* at 1529–30. "An expressive harm ... results from the ideas or attitudes expressed through a governmental action, rather than from the more tangible or material consequences the action brings about.... [T]he very meaning they convey demonstrates inappropriate respect." Richard H. Pildes & Richard G. Niemi, *Expressive Harms, "Bizarre Districts," and Voting Rights: Evaluating Election-District Appearances after* Shaw v. Reno, 92 MICH. L. REV. 483, 506–7 (1993).

[41] Jean Hampton, *Correcting Harms versus Righting Wrongs: The Goal of Retribution*, 39 U.C.L.A. L. REV. 1659, 1693 (1992).

[42] JOEL FEINBERG, HARMLESS WRONGDOING 12 (1988).

result of an accident, negligence, or an intentional act, the amount of compensatory damages remains the same.

Additional factors explain why the social meaning of civil liability is different from that of the criminal sanction. First, criminal defendants are afforded constitutional procedural protections such as proof beyond a reasonable doubt and the right to counsel. The absence of such procedural protections in civil proceedings expresses the seriousness of criminal punishment relative to civil liability. Second, a finding of civil liability is not accompanied by the risk of imprisonment or the collateral consequences of a criminal conviction. Accordingly, civil defendants are not humbled to the same extent as are criminal defendants. Criminal punishment expresses blame and reprobation, a message that is largely absent from an award of compensatory damages. In fact, far from being humbled or stigmatized, compensatory damages express to wrongdoers that they are privileged to act, subject only to possible payment later in the form of damages. Thus, the compensatory damages remedy allows wrongdoers to convert property rules into liability rules at will. Finally, even the players in the criminal justice system recognize the symbolic – and practical – difference between a judgment of guilt and a finding of liability, explaining why criminal lawyers often attempt to negotiate a civil settlement in lieu of criminal punishment. Although compensatory damages may sometimes express condemnation, they are not the socially conventional way of doing so.

The bulk of my discussion thus far has addressed the compensatory damages component of tort liability. However, an award of punitive damages is also possible. Punitive damages have been described as quasi-criminal punishment and are reserved for culpable actors. The Supreme Court recognized that "unlike compensatory damages, ... punitive damages are specifically designed to exact punishment in excess of actual harm to make clear that the defendant's misconduct was especially reprehensible. Hence, there is a stigma attached to an award of punitive damages that does not accompany a purely compensatory award."[43]

Punitive damages are a conventional device for expressing condemnation. However, the relative strength of that condemnation is weak compared to that of the condemnation expressed by the criminal sanction. Punitive damages carry neither the possibility of imprisonment nor the

[43] *See* Pac. Mut. Life Ins. Co. v. Haslip, 499 U.S. 1, 55 (1991) (O'Connor, J., dissenting).

collateral consequences of criminal punishment. Moreover, public perception of punitive damages as disproportionate punishment has diluted its condemnatory power. Finally, courts can reduce punitive damages awards at their discretion. If reduced, the resulting damages may no longer humble and shame the offender. Indeed, the reduction may even vindicate the wrongdoer.

In sum, compensatory damages do not express punishment, and the social meaning of punitive damages is at best ambiguous. Use of the civil sanction, as opposed to criminal punishment, expresses that the offender's behavior does not deserve denunciation by the state. Thus, the state's failure to charge researchers for crimes expresses an inappropriate attitude toward the victim and the offender when compared to its willingness to charge the lay public with crimes for committing similar acts outside the medical research context. Arguably, these messages are exacerbated by the too-frequent use of the criminal sanction as a normative response to wrongful conduct. I do not advocate overcriminalization. However, legislative eagerness to propose and pass new criminal laws and the use of tough-on-crime rhetoric send a message that the criminal sanction is the only means of expressing societal condemnation. Consequently, overcriminalization has constructed a social reality that only criminal sanctions are capable of truly punishing offenders and vindicating victims.

Institutional Sanctions

Institutional sanctions also provide a means for protecting against misconduct in human experimentation. Both the FDA and the National Institutes of Health (NIH) play a role in protecting human subjects. FDA regulations govern clinical trials of drugs and devices for FDA approval. Researchers who fail to comply with FDA regulations, such as informed consent requirements, may lose their permission to work with investigational drugs.

The NIH protects human subjects by conditioning its coveted research grants. Recipients of NIH funds must sign an assurance of compliance with human subject protection rules, including mandatory informed consent procedures. Failure to comply with these requirements can result in withdrawal of current funding and ineligibility for future grants.

Institutional sanctions can cause embarrassment, stigmatization, and reputational losses and even affect a researcher's ability to work in his chosen field. However, as serious as these consequences may be, they do not necessarily express moral condemnation. Although an offender may feel punished when his privilege to work in an industry is withdrawn, institutional sanctions are not unambiguously punishment and can even be understood as purely remedial.

The following hypothetical illustrates the notion that institutional sanctions are not punitive. Imagine a doctor who rapes his patient while she is under anesthesia. Rather than prosecuting this doctor, the state revokes his license. Most people would not consider this sanction a sufficient expression of moral blame. Thus, the failure to impose both criminal sanctions and professional sanctions sends the message that researchers' misconduct does not warrant the most serious sanction.

The criminal brand has symbolic, practical, and expressive significance that other sanctions do not. It is rife with notions of censure and blameworthiness and justifies the imposition of punishment, which includes not only the potential loss of liberty, but also a host of collateral consequences. The use of any sanction short of criminal punishment risks causing expressive harm because the message is that what was done to the victim does not deserve criminal punishment and its collateral consequences. In other words, it is acceptable for this offender to treat this victim in this manner.

The Utility of Criminal Punishment

Criminal punishment expresses moral condemnation in a way that alternative sanctions do not. Imposing criminal punishment will also further instrumentalist goals, such as deterrence and moral education.

Deterrence

Punishment can deter by vindicating the value of the victim through protection. This protective function works by issuing a "sting" that the offender feels upon engaging in a prohibited act.[44] The desire to avoid this pain in the future is how deterrence is achieved.

[44] Michael S. Moore, The Moral Worth of Retribution, Responsibility, Character, and the Emotions: New Essays in Moral Psychology 140 (Ferdinand Schoeman ed., 1987).

Determining how best to deter misconduct in human subject research is important because the protection of human subject autonomy essentially falls upon the individual researcher. In theory, institutional bodies such as the FDA, NIH, and Institutional Review Boards (IRBs) police misconduct by approving research protocols and conducting periodic audits. In practice, resource constraints make any consistent effort to ensure that human subjects are protected illusory. Since these institutions cannot audit even a small subset of human subject research, they rely upon researchers to provide truthful information in the study protocol when seeking approval to conduct research, to comply with follow-up reporting requirements, and to follow informed consent requirements. Thus, the lack of consistent and reliable institutional oversight of human subject research fails to provide adequate deterrence incentives.

Researchers are essentially left to police themselves, and historically, they have failed in their efforts. It took a law student to bring an end to the Tuskegee syphilis experiments, the FDA to stop Dr. Kligman's experiments at Holmesburg Prison, and the suspicions of a patient and his lawyer to discover Dr. Golde's mining of Moore's body. These are only a few instances of ineffective self-policing.

The threat of criminal punishment would likely have important deterrent effects on researchers. Currently, a researcher engaged in calculated risk taking knows that if he violates human subject protections, the likelihood of discovery is minimal and even if discovered, he will not be prosecuted. At most, he may pay compensatory damages or face temporary restrictions on his research. The "sting" of criminal punishment, including the stigma of being branded a criminal, risk of imprisonment, and message of disapproval, denunciation, and reproach, is more serious than that provided by alternative sanctions. The fear of being labeled a criminal will likely be felt strongly by researchers because they are a class that is prone to view themselves as different from the common criminal. Hence, the consequences of criminal punishment can be expected to deter more effectively than other sanctions even if the possibility that culpable acts will be discovered continues to be small.

Moral Education

Punishment can also be an effective moral educator. The infliction of pain serves an educative function because it "interferes with the offender's pursuit of his interests, draws his attention to the crime and society's condemnation of it, and conveys to him that certain actions are 'fenced off in virtue of what we take to be their immoral character.'"[45] The criminal law's educative and socializing role is arguably necessary to teach researchers that violations of autonomy and dignity are wrong despite the potential utility of the research.

There is evidence that research community norms may serve to facilitate misconduct. First, researchers have been resistant to attempts to place mandatory limits on their research. For example, many researchers objected to the binding nature of the Nuremberg Code as an appropriate guide for their behavior. Yet, as Naomi Duke articulates in an earlier chapter, the code was created in response to the atrocities committed by Nazi doctors during the Second World War and forms the basis for the protection of human subjects in the United States today. It establishes a set of mandatory, explicit, and uniform ethical guidelines and standards to govern the conduct of medical research on humans. Researchers rejected the code as "a good code for barbarians but an unnecessary code for ordinary physicians."[46] They thought that the code's "legalistic" demands were unnecessary and unduly burdensome to research.

Second, the research community appears to resist efforts to investigate allegations of misconduct effectively. For example, after Dr. Kligman's actions at Holmesburg Prison came to light, attempts were made by the American Academy of Dermatology to discover more information about his research at the prison. The academy created a task force that sent letters to the researchers involved in the experiments asking for comments. The letters referenced the atrocities at Nuremberg. When academy officers learned of this, they were furious. They not only immediately informed the task force that it had not been authorized "to suggest that [the] experiments may have been in violation of the Nuremberg Code," but also immediately sent apologies to each researcher who had received the letter. Finally, the research community tends to defend culpable researchers and downplay the harm.

[45] Jean Hampton, *An Expressive Theory of Retribution*, *in* RETRIBUTIVISM AND ITS CRITICS 1, 21 (Wesley Cragg ed., 1992).

[46] Jay Katz, *The Consent Principle of the Nuremberg Code: Its Significance Then and Now*, *in* THE NAZI DOCTORS AND THE NUREMBERG CODE: HUMAN RIGHTS IN HUMAN EXPERIMENTATION 226, 228 (George J. Annas & Michael A. Grodin eds., 1992).

Research norms are in need of modification – a need that can be well addressed by criminal sanctions. The criminal sanction can shape or even change norms or preferences within a community because people learn what is morally blameworthy in part through what is punished. The sanction teaches people, both potential offenders and the community at large, what the public morality is, whether or not they fully internalize it. Criminal punishment can be used self-consciously "to change beliefs, attitudes, and personal values and goals; [and] can effectuate policy considerations by influencing what a person thinks he ought to do or what he wants to do in a particular situation."[47] Some scholars even argue that the criminal category is not about public morality at all, but "[r]ather, ... a set of techniques to be manipulated for social ends."[48] Changing social norms can, in turn, "influence choices ... by altering the effects of reputational incentives and consequences for self-conception."[49] If the criminal sanction is successful in shaping social norms, then behaving in a manner inconsistent with them will result in "public disapproval," which in turn will produce embarrassment and shame.

To the extent that idealization bias and social benefit bias affect public views about researcher misconduct, criminal punishment can help "rekindle in the public a sense of the immorality of the defendant's acts."[50] Its power to express moral condemnation may more effectively deter misconduct and change both researchers' and society's views concerning bad acts. Criminal punishment can help overcome the idealization bias and social benefit bias that currently appear to exist in the context of human subject experimentation.

Scrutinizing Criminal Punishment

Criminal punishment may be the only sanction that can punish culpable medical actors engaged in intentional misconduct that violates individual rights to autonomy, dignity, and self-determination. I end this chapter by considering some preliminary questions and concerns that use

[47] Cass R. Sunstein, *Social Norms and Social Roles*, 96 Colum. L. Rev. 903, 923 (1996).

[48] Harry V. Ball & Lawrence M. Friedman, *The Use of Criminal Sanctions in the Enforcement of Economic Legislation: A Sociological View*, 17 Stan. L. Rev. 197, 211 (1965).

[49] Sunstein, *supra* note 47, at 916.

[50] Ball & Freidman, *supra* note 48, at 217, 222.

of the criminal sanction may raise, although I do not intend to resolve them here.

Punishment raises the specter of overdeterrence. With regard to the forms of misconduct discussed in this chapter, there exists little difficulty in distinguishing bad acts from good ones. However, if use of criminal punishment is extended to police other forms of research misconduct, this question of overdeterrence will require further scrutiny. The argument against criminal punishment, then, is that when there exists difficulty distinguishing between acts we want to encourage and those we do not, it is more appropriate to price the behavior through fines rather than to prohibit the behavior with criminal penalties.

Another concern with criminal punishment is that vigorous enforcement and stringent penalties may make it difficult to discover unlawful acts in human subject research. Recent work in the area of system justification theory posits that these responses may cause system justifying behaviors – behaviors among actors in the system that inhibit detection and prevention efforts. Empirical research into the culture and practices of the research community will be necessary before any prediction can be made about the effect punishment will have on researcher motivations. However, if criminal punishment will result in increased difficulty in ferreting out research crime, this is an important question to consider.

If criminal punishment is deserved in appropriate circumstances, then serious thought must be given to the amount of punishment necessary to humble the wrongdoers. If researchers are prosecuted under existing criminal statutes, do the sentencing schemes map well with what the appropriate sentence should be? In some cases, the punishment provided by existing criminal statutes may be too severe, and in others, too lenient.

If new crimes or sentencing schemes are appropriate, then there are institutional problems to consider. The existence of idealization bias and social benefit bias creates a chicken-and-egg problem. The biases may result in the failure to impose punishment, but imposing punishment may be necessary to change the existing biases. Punishment can reduce the efficacy of these biases, but the existence of them may make prosecutors unwilling to proceed with criminal prosecutions. Additionally, the biases may also affect legislators' willingness to pass criminal legislation or sentencing schemes to punish researchers, especially because one can expect significant resistance from the medical profession to criminal sanctions directed specifically at them. How do we address this? Perhaps the first step is at least to recognize the problem.

Conclusion

The fact that human subject research is socially beneficial should not mean that culpable acts are unpunished. Criminal punishment in appropriate instances would send a clear, expressive message that doctors are not privileged to treat human subjects in a manner inconsistent with their inherent value as human beings. Punishment can reassert acknowledgment of the victim's worth in the face of a denial. Proper punishment will cause suffering in the offender and demonstrate to researchers that their actions are worthy of stigma, ridicule, and shame and in this way, perhaps change the attitudes of the relevant community. This, in turn, will restore the proper balance between protecting human dignity and autonomy, and allowing socially beneficial research to continue. It will also likely make the self-policing nature of the existing regulations more effective. Punishment will help change the existing biases, and that can in turn change the existing norms and place the protection of individuals front and center instead of allowing them to be used as guinea pigs in favor of broader societal goals. If we are serious about protecting individual autonomy and dignity in research, consideration of criminal punishment is an important step.

10 Liberalizing Tort Law

Michele Goodwin

On the one hand, technologies based on human biologics, including organ and tissue transplants, innovative pharmaceuticals derived from cell lines, assisted reproductive technologies, and novel devices shaped from human bones and tissues, expand medical technologies and sophisticated research, inspiring robust demand utilization. On the other hand, despite ubiquitous application of human biologics, optimizing their legal designation remains a significant problem linguistically and legally. In an earlier chapter, Donna Dickenson points to this problem. For example, Congress regulates organ transactions criminalizing any payments or gifts to donors but leaves reproductive biological "donations" to the private market. The processing and selling of human tissues constitute a considerable market share of the billions of dollars in revenues generated by biobanks; companies buy, sell, trade, and barter human tissue as if it were currency. However, individuals may not sell their human tissues (or that of their deceased relatives) at death, lest they risk criminal prosecution.

Inconsistent approaches to the liberalization of human biologics create numerous problems, including advantaging frequent corporate players while disadvantaging the one-shot individual donors. The social and political diagnostics explaining the problems in this sphere vary. Corporations maximize economic opportunities, sometimes violating the spirit of legislation prohibiting the commercialization of human biologics by taking advantage of porous legal loopholes, while individuals are disadvantaged or excluded from full or equitable participation in most human biological markets - blood, plasma, and reproductive biologics stand as exceptions. In other words, the legal status of human tissues varies across a tenuous sphere; some become cleared for commercialization and others not.

Neither science nor cultural attitudes nor legislatively articulated legal principals explain the disparities.

Importantly, this failure to reconcile the legal statuses of human biologics creates externalities across a spectrum, from misaligned market dynamics to human rights violations and exploitation. Conceptually and legally, there is a problem in the ordering of human body parts. Indeed, less clear are the optimal designations for these now-essential human biologics, despite important legislative and social justice reasons for reconciling the status of human body parts. Promoting the public health, protecting human rights, advancing conceptions of dignity, liberalizing trade, disentangling information asymmetries, and reconciling the common law rank among the most urgent explications for optimizing body part designations. Yet, conflicts emerge when considering not only the designation of human body parts, but also who should decide: legislative bodies, the executive, administrative agencies, or the judiciary.

Failure to explore the pertinent normative and political economy questions related to the designation (and ownership) of the human body results in the dark side of variation, where simultaneously operating regimes sometimes function in competition, sometimes in cooperation, sometimes barely cognizant of the other. Equally disordered are the legal regimes that govern human biologics; sometimes the legal rules appear aligned, but most often a mishmash[1] of legislation and legal perspectives exists at local, state, and transnational levels. This lack of legal organizing and attentive ordering has real world implications for individuals injured through the acquisition, trade, theft, implantation, and harvesting of human biologics.

Courts warily echo Roy Hardiman's observation twenty-five years ago: "A direct consequence of recognizing property rights in human tissue is the application of traditional property law doctrine to the human body."[2] Years prior, judges reasoned that recognizing property interests in the body could lead to untenable externalities, including individuals' inadvertently stifling American research by refusing to donate or holding out for huge sums, crowding out altruistic systems, driving potential altruists out of the

[1] Guido Calabresi, *An Introduction to Legal Though: Four Approaches to Law and the Allocation of Body Parts*, 55 Stan. L. Rev. 2113 (2003).

[2] Ray Hardiman, *Toward the Right of Commerciality: Recognizing Property Rights in the Commercial Value of Human Tissue*, 34 U.C.L.A. L. Rev. 207 (1986).

"market," and denigrating personhood.[3] Similar ambivalence remains. Yet the failure to optimize the designation and status of human body parts directly results in ambiguity, vagueness, and real social and legal harms. For example, when human tissue is misappropriated, which civil theories of law should be applied: conversion, accession, abandonment, bailment, assault, battery, negligence, or strict liability? This question remains largely unresolved due to judicial deflection on the broader point of human "ownership."

What explains judicial reluctance to acknowledge the introduction of property values to transactions involving the human body? That judges are slow to adopt the language or conceptual application of property principles to the human body is not simply a matter of judicial discretion. Indeed, this formalism hampers the development and advancement of property theory. That is not all; other externalities result from an uncritical commitment to judicial formalism in this domain, including stymieing the advancement of property and tort law doctrine, particularly in light of the human body's various commercial uses and applications. Ultimately, however, formalism may contravene civil protections. This chapter takes up these matters to explain how judicial formalism in the human biological realm undermines the development of common law.

This chapter advances the dialogue and debate on status in the human body. I briefly argue that fuzzy signaling dominates judicial responses to questions of nomenclature in the human body. That section emphasizes an important fact: market realities already exist in the human body and the judiciary's ambivalence about that topic will not signal legislative action; nor will it create structural incentives or pecuniary disincentives to motivate "bad actors" to behave differently. Next, the chapter unpacks elastic concepts in the body to demonstrate the problematic adherence to formalism by U.S. courts. Both conceptions draw from important cases involving the fluidity of body part designations and acquisitions. The chapter then scrutinizes the value and risk of expressive minimalism to the claims upon which the sections are developed.

The majority impliedly [find] three "reasons to doubt" that Moore retained a sufficient ownership interest in his cells.... The majority's first reason is that "no reported judicial decision supports Moore's claim, either directly or by

[3] Moore v. Regents of the Univ. of Cal., 793 P.2d 479 (Cal. 1990).

close analogy." Neither, however, is there any reported decision rejecting such a claim. The issue is as new as its source – the recent explosive growth in the commercialization of biotechnology. (Justice Mosk[4])

Lofty Formalism

More than sixty years ago, Judge Charles Clark wrote that the function of courts "cannot be limited to a mere blind adherence to precedent."[5] He cautioned fellow jurists against what the scholar Martha Nussbaum might refer to as "lofty formalism."[6] Clark warned that judges should avoid clinging to precedent simply for the sake of it and "artfully" dodging new doctrine.[7] He recognized the value of judges' fully exercising their mental powers and "discovering and applying" new trends in law as the technology and policies of the time demanded.[8] Clark's pragmatic advice to fellow colleagues on the bench remains timeless. In prior works, I have criticized judicial fidelity to formalism and the risks associated with unquestioning adherence to precedent. In few areas of the law is this criticism more relevant than the commercialization of biotechnology and the human body, where science outpaces law and greed engenders the type of coercion, fraud, and exploitation eloquently explained in Song Richardson's earlier chapter in this book. Yet, the proper role of courts in addressing these dynamic issues remains ambiguous and unsettled. Song Richardson offers a turn to the criminal law as an approriate response and sanction.

However, legal scholars barely take note of the entrenched judicial formalism in human biological exchange. Of nearly one thousand law review articles studying, citing, and describing the iconic case of the field – *Moore v. Regents of the University of California*[9] – barely 8 percent reference the probative and quite relevant dissent that advances three issues relevant to this chapter: human ownership in the body, judicial formalism, and the rapid

[4] *Id.* at 50 (Mosk, J., dissenting).

[5] Spector Motor Serv., Inc. v. Walsh, 139 F.2d 809, 814 (2d Cir. 1943). *See also* Benjamin N. Cardozo, The Growth of the Law 56–80 (1924) (charting the evolution of decision making from pure adherence to precedent to a less rigid and more flexible approach commonly associated with shift from naturalism to pragmatism).

[6] Martha C. Nussbaum, *Foreward: Constitutions and Capabilities: "Perception" Against Lofty Formalism*, 121 Harv. L. Rev. 4 (2007).

[7] *Spector*, 139 F.2d at 814.

[8] *Id.*

[9] 793 P.2d 479 (1990).

expansion and commercialization of human biologics. Importantly, Justice Mosk's dissent in *Moore* urged that embryonic legal issues for which no germane precedents exist demand rigorous review and where necessary an expansion of the common law to address nascent areas of law appropriately. In limited instances, courts have taken up Mosk's challenge, specifically in embryo adoption cases, where property interests and the commercialization of human biologics collide. Nevertheless, even within the contexts of assisted reproductive technologies, tort law has yet to develop fully.[10] Thus, basic tort principles have yet to become comprehensively instantiated in judicial opinions evaluating human biological disputes.

This embrace of formalism represents more than minimalism or oversight, but a problematic principle in contemporary jurisprudence. In application, this entrenched formalism results in expressive minimalism, which risks the appropriate and necessary advancement of tort law doctrine. The cases visited in this domain test our capacity to understand whether life is appropriately described as being beyond the definition of property, as well as the disputed assumptions about life's being commodifiable, patentable, destroyable, and conscriptable. Quite simply, expressive minimalism too frequently governs judicial approaches to the commercialization of human biotechnologies, thereby stymieing the proper development of the common law.

What motivates judicial formalism, expressive minimalism, or low-level signaling in human biotechnology cases might be explained by four factors: information asymmetries; entrenched normative views of the body as a noncommercial, altruistic source; a positivist commitment to conventional approaches to the rule of law; or the expectation that legislatures, including Congress, demarcate appropriate boundaries and define punishable conduct in the human biotech realm. Individually and collectively, these factors may influence the development of law. Specifically, these factors may explain the incoherent jurisprudence that fastens old law to dynamic, new human commercialization cases.

My analytical hunch is that rather than motivating legislative action or imbuing the bench with greater wisdom or resolving information asymmetries, formalism in the human biotechnological realm perpetuates misalignment or fuzzy signals to legislators and litigants. These fuzzy signals

[10] *See* Michele Goodwin, *A View from the Cradle*, 58 Emory L. J. 1039 (2010).

manufacture manifestly unclear messages to the legislature. Indeed, fuzzy signals, like broken transmissions across communication technology, discombobulate messages, distort the imagined and real, and, ultimately, dissolve into indecipherable and difficult to read codes. In most cases, when signals become fuzzy, channels reboot. Rarely is there incentive to listen through fuzzy noise. The false presumption relied on by those who regard judicial minimalism (or fuzziness) as directly signaling the legislature is a miscalculation that legislative bodies are inclined, motivated, or incentivized to listen to judicial formalism or that legislatures understand the messages that courts intend to send.

If this is correct, expressive minimalism will not result in legislative action. Fuzzy signals from the judiciary will not promote the development of responsive public policy in contemporary human commercialization cases or those to come. My claim is not that legislators lack the capacity to shape public policy without judicial guidance. Rather, because there are times that legislatures will be captive to collective action, pressured by special interest, and responsive to economic interests, they may not serve as the best source of law in tort law conflicts emanating from biotechnology disputes.

Nowhere is fuzzy signaling more apparent than in how and for what purposes courts define the body. Nevertheless, market realities in the body already exist,[11] and judicial failure to recognize this results in perverse externalities, including a profoundly undeveloped nomenclature, the exploitation of human subjects, a loosely monitored but robust market in buying and selling purloined human tissues,[12] and an expanding, conflicting common law on the status of reproductive biologics, such as sperm, ova, and embryos. How human "parts" are acquired is far more troubling than the fact that commercialized tissue markets exist. Acquisition occurs through coercion and fraud (i.e., tissues donated for altruistic purposes, but later

[11] Medical researchers, for example, participate in the human tissues market when they obtain and use cells, tissues, and organs to advance the development of patents, which will inure benefits (financial or otherwise) to them and their institutions. *See, e.g.*, Donna Dickenson, *Consent, Commodification and Benefit-Sharing in Genetic Research*, 4 Developing World Bioethics 109 (2004).

[12] Incidences of body part thefts have been prosecuted in New York, Philadelphia, New Jersey, Florida, and other states. *See* Robert Smith, *Four Indicted in Case of Tissue Theft* (National Public Radio broadcast Feb. 23, 2006), *available at* http://www.npr.org/templates/story/story.php?storyID=5230544.

sold by the recipient), funeral homes and crematoriums desecrating and selling body parts, and misappropriation from some physicians, scientists, and researchers.[13]

Notwithstanding a rather robust human biologics industry, some scholars conclude that to place a financial value on the body is to diminish its personhood and pollute its legal, social, and moral status. Margaret Radin's iconic scholarship in this domain advances the concept that the human body is a sacred entity, and its status as such is violated by any association with financial evaluations and market terms and conditions.[14] An extrapolation of Radin's theory is that the body should remain inalienable, notwithstanding the various uses governments and private entities find for it, lawful or not. Other legal and social commentators invoke the horrific slave experience in the United States to buttress anticommercialization claims and to demonstrate in stark, graspable terms the significant consequences of placing financial value on human beings. To suggest that their concerns are less relevant to contemporary biotechnology invites remonstration from varied ideological corners wedded to anticommodification, incommensurability perspectives, which are not altogether difficult to understand.

Yet, as prior chapters discuss, the human body and its constituent parts are the subject of trade, trafficking, bartering, black markets, conscription, and, importantly, significant profit. Who gains utility and benefits from and who is harmed by these exchanges vary by context and even court.

Risky Exchanges and Conceptions

Information Asymmetries

Moore v. Regents of the University of California,[15] is perhaps the most recognized body part appropriation case by law students and legal scholars.

[13] *See* Dickenson, *supra* note 11, at 110 (discussing one researcher's misrepresentation to a certain population in New Guinea that she wanted blood samples to check for insects, when she actually wanted the samples to enhance research in pursuit of a parent, and another set of researcher's misrepresentations to Chinese villagers that they would receive medical care in exchange for DNA samples).

[14] Margaret Jane Radin, Contested Commodities (1996); Margaret Jane Radin, *Market-Inalienability*, 100 Harv. L. Rev. 1849 (1987).

[15] 793 P.2d 479 (Cal. 1990).

Indeed, several chapters in this book refer to it. On October 8, 1976, Dr. David Golde, an employee of the University of California at Los Angeles Medical Center, informed Mr. Moore "that he had reason to fear for his life, and that the proposed splenectomy operation ... was necessary to slow down the progress of his disease."[16] Moore consented to the operation. If taken as true that Moore's life depended on the surgery, the legal and moral implications of the physician-patient relationship ex ante and ex post the operation warrant consideration. Golde's conduct prior to the operation appears to conflict with his fiduciary obligations to Moore (if the doctor's financial motivations were alive at the time of the operation).

Yet, this view of the case is not shared by all. Some legal scholars claim the legal questions related to property and status of body parts are rendered less significant by the necessity of Moore's operation. An extrapolation of that argument suggests that the urgency that dictated Moore's operation served to immunize his physician from subsequent liability. Framed that way, so long as the operation was necessary, the physician did not cause any additional or unnecessary harm to Moore. Body parts destined for incineration became valuable research tools and resources, which ultimately benefited patients.

However, ethical and legal concerns dominate this case, even if Moore's initial contact with his doctor was triggered by medical urgency. Days within meeting Moore, Dr. Golde and Shirley Quan, a researcher at UCLA, formed a partnership with the intent to make "arrangements to obtain portions of [Moore's] spleen following its removal and to take them to a separate research unit."[17] Over the next few years, Golde subjected Moore to additional tests (extracting blood, sperm, bone marrow, and other fluids), fraudulently inducing him to commute to Los Angeles from Seattle under the pretense of medical necessity.[18] Nearly three years later, according to the court record, "Golde established a cell line from Moore's T-lymphocytes."[19]

[16] *Id.* at 481 (internal quotation marks omitted).

[17] *Id.* (internal quotation marks omitted).

[18] *Id.*

[19] *Id.* The particular lymphocyte derived from Moore's spleen is described as "a type of white blood cell. T-lymphocytes produce lymphokines, or proteins that regulate the immune system. Some lymphokines have potential therapeutic value. If the genetic material responsible for producing a particular lymphokine can be identified, it can sometimes be used to manufacture large quantities of the lymphokine through the techniques of recombinant DNA." *Id.* at 482 n. 2.

In 1981, the Regents applied for a patent on the cell lines and listed Quan and Golde as "inventors," the royalties and profits from which would be shared by the inventors and Regents. It was projected that billions of dollars would be recouped from the exploitation of Moore's spleen and other tissues.[20]

Without an appreciation for "what" the legal statuses of Moore's cells, sperm, and spleen were, the California Supreme Court justices were ill equipped to define what the legal remedy should be. The court, finding that there was no other judicial or legislative guidance that would treat Moore's spleen and the cell line as property, dismissed his conversion claim.[21] To suggest, as the court did, that his biological materials were sui generis, addresses only Moore's health condition, but provides little guidance as to the plaintiff's legal status. The court erected an unnecessary barrier, suggesting that there was no possessory interest in Moore's cell line. On this fact, the court may have been incorrect. In fact, Dr. Golde possessed an interest protected by law. But why didn't Moore?

The *Moore* court deflected, dismissing virtually all of the plaintiff's claims and rejecting the concept of *self*-ownership in one's body.[22] The court cautioned that Moore had no interest in his cell line subsequent to Golde's creation of a patent. Importantly and quite problematically, the court overlooked the central point of Moore's claim, that he had a protected legal interest in his cells, tissues, and blood *prior* to the unauthorized exploitation and harvesting by his doctors and before the patent was issued. Yet, the timing of the patent is a false time stamp and mistakenly applied by the

[20] Jennifer Lavoie, *Ownership of Human Tissue: Life After* Moore v. Regents of the University of California, 75 VA. L. REV. 1363, 1366 (1989).

[21] *Moore*, 793 P.2d at 488. Moore's original complaint brought forth thirteen causes of action. The court observed, "each defendant demurred to each purported cause of action. The superior court, however, expressly considered the validity of only the first cause of action, conversion." *Id.* at 482. The court reasoned that the other causes of action, including (1) lack of informed consent, (2) breach of fiduciary duty, (3) fraud and deceit, (4) unjust enrichment, (5) quasi-contract, (6) bad faith breach of implied covenant of good faith and fair dealing, (7) intentional infliction of emotional distress,(8) negligent misrepresentation, (9) intentional interference with prospective advantageous economic relationships, (10) slander of title, (11) accounting, and (12) declaratory relief, were defective. *Id.* at 482 n. 4

[22] *Id.* at 488 (holding that the tort of conversion does not apply to his "biological materials"). However, the holding in *Moore* does not signify that harm has not occurred or that an injury has not been sustained. Rather, the court does indicate that damages might be difficult to calculate.

court; a patent does not cut off past interest or, according to Justice Mosk, present or future rights. Nor does the ex post creation of a "new" thing derived from a fraudulently or illegally obtained preexisting thing waive liability in intentional or negligent torts.

A simple thought experiment highlights the problematic reasoning undergirding the California Supreme Court's holding in *Moore*. Consider, for example, that a significantly uninformed possessor of "*x*," a valuable good, may nevertheless bring a successful suit for fraud and/or fraudulent inducement if she is coerced, compelled, or otherwise induced to surrender her good(s) under false pretense. This is the essential issue in *Moore*. The use of tricks or deceit to induce one to act to her disadvantage is a fraudulent, tortuous act.[23] Knowledge of *x*'s value prior to the fraud is not necessary for a plaintiff to recover. Generally, actions in fraud do not accrue until the time the facts giving rise to the cause of action are discovered or should be discovered with the exercise of due diligence. Such are the scenarios with art heists and other sophisticated frauds; never would such goods be recoverable if thieves could claim ownership simply by extending possession until "ownership" in the rightful possessor is time-barred. In other words, even the least informed plaintiffs are entitled to tort law protections for the fraudulent misappropriation of their property just as the most sophisticated who are defrauded of their valuable possessions.

That Moore lacked the sophistication to convert the value of his biologics to their highest commercial profit or most innovative use is a seductive distraction, but immaterial to his tort claims. To assert that no value exists in *x* simply because the possessor lacks the capacity to maximize *x* or fully capitalize on *x*'s value would undermine basic free market and tort law principles. Recovery for fraud and fraudulent dispossession are not dependent on the deceived's knowing the items' value prior to fraudulent dispossession. Neither do claims of conversion rely on that type of special knowledge or capacity to predict future harms. Similarly, the inability to

[23] *See, e.g.*, Hunter v. Up-Right, Inc., 26 Cal. Rptr. 2d 8, 16 (Cal. 1993) (stating that "[f]raud ... has long been recognized as an independent tort.... [A] defendant crosses the boundary of mere bad faith and commits fraud when he induces a plaintiff to reasonably rely on these deceptions to his detriment, and damages result"); *see also* Hinesley v. Oakshade Town Cent., 37 Cal. Rptr. 2d 365, 367 (Cal. Ct. App. 2005) (stating that fraud in the inducement is "a subset of the tort of fraud," occurring "when the promisor knows what he is signing but his consent is induced by fraud").

convert a possession to its most innovative use does not diminish a viable fraud claim. A key element in proving fraud is an actual injury,[24] which in this case included financial and physical harms as Moore frequently submitted to his doctor's orders, including traveling to California from the state of Washington for invasive medical tests and extractions of tissue, spleen, blood, plasma, and semen under the purported guise of treatment.[25]

The *Moore* case highlights the importance of optimizing designations in the human body, because a key point of confusion in body part theft cases involves assigning value to raw human biological materials. Courts struggle with this issue. Defendants tend to argue and courts presume that raw human biologics lack "value" or that price points associated with an organ, bone, or cell line represent fees for processing or transportation and not actual values or prices. However, claims that Moore's biologics lacked market value were simply inaccurate even in the 1980s – as blood and semen markets existed in the private sphere and hospitals, research clinics, and biobanks regularly traded cell lines and other biologics.[26]

A more probing analysis reveals vast networks of trading in human tissue, skin, bone, and other biologics that are decidedly nonaltruistic and resource driven. Sometimes the fees associated with those trades are couched in euphemisms, such as "processing" or "transportation" fees, and other times, the terminology and costs are explicit.

Blood Shield Law Model: Body Part as a Service

In February 2006, the Brooklyn district attorney, Charles Hynes, charged four grave pillagers with "medical terrorism." Hynes claimed the body-robbing scandal was "unique in its utter disregard for human decency."[27] It was the latest horrific episode in the ongoing tissue transplant industry saga.

[24] "The elements of fraud are (a) a misrepresentation (false representation, concealment, or nondisclosure); (b) scienter or knowledge of its falsity; (c) intent to induce reliance; (d) justifiable reliance; and (e) resulting damage." *Hinesley*, 35 Cal. App. 4th at 294.

[25] *Moore*, 793 P.2d at 481.

[26] *See* Rebecca Skloot, The Immortal Life of Henrietta Lacks (2010). For example, Invitrogen, a biotech company, sells products made from Lacks's cells for anywhere from $100 to $10,000 per vial. *Id.* at 194. It has been estimated that "one human body can bring in anywhere from $10,000 to nearly $150,000." *Id.* at 322.

[27] Anthony M. DeStefano, *The Body Snatchers: Funeral Home-Based Ring Charged*, Newsday, Feb. 24, 2006, at A3.

The indictment alleged that a New Jersey dentist, Michael Mastromarino, and codefendants robbed more than a thousand bodies of bones, ligaments, heart valves, organs, and other valuable tissues. The defendants subsequently admitted to stuffing the bodies with plastic tubing to deceive relatives and mourners.[28]

Detectives and investigators unmasked Mastromarino's surreptitious scheme, but only after thousands of body parts, some from diseased corpses, were introduced to the market and sold for transplantation to hospitals, doctors, and patients throughout the United States[29] and internationally.[30] Tissue, similar to blood transfusions, can transmit hepatitis, HIV, mad cow disease, bacteria, and various other communicable diseases to the unsuspecting transplant recipient.[31]

The *Moore* case and Mastromarino's business highlight various problems that attend human tissue transplantation and the reconstitution of body parts beyond the question of ownership. First, are warranties appropriate for reconstituted, processed, or restructured body parts? Second, what is the appropriate recourse in cases involving the purchase and sale of insalubrious tissues? Third, how should courts or legislatures frame remedies for injured plaintiffs – through tort or contract law? What is the role of property law in these domains? Some of these problems are illuminated in disturbing narratives, including those of Brian Lykins, Bonny Gonyers, Ken Alescu, Sydney Steinberg (a five-year-old who died from a heart valve infection possibly linked to Cryolife, the supplier of the body part that she received), and similar cases.[32] In each instance, plaintiffs suffered injuries connected to the implantation of infected human tissue. Severe injuries and even deaths occurred not as a result of surgical malfeasance, but of diseased tissues that spread deadly bacteria within the transplant hosts' bodies.

[28] *Id.*

[29] *Id.*

[30] Daryl Passmore, *The Body Business*, SUNDAY MAIL (Australia), July 1, 2006, at 57.

[31] Mastromarino subsequently pled guilty to numerous charges of enterprise corruption, reckless endangerment, and body stealing in New York. Alan Feuer, *Dentist Pleads Guilty to Stealing and Selling Body Parts*, N.Y. TIMES, Mar. 19, 2008, at B6. In Pennsylvania, he pled guilty to charges involving his business arrangement with three Philadelphia morticians. Joseph A. Slobodzian, *Body-Parts Mastermind Pleads Guilty*, PHILA. INQUIRER, Aug. 29, 2008, at B01.

[32] *See* Sandra Blakeslee, *Recall is Ordered at Large Supplier of Transplant Tissue*, N.Y. TIMES, Aug. 15, 2002, at A1 (discussing the FDA's order for Cryolife to recall all soft tissues it had sold).

Given the failure to optimize designations in the human body, what remedies exist or should exist for these injured parties? Few court cases provide guidance on these issues and those that shape this field or answer the question offer reason for concern. *Cryolife, Inc. v. Superior Court*[33] and *Condos v. Musculoskeletal Transplant Foundation*[34] offer relevant, but troubling guidance. Importantly, each case relied on fuzzy signaling to arrive at conclusions that undermine the goals of optimizing designations for human body parts. In both cases courts ruled that human biologics sold for transplantation do not constitute products or goods, but rather services, thereby disadvantaging duped patients by restricting if not completely foreclosing all potential civil remedies. The *Condos* and *Cryolife* rulings conclude that tissue banks should not be held liable for placing contaminated tissues into the stream of commerce even if their products cause the deaths or life-threatening illnesses to consumers.

Courts appear wary to do the heavy lifting and shaping of new law, despite the Center for Disease Control's (CDC's) investigations revealing numerous problems at tissue bank laboratories and warehouses, and the very direct links between deaths and illnesses of consumers and cadaver sources used by the companies that process and sell body parts that they purchased. In other words, recent jurisprudence unwisely places the burden on patients and doctors to guard against implanting contaminated body parts.[35] With this type of fuzzy guidance from courts, how are patients, often the least informed, to police this process?

Despite prior lawsuit settlements against Cryolife, the Court of Appeals of California determined in 2003 that Cryolife and arguably other tissue banks are immune from product liability when the body parts they place into the stream of commerce injure patients.[36] According to the Court of

[33] 110 Cal. App. 4th 1145 (Cal. Ct. App. 2003).

[34] 208 F.Supp.2d 1226 (D. Utah 2002).

[35] *See id.* at 1230; *Cryolife*, 110 Cal. App. 4th at 1154–60; Johnson v. Super. Ct., 101 Cal. App. 4th 869, 886–89 (Cal. Ct. App. 2002) (limiting the recovery of parents seeking damages because sperm bank failed to disclose that purchased sperm was from a donor with a history of kidney disease, which their daughter later inherited); Lenahan v. Univ. of Chi., 808 N.E.2d 1078, 1087 (Ill. App. Ct. 2004) ("Plaintiffs failed to allege facts sufficient to show that the defendants knowingly and voluntarily participated in a common scheme to commit any tortious acts in relation thereto").

[36] *See Cryolife*, 110 Cal. App. 4th at 1155 (concluding that the California Health and Safety Code "provides statutory immunity from strict liability to tissue banks subject to regulation").

Appeals of California, Cryolife's immunity arises from the fact that buying, collecting, processing, storing, and selling body parts are collectively and essentially a "service" and that the parts sold are not "goods."[37] The *Cryolife* holding invites scrutiny as to the normative ordering of human body parts. For example, how should body parts be classified and what ought their legal statuses be?

The court's conclusion that body parts are a *service* rather than facilitate the *performance of a service* precluded the plaintiff's recovery and is a striking feature of the case.[38] On the one hand, few people would consider his or her knee, heart, hip, or spine a service – these are tangible, biological parts. On the other hand, tissue banks refuse to designate knees, bones, and other biologics as goods, which could potentially expose their shareholders to liability if contaminated cadaver tissues reach the stream of commerce. This tension and incoherence in the law expose the need for optimized designations and understanding of the legal and social status of body parts and tissues. In the changing function and use of body parts, common understandings as to bioparts' postharvesting classification should also evolve. In other words, what Cryolife *processes* describes its service; what it *produces* through that processing is a good or product for which it receives value.

The relevance of this point proved significant to the court's analysis of *Cryolife* and whether the plaintiff could pursue a strict liability claim for punitive damages against the tissue bank. Ultimately, the Court of Appeals of California was not persuaded by the plaintiff's claim that *Cryolife* did not fit within the legislative exemption provided for blood banks.[39] California and a majority of states enacted blood shield immunity statutes during the 1950s and throughout the subsequent two decades to shield organizations that collected and processed blood from strict liability claims.[40]

Indeed, Cryolife's contention that the Health and Safety Code provisions of California, which define the status of tissue banks, barred plaintiffs from strict liability claims against tissue banks proved successful.[41] The statute,

[37] *Id.* at 1154.

[38] *Id.* at 1154–55.

[39] *Id.* at 1153–54.

[40] *Id.* at 1153.

[41] *Id.* at 1153–54; *see also* Cal. Health & Safety Code § 1635.2 (West 2007).

however, does not explicitly provide such an exemption or immunity to tissue banks. Rather, Section 1606, the codification of the blood shield law, provides in pertinent part:

> The procurement, processing, distribution, or use of whole blood, plasma, blood products, and blood derivatives for the purpose of injecting or transfusing the same, or any of them, into the human body shall be construed to be, and is declared to be, for all purposes whatsoever, the rendition of a service by each and every person, firm, or corporation participating therein.[42]

Ultimately, the court agreed with Cryolife's nuanced definition of its business. The tissue bank claimed that its business status, although for-profit, is similar to that of blood banks – which traditionally operate as charitable, not-for-profit organizations – within the definition of the blood shield immunity law.[43] Both sections of the law (1606 and 1635.2) describe the banks as providing services; however, only the blood shield statute provides an immunity provision – and only for blood banks.[44] Despite the "difference in language of section 1606 and section 1635.2,"[45] the court held that the legislature must have intended to shield tissue banks from strict liability claims.

The court's novel interpretation of lawmakers' legislative intent is not supported by any legislative history or legislative comment; nor does the court point to comment sections from the Health and Safety Code. Substantively, the court's holding reasons that in 1991, the legislature should have known or predicted that in 2003 "tissue banks [would be] paid for their activities in connection with providing human cadaver tissue for medical use" and thus must have "intended tissue banks to be immune from strict liability."[46]

However, the court's effort to be guided by the legislature is undermined by its jurisprudence. To explicate, the court extends immunity protection to tissue banks when the statute that it relies upon does not grant that type of protection to the industry. The court gives a new and unusual interpretation of the tissue bank statute, which does not provide any immunity language, without an effort to investigate or explain whether the legislature actually

[42] Cal. Health & Safety Code § 1606.
[43] *Cryolife*, 110 Cal. App. 4th at 1150.
[44] Cal. Health & Safety Code § 1606.
[45] *Cryolife*, 110 Cal. App. 4th at 1155,
[46] *Id.*

intended for tissue banks to be immune from strict liability lawsuits. It is more common to look at the legislative history, or at least to examine the record of the legislative committee enacting the statute, when a case is under de novo review. Had the court examined the legislative history of the blood bank statute and the later tissue bank regulations, it might have discovered that the public policy rationales for blood bank immunity were quite unique to that industry.[47]

Unlike blood suppliers, tissue banks operate under different business, tax, and social models. For example, some tissue banks supply heart valves, while others focus on cosmetic services, such as products to enhance lips, penis size, cheekbones, and other nonessential elective medical products. Moreover, the technology is available for highly sophisticated testing of tissues before they enter the stream of commerce, unlike the developing science of blood testing in the 1950s (when immunity statutes were first drafted).

The *Cryolife* ruling creates a problematic precedent, which undermines patient recovery and constrains the advancement of tort law jurisprudence in the biotech realm. The court too easily dismissed the plaintiff's claim that he received a defective product and not a service. Minvielle's surgeon successfully implanted a contaminated body part. The service received was perfectly fine. The product was the problem. The court made a significant error in expanding the protection of blood shield statutes (promulgated more than forty years prior)[48] to an industry neither so altruistic, nor anticipated by state legislatures in the 1950s and 1960s. Ironically, the court concludes its dismissal of the plaintiff's strict liability claim against the tissue

[47] Blood banks in the 1950s were mostly not-for-profit and often connected with hospitals. Legislatures treated the collection, processing, storage, and administration of blood as a service and not as a sale subject to warranty because blood banks were organized around altruistic principles, which were consistent with their not-for-profit status. The legislative intent was to promote the procurement of blood and protect blood banks from the possibility of frivolous (and more serious) lawsuits. Blood supply was vital as a domestic and military issue given cold war aggressions and wars in Korea and later Vietnam. Blood banks were not in the position to warrant the quality of blood that donors provided despite the fact that they processed, transported, and administered blood; they were limited by the available science at the time. Nor was the technology available to perform sophisticated blood analyses. Thus viruses transfused through blood were often undetectable during this era.

[48] 1991 Cal. Legis. Serv. Ch. 801 (A.B. 2209) (West). The 1606 statute discussed in *Cryolife* goes back more than forty years.

bank by quoting from an earlier blood shield law case, *Hyland Therapeutics v. Superior Court*,[49] to support its rationale that the California legislature intended for blood banks to be free from fault:

> We concur in the perception that "legislatures have determined that the production and use of human blood and its derivatives for therapeutic purposes should be encouraged; and for this purpose those who provide these products, and who are themselves free from fault, should not be required to bear the economic loss which might otherwise be imposed under the rules of strict liability which are applicable to sellers of commercial products generally."[50]

The ruling indicates that the status and designation of the body can change from one handler to the next, perpetuating a problematic public policy. The courts recognized ownership or property interests in the transplanted body parts. However, the relevant question is, *Who is the possessor or owner of body parts in the stream of commerce?* One way to interpret these transactions that seems fairly consistent with the holding is that the patient owned the tendon he purchased. The tissue banks "owned" the tissues prior to selling them. However, it appears from the logic of *Cryolife* that as soon as the good leaves the warehouse of the tissue bank, the body part becomes a "service." Thus, this case and others illuminate inconsistent treatment vis-à-vis the status of body parts.

Conceptual Problems

Inconsistent approaches to the designation of human biologics create numerous problems, including information asymmetries, entrenching hierarchies between researchers and their patients, as well as advantaging corporations while disadvantaging patients. The social and political diagnostics are troubling; corporations maximize economic opportunities, sometimes violating the spirit of legislation prohibiting the commercialization of human biologics by taking advantage of porous legal loopholes, while individuals are disadvantaged or excluded from full or equitable participation in most human biological markets. Back end protections of biobanks, shielding such organizations from liability under blood shield laws, further expose the incoherence of the field.

[49] 175 Cal. App.3d 509 (Cal. Ct. App. 1985).
[50] *Cryolife*, 110 Cal. App. 4th at 1156.

That human body parts vary by designation depending on the "holder" proves a fallible legal concept. Conceptually and legally, ordering of human body parts according to their possessor creates the types of inconsistencies in laws that incentivize coercion and exploitation. The cases described herein and throughout the book reflect solid slices of the field and highlight real concerns. First, this stunted lexicon in body part cases that refers to virtually all exchanges as "donations" provides very little useful guidance to a burgeoning field. Incompatible concepts and misleading jargon describe new and distinctively different practices. For example, when a hospital sells a placenta to a cosmetic company, that transaction defies the language of "donation" and the concept of altruism. The placenta is not a "donation" from the mother; nor is it a "gift" from the fetus or the third party hospital.

Second, failure to resolve and optimize human body part designations effectively creates perverse externalities in essential medical therapies. Ironically, market equilibriums exist in nontherapeutic human biological spheres, but not where tissues and organs are most needed. Reproductive markets flourish, while thousands die waiting for altruistically transferred kidneys. Congress remains wedded to the notion that organs carry only altruistic value. It is no wonder then that almost 100,000 Americans wait for kidneys on the national transplant waiting list.[51] More than seven thousand will die this year, and thousands more will be removed from the waiting list as a result of rationing constraints. That burden will be borne by the elderly and sickest patients. Neither courts nor legislators provide compelling reasoning for the disparate treatment between commercialized reproductive biologics and organs.

Last, how should markets be liberalized to capture commercialized human biologics adequately? This is a present condition – not an imagined world. Tort law will inevitably be appealed to for solutions.

Each year more than one million allograft surgeries are performed in the United States.[52] However, when harvested bones from cadavers enter the marketplace through sales to biotech companies, legislators, courts, agencies, and the industries lack a common parlance. This creates information

[51] As of July 2012, there were 92,842 candidates on the United States waiting list for a kidney. *National Data*, Organ Procurement & Transplantation Network, *available at* http://optn.transplant.hrsa.gov/latestData/step2.asp (accessed July 11, 2012).

[52] *See* Allograftinfo.com, *available at* http://www.allograftinfo.com/faqs.html (accessed July 11, 2012).

asymmetries and incoherence across a sphere that involves regulators, purchasers, sellers, patients, hospitals, and doctors. Optimizing the designations will allow for greater ethical, medical, and legal clarity. Indeed, at any given time, these human biologics might have conflicting designations: commercial, service, patented, inalienable, property, and product. Each term has meaning and implies social values, cultural understandings, and legal statuses, each of which is significant to judicial interpretation.

The assumptions that crowd social and cultural understandings about the human body, including that it lacks value, no longer make sense because those conceptions are no longer credible or relevant. Judicial minimalists necessarily err when they ignore exogenous sources, instead choosing to concentrate on adhering to traditional norms,[53] lest they be viewed as unmindful of their role, radical, or even judicially activist. In essence, judges do not believe it is their role to *change* the law to respond to biotechnology. Yet, rather than clarifying the law, a fuzzy picture develops.

Minimalists argue that it is the legislature's role to introduce *new* meaning to the law; the courts simply sort out the statutory "mishmash."[54] Guido Calabresi suggests that the formalist approach "does not contemplate the introduction of new or modified values into the scheme as part of the[ir] role."[55] Thus the court's function to hear the new biotechnology cases with an objective ear is usurped not by judicial indifference to plaintiffs, but rather by a defense "of the values it finds embedded in the system."[56] In strictly adhering to minimal expressionism, judges ignore the independence of the bench and its secondary function, which is to sort out the mishmash. Obsequious loyalty to doctrine necessarily inures heightened blindness to external factors and, in the face of biotechnological harms to plaintiffs, may undermine the perception of the judiciary. At risk will be injured patients' perceptions of the judiciary as an independent, fair, and competent arm of the government.

[53] Calabresi, *supra* note 1, at 2115.

[54] *See, e.g.*, Moore v. Regents of the Univ. of Cal., 793 P.2d 479, 494 (Cal. 1990) (noting that "it is inappropriate to impose liability for conversion based upon the allegations of Moore's complain [because] problems in this area are better suited to legislative resolution").

[55] *See* Calabresi, *supra* note 1, at 2115–16 (explaining four dominant legal schools of thought: doctrinalism or autonomism, "law and . . . ," legal process school, and law and status).

[56] *Id.* at 2116.

Conclusion

Michele Goodwin

This book illuminates a difficult truth: altruism is vulnerable to and sometimes captured by the negative dynamics that its adherents passionately oppose in markets. At the heart of these authors' observations is a sturdy mindfulness about the comparative choices available to courts, industries, patients, consumers, doctors, and even third parties. Corruption, greed, pressure, and dishonesty flow alongside and sometimes overlap and intertwine with the noblest philanthropic intentions in altruistic human body part exchanges. These negative externalities may be more difficult to track in human biological exchanges, but they exist nonetheless. For example, in the past decade, major research universities have been implicated in the selling of donated human bodies and body parts for research. Indeed, Ernest Reid, a body part broker who clandestinely operated a chop shop at the University of California-Los Angeles Hospital, profited handsomely by selling body parts to Fortune 500 companies.[1] Los Angeles prosecutors claimed that he profited more than $1.5 million during a four-year period when he paid Henry Reid, a UCLA official, to give him access to bodies that were donated for medical research. Such startling events are not as rare as we would hope.[2]

More recently, an eight-month investigation by a group of journalists from around the globe exposed the tentacle-like reach of the human body trade that is purportedly based on altruistic "donations." The reporters picked up on a story from the Ukraine in early 2012 that bones, tissues,

[1] Jack Leonard, *Businessman Found Guilty in UCLA's Willed Body-Parts Program Scandal*, L.A. Times, May 15, 2009, *available at* http://articles.latimes.com/2009/may/15/local/me-willedbody15.

[2] *Id.*

and other human remains were "crammed into coolers in a grimy white minibus."[3] Police investigators discovered stacks of cash, stuffed in envelopes, and autopsy records "written in English." The reporters learned that what security guards and police stumbled upon was not the macabre work of a mass murderer, but instead, "part of an international pipeline" destined for a subsidiary in Germany, owned by a U.S. biobank, based in Florida – RTI Biologics. For its part, RTI refused to comment or respond to reporters, but its public statements reiterate a common theme – altruistic procurement: "RTI honors the gift of tissue donation by treating the tissue with respect."[4] What investigators uncovered were bodies pillaged of parts, strewn about morgues.

As it turns out, human body parts presumed discarded at hospitals and clinics are often sold, traded, or surrendered for fees and profits postoperatively. Frequently, patients are the unwitting participants in this murky business. Sometimes individuals are directly exploited, such as in the cases of John Moore and Henrietta Lacks, patients whose illnesses required medical treatment. In both cases, the sick patients' bodies were mined for unique cells and tissues. Moore and Lacks suffered medical, economic, and legal exploitation by physician-researchers whose conflicting business and research interests trumped basic fiduciary protocols and duties owed to their patients. Henrietta died penniless and destitute although researchers at Johns Hopkins (and around the globe) benefited from the financial and reputational value gained by harvesting and manipulating her tissues. In other cases, significant information asymmetries exist.

Hospitals profit from patients' ignorance and naiveté. To capture the scale and scope of the biological market, consider that in the wake of births millions of patients leave behind or discard valuable body parts, such as placentas, foreskins, umbilical cords, and other tissues they presume will be destroyed by hospitals. Yet, hospitals generate significant profit from patients' ignorance, collecting these inches of flesh and selling them to companies like Bio Surface Technology, Advanced Tissue Sciences, and other biobanks. According to Thomas Tully, the former president of

[3] Kate Wilson et al., *Skin, Bones and Tissue for Sale: How the Dead Are Being Used for Grisly Trade in Human Body Parts*, MAILONLINE, July 17, 2012, http://www.dailymail.co.uk/news/article-2175006/Skin-bones-tissue-sale-How-dead-used-grisly-trade-human-body-parts.html (last accessed Dec. 28, 2012).

[4] *Id.*

Organogenesis, "From one foreskin, our scientists say they could replicate enough times to where it covers a football field."[5] Body parts such as these are used to make useful products such as insulin and wound dressing, as well as cosmetics and hair creams. But are parents informed that their sons' foreskins will be sold postoperatively?

It turns out that very little about the industry is altruistic as companies sell to the highest bidders, a process that more commonly shuts out the not-for-profit burn banks.[6] Throughout these transactional chains, hospitals and biobanks profit from body parts that were never altruistically donated – in the purest sense. But rather, they capitalize on patient ignorance and emotion: grief, sorrow, or joy – all of which serve to distract patients and their family members at hospitals. This could hardly be described as good-faith altruism, but it passes as such in an era where biotechnology outpaces regulation and judicial wisdom.

The Global Body Market challenges the notion that altruism represents an unburdened institutional choice in an age when the human body is conscripted, sold, bartered, donated, processed, and destroyed. To the contrary, sometimes the less desirable or even pernicious aspects of markets map onto and dominate altruistic exchanges. The compelling biographies of Henrietta Lacks and John Moore illume the darker, more complicated aspects of altruism where patients become the unwitting participants in human research that may advance technology, but will inure enormous profits to the researchers who conscript their cells, tissues, organs, and other body parts.

Where are the limits? Just as with other institutional choices in the disposition of human body parts – namely, markets – altruistic exchanges are encumbered by bias, controversy, pressure, and coercion. On inspection, altruism operates under the same political constraints, opportunities, dynamics, and interests that attend other institutions, including markets. This book analyzes those constraints in various body part regimes and their unintended endogenous and exogenous effects, including an underdeveloped and inaccurate nomenclature that deems all goods that flow from the body as "gifts" and "donations" even when they are paid for and could hardly be described as charitable contributions.

[5] Ronald Rosenberg, *Companies See $1.5b Market in Replacement Skin Products*, Bos. Globe, Oct. 19, 1992.

[6] Wilson et al., *supra* note 3.

Noncompensated body part exchanges, such as organ donations in the United States, veil the economic exchanges that attend every step of human biological sharing, covering the fact that very little in this domain is truly altruistic. Those who benefit from these misapplied designations are the frequent players, those whom Marc Galanter might describe as the "haves," who typically come out ahead.[7] Corporations that surreptitiously and mysteriously collect "donated" tissues and body parts benefit significantly from global body part regimes. Companies profit from governments' disallowing any selling of human body parts, understanding that such laws are intended for unsophisticated laypeople – and not for businesses. Patients also benefit, but only if the mysteriously obtained parts are healthy and useful. Otherwise, their fates are left to well-intentioned, but nevertheless uninformed courts, reluctant to introduce new theories, concepts, values, and principles to the common law jurisprudence on the body. To them, a human body has no property value and therefore cannot be the subject of tort litigation. Not even the criminal law provides an adequate response to the egregious cases of body-part theft – *from the living!*

Those harmed by the government's unequivocal adherence to altruistic exchanges tend to be the less frequent, one-time players. Patients who need organs, but are shut out because too few enter altruistic procurement regimes are among those most disserved and injured by government policies wedded to altruism. For their part, legislators cling to a deeply romanticized view of altruism, which ignores the calculated economic interests of companies, doctors, and hospitals that facilitate the "altruism" they demand. When these matters are called to their attention, politicians are ultimately conflicted about the plight of these patients and what to do about their suffering. Patients in need of organ transplants endure for years on waiting lists, tethered to dialysis machines or bedridden for months that morph into years.

Only those with the tenacity of athletes and the luck of lottery winners actually achieve receiving an organ in the U.S. transplant system. Others are removed from the lists, die, or enter the black markets. These patients suffer needlessly under the constraints of altruism, while procurers of human reproductive materials are less encumbered by government restrictions.

[7] Marc Galanter, *Why the "Haves" Come Out Ahead: Speculations on the Limits of Legal Change*, 9 LAW & SOC'Y REV. 95 (1974).

Less regulation is not necessarily the answer, nor the driving theme of this book. Instead, the goal is to grapple candidly with the darker elements of altruism and to concede honestly when altruism simply demands too much.

Inconsistent approaches to the liberalization of human biologics will continue to create problems and perpetuate the lack of transparency and clarity that pervades the culture of human body part exchanges. How nation-states advance human flourishing and health is now deeply interwoven with how their governments manage human biological exchanges. From the building blocks of families to the protection and promotion of health, the uses of human body parts are crucial to these arrangements. Yet, despite their ubiquitous application from medical and dental treatments to pharmaceutical medicines and cosmetics, optimizing the appropriate legal, medical, and linguistic designations for human body parts remains a significant problem. Until this problem is resolved, altruism will remain a lofty, but unreliable measure for human sacrifice and compassion.

Journal Acknowledgments

Jamila Jefferson-Jones, *The Exchange of Inmate Organs for Liberty: Diminishing the "Yuck Factor" in the Bioethics Repugnance Debate,* 16 J. GENDER RACE & JUST. (2012).

Michele Goodwin, *My Sister's Keeper? Law, Children, And Compelled Donation,* 29 W. NEW ENG. L. REV. 357 (2007).

Michele Goodwin, *Expressive Minimalism and Fuzzy Signals: The Judiciary and the Role of Law,* 84 CHI.-KENT L. REV. 19 (2009).

Index